maverick's

by
Matt Warshaw

foreword by
Daniel Duane

the story of big-wave surfing

CHRONICLE BOOKS
SAN FRANCISCO

Library of Congress Cataloging-in-Publication Data available.
ISBN 0-8118-2652-X
Printed in Hong Kong.

Herter Studio
432 Elizabeth Street
San Francisco, California 94114
415 282 8143   415 285 1659 fax

Producer and Creative Director
    Caroline Herter
Project Editor
    Jeff Campbell, *Ripple Moon Studio*
Design and Art Direction
    Martin Venezky, *Appetite Engineers*
Commissioned Photography
    David Perry, *David Perry Studio*
Photo Editor
    Kelly Duane
Proofreader
    Carolyn Keating
Indexer
    Ken DellaPenta

Distributed in Canada by
    Raincoast Books
    8680 Cambie Street
    Vancouver, British Columbia
    V6P 6M9

10   9   8   7   6   5   4   3   2   1

Chronicle Books
85 Second Street
San Francisco, California 94105
www.chroniclebooks.com

Dedicated to MARC THEODORE and the twenty-five years
we've been riding waves together. Let's go for another fifty.

I first saw Maverick's IN 1994, while driving

home to Santa Cruz from San Francisco. Enormous, mile-long wave bands were rippling the blue horizon, and I'd just heard of a new big-wave break, so I took a few wrong turns, drove in circles around a local airstrip, and finally found my way to the preposterously named village of Princeton-by-the-Sea, a grassy collection of boatyards and cottages. There were a few obvious surfer cars in the dirt parking lot, but nobody to tell me which way to walk—none of the teeming crowds that now appear on every good day—so I scrambled up a grassy hill, toward an old Cold War radar dish, and saw a reasonably big wave about to break. A flock of tiny shorebirds rose slowly, perilously up the face, no more than specks on a ten-foot wall. I couldn't see a single surfer. The wind blew off-shore in clear December skies and a gull passed above, and then one of those shorebirds stood up and took off. It was a surfer after all, on an eleven-foot board, on a wave face that approached thirty feet.

The pleasures and struggles of "outdoor sports" express the very essence of the way we are—or at least the way we were—in the world. Hunting, of course, the pursuit of food; hiking, horseback riding, and river rafting, all the rigors of travel. Human pride and exuberance turn every indispensable craft and skill into a form of expression, such that mountain peoples have long venerated those who move confidently over rock walls and snow-filled couloirs. Likewise, coastal people: sailing, of course, and also sea kayaking, and spear and game fishing. But no tribe has ever depended on the man who could surf down a marlin with a spear in hand, or use a wave to get from one village to the next. Surfing expresses, rather, a pure yearning for visceral, physical contact with the natural world.

Everywhere along the docks and beaches and bluffs—as Melville once observed of Manhattan—we find people like ourselves, gazing into the void, both calmed and expectant, and what do we see there, if not waves? No wonder that Polynesians, reminded all their lives of the power and variety of the surf, made a venerated sport of playing in it, nor that twentieth-century seaside cultures would celebrate that same atavistic mastery. Hanging five in a protected bay or standing tall in the barreling vortex, the surfer doesn't perfect something we need done anyway;

the surfer demonstrates something we dream of—looking out to sea at all that booming energy and just, well, doing something about it, and something as marvelous as the energy itself. Thus the smiles on the lips of onlookers: surfing, alone among sports, generates laughter at its very suggestion, and this is because it turns not a skill into an art, but an inexplicable and useless urge into a vital way of life.

Upon realizing that those shorebirds were surfers, I walked around the headland until I found a small crowd of men and women with a better view. They were all surfers themselves—a few were surf photographers—and they shared a reverential quiet. There were several reasons for this, in addition to the natural taciturnity of surfers. The first was surprise. For decades, big-wave surfing had meant one thing: Oahu's Waimea Bay, in the winter. Todos Santos, off Baja, was a kind of runner-up, K2 to Waimea's Everest—though the analogy isn't quite right. To understand the discovery, in the early 1990s, that the world's greatest big-wave break lay just outside San Francisco, imagine, next week, a climber stumbling upon a mountain both bigger than Everest and harder to climb, right outside Denver.

The silence that day also had to do with the waves themselves, appearing first as deformations in the surface of the sea, bending and warping their way toward the lineup. The black dots that were grown men on huge boards inched aside like ants avoiding a bus. When the waves stood up to break, a dark hole opened in the trough and the lip hung in space and the detonation was, in words William Finnegan once used to describe Ocean Beach, a "basso profundo of utter violence." All good, strong surfing waves look dangerous—like they could knock you down and kick you around—but Maverick's looks like it could kill you, for real. And it can. The surfers in the water that day weren't just gazing at peelers and wanting to play; they were looking at the sea at its most severe—the kind of surf that destroys bridges, sinks ships, and rearranges coastlines—and they were putting themselves deliberately in its path. Maverick's is, in other words, the wave beyond, the place outside the bounds of mortal experience. It expresses our yearning for contact, all right, but at its most extreme—a deliberate flirtation with death in exchange for a firsthand taste of the storm.

Another reason for the quiet I shared on the cliff at Maverick's, in December of 1994, had to do with something the others had seen shortly before I arrived—a truly horrifying wipeout on a wave at least thirty feet high. The first act had just transpired in the foundational legend of Maverick's, a story that would play out over the next five days and end in very real tragedy, and a story that, in Matt Warshaw's able and experienced hands, will be a part of American sports history forever.

Daniel Duane
San Francisco, 1999

a lmost

150 years ago, NEAR THE END of big-wave surfing's long, sun-warmed prehistory, a tsunami wave roared into the northeast coast of Hawaii, peaked at some impossible height against the beachfront hills and cliffs, then abruptly reversed direction and pulled much of the landscape out to sea, including a man named A'a Holaua and his small wood-frame house. Tsunami waves travel in sets, like regular ocean waves, and as the second enormous swell lifted up, Holaua ripped a plank from the side of his house, positioned himself beneath the curl, shot down the face, and rode to shore.

Surfer magazine says it happened on April 2, 1862, on the Big Island of Hawaii. Surfing historian Ben Finney claims it was Kauai in 1868. Exactly where and when A'a Holaua's tsunamic encounter took place, *if* it took place—such questions, in the operatic world of big-wave surfing, don't really matter. Myth and legend are the animating forces here, more so than truth and veracity. Surfers raise a skeptical eyebrow at A'a Holaua's story, like anyone else—but they indulge it, too, because it's a nicely exaggerated version of *their* story, that of ease and triumph in an environment that most people see as frightening, dangerous, and hostile. A 1948 oil painting of Holaua's wave by American artist C. P. Cathcart underscores the point. With the natural forces raging around him, Holaua doesn't just *survive*. He doesn't get washed ashore, or even sled along on his stomach. As rendered by Cathcart, Holaua charges for land standing up—and with rakish good form, too, in loose-fitting cut-offs and crouched in a hot angle across the wind-whipped incline, damn the looming rocks and uprooted palm trees. It's a vanquisher's stance. It's Beowulf gone tropical.

Holaua's ride, with its constituent elements of spontaneity and adventure, style and daring, helps explain why big-wave riders—and surfers in general—resist having their sport even labeled as "sport." Surfing isn't played as much as it's romanced, and this notion has turned surfers into chronic elitists. *We're out here having a great time,* holds a long-cherished tenet of the surfing philosophy, *while the rest of you dummies are stuck in there doing whatever.* But surfing can be positioned as an outlier to the larger community of sport by more direct means, too. It has no regulation playing field, for starters. No written rules. Few statistics or records. It isn't unquantifiable, exactly. But most scores, tallies, and figures, when applied to surfing, dissolve easily.

Big-wave riding has a particularly strange relationship to the world of numbers. Some data are hard and utilitarian: surfboard measurements are precise to a thirty-second of an inch; tide measurements, wind speed, and swell interval are monitored by big-wave surfers like the scrolling figures on the NYSE board. Other readings are illusory—or flat-out deceptive. A twenty-second wipeout, for example, doesn't sound especially awful. But to the out-of-breath, sensory-deprived big-wave rider planted deep inside a fissioning underwater whorl, one moment follows the next at ever-longer intervals until time seems to open to infinity. Panic usually hits at thirty seconds, even for an expert. At fifty seconds, most surfers will be unconscious.

Numbers and number-assigned values have even less meaning when surfers evaluate and judge wave height. A twenty-foot wave, trough to crest, as reasonably determined by the layperson, will be identified by the big-wave rider as ten or twelve feet. A thirty-footer is called fifteen or eighteen. Forty becomes twenty, or maybe twenty-five. Fifty is *still* twenty-five. And it gets stranger. Remove a ten-foot wave from the North Shore of Oahu and graft it onto a beach in Florida, and the local surfers would probably call it eighteen feet. In southern California it would be fifteen feet. In northern California, twelve. The idea, in general, is to play it cool by playing size down, and the seventy-foot-high waves that are now being ridden are labeled— with straight faces, by professionals—as thirty or thirty-five feet. Not that a more rigorous and exacting assessment would make any real difference. "Waves aren't measured in feet," as pioneering big-wave rider Buzzy Trent said, "but in increments of fear."

And Trent's right. Measurements and numbers (and to a lesser degree names, dates, and places) in big-wave surfing are mainly used as supports, like cotton-candy sticks, to catch and hold the diaphanous story-building strands of fear, mortality, triumph, folly, and courage that circulate so freely through the big-wave world—which itself was spun off from a centuries-old Hawaiian surfing mythology that includes demigods and talking animals, kings, queens, and warriors, kidnapping and ritual human sacrifice, chants and prayers, temples and consecration, inter-island murder plots and life-endangering passion. "Promise me you will never kiss another woman," the Bird Maiden said to Kahikilani, the prince from Kauai who, according to the ancient story, had sailed a hundred miles from his home to try the big waves on Oahu's north shore. The two lovers had spent several happy months together, but now the surf was up. Kahikilani grabbed his board, pledged his fidelity, and hit the beach—and afterward his big-wave excitement was such that he kissed a beautiful woman who'd been admiring him. Spying birds flew to the Bird Maiden and reported what they'd seen, and when Kahikilani returned later that day she turned him to stone.

"We're dysfunctional," says Hawaiian big-wave rider Ken Bradshaw, sitting on the front porch of his North Shore house, just yards from the same sandy bay where Kahikilani rode his last wave. "We have just barely functional relationships with other people—at best." This, of course, is part of the big-wave mythology as well, the modern adaptation, which presents the surfer as nobly maladjusted. Bradshaw squints out at the surf and makes another doleful comment, this one perhaps closer to the truth. "It's created junkies out of most of us. Surfing junkies, right? Our whole lives, we drop everything to go surfing, and we always will."

Here he pauses for a self-accepting and vaguely defiant little smile. He shrugs. "That's what we do. That's who we are."

In the EARLY NINETIES, a central California break called Maverick's made its public debut, and big-wave surfing was revised and redecorated. What had traditionally been framed by translucent aquamarine water and soft coral sand beaches was now being offered in steely blues, browns, and grays against a backdrop of steep, dusky, fog-shrouded cliffs. Hawaiian big-wave riding is frightening, even terrifying, but always tropically warm, and often sensual—a bare-skin pastime where the scent of plumeria occasionally drifts through the lineup. Maverick's is severe. Always. Even when the sun is out it sparkles coldly, and surfers protect themselves against the chill water and air with head-to-toe rubber wetsuits. Broken waves rush across a wide, jagged rock barrier. Decaying strands of kelp twine into a soft and slippery frieze along the high-tide line. Maverick's, a product of the north, has the presence of an ice-sculpted fjord, with seemingly no geologic connection whatsoever to the lava-layered reefs of the tropics and the sport's balmy Polynesian roots. Few big-wave riders—none, probably—would choose the Maverick's aesthetic over the Hawaiian. But everyone understands that Maverick's presents a surfing challenge like no other—and challenge, above all other big-wave attributes and attractions, drives the sport.

Surfer magazine introduced Maverick's to its readers as a "voodoo wave" in 1992, not long before a San Francisco weekly newspaper ran a full-bleed Maverick's photo on the front page and an enormous headline reading "Meet the Monster." Maverick's quickly became a new repository for big-wave myth and legend, and the sense of foreboding that radiated from this tiny, mid-California knob of coastline was further detailed in the accounts of a few dozen Bay Area surfers who were by then riding the break—except their own descriptions emphasized the beauty of Maverick's as much as the danger.

Distinctions between the two, though, were often hard to make. When visiting Hawaiian big-wave pro Mark Foo drowned at Maverick's on December 23, 1994, on the sunniest, smoothest, warmest day of the season, beauty and danger fused into a single entity. Maverick's legend took on an even darker presence as it moved to the center of big-wave surfing's collective consciousness. And Foo took up instant lodging in the surf-world pantheon.

Foo also became the mainstream media's spectral escort into what had always been a fairly obscure and cloistered pursuit. Newspapers, magazines, and TV news and entertainment shows, nationally and internationally, produced feature stories on Foo and Maverick's, with the larger drama- and color-saturated world of big-wave surfing as a backdrop. Never before had the sport been so much with the general public. A new, richer, pervasive big-wave commercialization followed, and seven years after Foo's death the sport continues to be aggressively marketed, packaged, and sold. Big-wave contests, once rare, are all the rage. Big-wave videos (with Maverick's-only tapes as a popular subgenre) retail by the tens of thousands. Big-wave books are published. Big-wave stickers are fixed to car bumpers from Honolulu to New York to Sydney to Tokyo. Some of the displays are edifying, honorable, handsome. Others banal, trite, even degrading.

And yet big-wave surfing's vital, blood-pumping center seems protected from the gathered forces of commercialism. Mark Foo died at Maverick's with the cameras rolling, during what might fairly be called a business trip. But he would have been out there riding anyway—by himself, if necessary, unpaid and unwatched. Foo's surfing career drafted along behind his surfing pleasure.

Maverick's: The Story of Big-Wave Surfing traces the fault line between the private and public sides of big-wave surfing, between the ride itself and all its many and varied by-products—commercial, editorial, and artistic. Maverick's, as Foo well understood, is fertile ground for both grand adventure and commercial opportunity. And to one degree or another, the story has been the same throughout much of big-wave surfing's history.

Maverick's alternates between these two big-wave settings. Chapters 1, 3, 5, 7, and 9 focus on Maverick's. They are built along the latticework of feeling, emotion, and sensation connecting Maverick's riders to the break and to each other, and they trace the colossal five-day run of surf leading up to Foo's death. Big-wave surfing's twentieth-century history and culture are outlined in chapters 2, 4, 6, 8, and 10, with special attention given to those moments when the sport runs directly through the turbines of commerce, publicity, and trade.

Matt Warshaw
San Francisco, 1999

surfacing

december 19 1994

sixteen-year-OLD JAY MORIARITY from Santa Cruz was

so intent on paddling into his first wave of the day and pushing up into the correct stance—and he nailed it, feet spread wide across the deck of his board, head tucked, weight forward and low—that he didn't at first realize he'd lifted off the water and was now surfing through air, just ahead of the curl, thirty feet above sea level.

Moriarity, as the big-wave expression goes, didn't penetrate. The wave had pulsed and expanded as it rolled over Maverick's reef, passing quickly from canted to vertical to concave, at which point Moriarity should have been two-thirds of the way down the face, driving like a javelin for flat water. But a draft of wind had slipped under the nose of Moriarity's surfboard—and instead here he was, still in his best big-wave crouch, levitating near the wave's apex. Now the nose of his board lifted up and backward onto a near-perfect vertical axis, its brightly airbrushed underbelly exposed and sharply limned in the morning light. Beautiful and condemned. The crest hooked forward, and Moriarity's arms came up and spread out from either side of his board, creating a Maverick's tableau that couldn't be taken as anything other than a kind of crucifixion.

The religious metaphor is an easy one to make—since big-wave surfers themselves so often use spiritual terms to characterize and illustrate their sport—but it makes you wonder how God, or Lono, or any such divine presence, could have decided to flick Jay Moriarity, Maverick's youngest and sweetest surfer, into the abyss. He was *Jay*, no nickname, friendly, wholesome, and unjaded—as compared to Flea, Ratboy, Skindog, and a few of the other red-hot and moderately profane Santa Cruz surfers known collectively as the Vermin. Moriarity won sportsmanship awards at surf contests. Recalling his first day at Maverick's during a surf magazine interview, the Georgia-born teenager gushed with Mousketeer enthusiasm: "I felt like I had just conquered Mount Everest or won a Gold Medal in the Olympics! I really felt on top of the world!" For the past two years Moriarity had been openly thrilled with the practice and promise of riding huge surf. He fell asleep thinking about big waves, then dreamed big-wave dreams. When the surf was down, he drove to Maverick's to survey the angles and contours of the reef, like a Formula One driver walking the track before a race. He wrote essays about big-wave surfing. Over the summer he'd paddled thirty-five miles across Monterey Bay to help build stamina and strength. For a moment, in fact, while still airborne, unaware that he'd just launched into what would soon be described as the most spectacular big-wave wipeout on record, Moriarity had the confidence to tell himself, "No problem, this one's *made.*"

The previous EVENING, at about 9 P.M., halfway through his evening shift in the kitchen at Pleasure Point Pizza in Santa Cruz, Moriarity phoned the National Weather Service for the updated buoy and weather report. For the past few days, he'd been tracking a North Pacific storm, and his eyebrows went up in stages as he discovered that the surf was going to be bigger than he'd thought, and it was due to arrive in just a few hours. Moriarity had ridden Maverick's twice that season already, and twice the season before. Driven to distraction by the prospect of a fifth session tomorrow, he clocked out, drove to Pleasure Point, suited up, and hit the water for a soothing round of night surfing.

At 5 A.M. the next morning, Moriarity steered his mother's Datsun pickup north on Highway One out of Santa Cruz, a pair of ten-foot, eight-inch surfboards stacked diagonally in the truck bed, their back ends jutting out past the tailgate. An hour later he pulled off the highway near Pillar Point Harbor, just a few hundred yards north of the Half Moon Bay city limit. Maverick's wasn't visible, but out past the harbor jetty, Moriarity could see smooth, wide-spaced ribbons of swell moving toward shore. Big for sure. Maybe bigger than he'd ever seen it.

Another two dozen people—surfers from San Francisco, Santa Cruz, Half Moon Bay, and Pacifica, along with a few surf photographers and spectators—were also driving toward Maverick's in the predawn light. Most parked in the small dirt lot just east of the Pillar Point headland, but Moriarity parked near the harbor, where he was going to catch a ride on *Lizzie-Lynn*, a twenty-six-foot fishing boat hired by one of the photographers. Moriarity unloaded his car and jogged toward the dock, a surfboard under each arm and a nylon backpack hanging off one shoulder. The weather was dry and brittle, in the upper 40s, but a steady east wind made it seem colder. Moriarity wore a black sweatshirt, jeans, and sneakers, with a black wool watch-cap pulled down low on his forehead. He stepped aboard *Lizzie-Lynn*, nodding and smiling to photographer Bob Barbour and the boat captain as he set his boards down, then he brought both hands up to his mouth and blew, to warm them. The boat began to pitch and roll as it cleared the harbor entrance, but it was a short ride, and ten minutes later *Lizzie-Lynn* pulled into a deepwater channel adjacent to Maverick's, about seventy-five yards south of the breaking surf.

It was just past 7 A.M. Ten riders were already in the water, loosely clustered and sitting on their boards, alert but casual as they watched the ocean and waited. The surf had been relatively calm during the boat's approach. Now, almost on cue, a set of waves shifted through the water about a half mile past the surfers—all of whom snapped to attention like pointers. One of them dropped and began sprint-paddling to the west, recognizing that the advancing waves were going to break ten or twenty yards beyond the group's current position. The other surfers, in a pack, followed.

Moriarity watched the first wave track across the distant part of the reef, which served as a kind of anteroom for Maverick's-bound swells. The wave, shaped like a broad-based pyramid, grew steadily, then fringed along the crest as it intersected with the group of surfers, their arms like pinwheels as they clambered up the face and dropped, safe, down the back slope. No takers. Not even an exploratory sidelong look. Everyone vanished from sight as the wind aerated the uppermost few inches of water and spun out an enormous sunlit corona of mist, which trailed behind the wave like a cape.

The crest arced down and exploded across the flat water with a low-pitched ripping noise, as if the air itself had split open, and the wave transformed into a cyclonic thirty-by-fifteen-foot tube, through which the rural tree-lined cliffs of Moss Beach, two miles away, were briefly visible. The canopy then imploded and a geyser of water shot out from the now-shrinking mouth of the tube, like a sharply exhaled cloud of smoke. A "spitter"—the salacious and climactic big-wave moment. The wave rumbled on, still big, powerful, and noisy, but dissipating, until it washed over a stand of rocks thirty seconds later and poured into the nearby lagoon.

Jay Moriarity stood like a tuning fork on the deck of *Lizzie-Lynn*, staring, almost vibrating with nervous anticipation, three words looping through his mind—*huge and perfect, huge and perfect*. Then a pragmatic thought: *too much wind*.

Surfers welcome a gentle land-to-sea breeze—an "offshore" wind—because it brushes out the nautical flaws, chops, and burrs and casts the sea's littoral, or near-shore, field in a dreamy sort of brine-sparkle. The wind on this particular morning, though, was of a different order. A 20-knot easterly was being amplified through the nearby coastal range mountain passes, then amplified again as it whipped up and around each breaking wave. An incoming surfer, Moriarity knew, would be temporarily deafened by the noise and partially blinded by the saltwater spray blowing off the front of his board. You'd have to do part of the takeoff by feel, he told himself. And once into the wave, you'd have to get low and *stay* low to fight down through the wind. Don't straighten up. Penetrate.

As he ran down his tactical checklist, Moriarity watched Evan Slater wheel his board around and paddle into the second wave of the set. Slater got to his feet smoothly, but the wind flicked him sideways—just like that. He landed midway down the face on the small of his back, skipped once, twice, then disappeared as the tube threw out around him like a giant blown-glass bubble and collapsed.

"Oh my *God!*" someone on the boat yelled. Two or three others added yowling surfer-shouts, thrilled and shocked, and everyone scanned the wave's white-foaming aftermath until Slater's head popped up about a hundred feet shoreward from where he'd gone down. More wild shrieks of amazement—"That was in*sane!*"—voices tinged with nervous relief. *Lizzie-Lynn* had been in the channel less than two minutes.

Moriarity squatted down, unzipped his nylon backpack, and pulled out a full-length hood-to-ankle neoprene wetsuit, black with blue accents, plus a long-sleeve polypropylene undershirt, a pair of wetsuit booties, and a pair of webbed gloves. The ocean temperature was a skin-tightening 52 degrees, but with this layered outfit he might stay in the water for hours. Moriarity could get fully rigged-out in less than two minutes, but he stopped halfway through and told himself to slow down. Stripped to the waist, now unaware of the cold, he breathed in, counting slowly to five. Then a five-count exhale as the wind gusted and the arm pieces of his wetsuit fluttered around his knees. Another breath to five, then he lost patience, rammed his arms into the rubber sleeves, zipped up, grabbed his board, and slipped over the edge of *Lizzie-Lynn*, gasping as he hit the water.

As Moriarity PADDLED toward the Maverick's

lineup, Half Moon Bay's twelve thousand residents were getting showered and dressed, pouring coffee, reviewing the Monday morning headlines, and glancing outside to take note of the ongoing stretch of temperate weather. Commuters moved onto the highways, driving north to San Francisco, south to San Jose, east to Silicon Valley. Most of Half Moon Bay High's students were still sleeping through their first few hours of Christmas vacation.

What Half Moon Bay locals were not doing was paying any attention to the fact that Moriarity, Slater, and the rest were at that moment tilting against waves bigger than anything surfers had ever faced anywhere in the world outside of Hawaii. Maverick's would in the days ahead produce international headlines. It would eventually produce bigger surf. But that morning, December 19, 1994, the huge wind-sculpted waves were changing the big-wave surfing landscape—and doing so in showy, dramatic style.

That it was happening in near-seclusion was partly a matter of geography, as Maverick's is hidden from view behind Pillar Point's silt-and-sandstone headland and the adjacent boat harbor breakwater. But Maverick's was also relatively unknown: it had publicly debuted to the surf world just eighteen months earlier, in a six-page *Surfer* magazine feature story. For two years before that, it had been something of a shared secret among twenty-five or so northern California surfers. Before that, no one outside of Half Moon Bay had even heard of Maverick's, and it was ridden by only one person, a local carpenter.

In addition, Half Moon Bay wasn't a hard-core surf town, and never had been. San Francisco, twenty-five miles north, had long occupied a special niche in the surf world—partly due to the incredibly photogenic wave that breaks under the southern span of the Golden Gate Bridge, but more so because of the curious and pleasing fact that surfing could take root and flourish on the perimeter of such a famous, sophisticated urban center. Santa Cruz, meanwhile, fifty-eight miles south of Half Moon Bay, had a strong claim as the world's greatest surf city. High-quality surf breaks are strung together like beads along the Santa Cruz coastline, and the near-Homeric scope of local surf history goes back to 1885, when Edward, David, and Cupid Kawananakoa, three blue-blooded Hawaiian teenagers attending a local military school, crafted boards for themselves from redwood planks and tested the shorebreak near the San Lorenzo rivermouth—becoming not just the first surfers in Santa Cruz but the first surfers in America. Wetsuit magnate Jack O'Neill opened his first shop here in 1959. Tom Curren, three-time world champion and American surfing icon, opened his 1990 world title run with a contest win at Steamer Lane, Santa Cruz's best-known break. A few years later, Darryl Virostko, Josh Loya, Chris Gallagher, Peter Mel, Kenny Collins, Jay Moriarity, and other young Santa Cruz locals had collectively become the hottest regionally connected troupe of surfers in California.

Half Moon Bay, meanwhile, wasn't off the surfing map entirely in 1994. Some of the reefs north of town occasionally produced good, powerful waves, and the long crescent-shaped beach south of the harbor was a fallback when the surf was small. Two Half Moon Bay surf shops were doing slow but steady business. Local surf history, though, was thin and mostly unrecorded. Just a few people, for instance, knew the story of Maverick, the white-haired German shepherd who, one winter's day in 1961, tore into the water behind three Half Moon Bay surfers as they paddled out to try the distant waves off Pillar Point. One of the surfers, Alex Matienzo, who lived with Maverick's owner, thought the surf looked too rough for the dog. Matienzo paddled back to the beach, whistled Maverick in, and tied him to the car bumper. The waves ended up being too rough for the surfers as well; they soon returned to the beach without having done much riding, and left Pillar Point alone after that. Because Maverick the dog had obviously gotten the most out of the experience, Matienzo and his friends called the intriguing but vaguely sinister Pillar Point surf break "Maverick's Point"—or just Maverick's.

Surfing and surf culture hadn't yet made any real impression in Half Moon Bay, which by 1994 was known more for its weathered rows of cut-flower greenhouses and its neatly groomed acres of brussels sprouts, broccoli, and artichokes, for the horse stables, the stately Beaux-Arts city hall building, the sublime foothill views along Highway 92, and an elaborate and well-attended annual pumpkin festival appropriate for a city billing itself as "The Pumpkin Capital of the World." While strip malls had gone up near downtown and touristy seafood restaurants and nautical-themed gift shops were clustered by the harbor, local slow-growth advocates had been masterful at keeping large-scale commercialization at bay. They had shut down all attempts to widen Highway One and expand the

Half Moon Bay airport. Residents, for the most part, were happy to be at a friendly but distinct remove from San Francisco.

Half Moon Bay, the oldest city in San Mateo County, nonetheless has a long and interesting mercantile connection to the sea. Portuguese whalers, in the late nineteenth century, dragged California grays and humpbacks onto the sandy hook of beach just inside Pillar Point, where they rendered slabs of blubber in enormous iron cook pots. Wooden ships were often gutted on the nearby reefs, some producing horrible scenes of splintered planks and floating corpses, others bringing sudden windfall. "Locals rushed to the scene," writes June Morrall in *Half Moon Bay Memories,* describing the gently beached and evacuated *Columbia* steamer, which ran aground in 1897, "and stripped luxurious staterooms of their white and gold molding. Others removed copper wire and within days every yard in the vicinity proudly displayed a new copper wire clothesline."

During Prohibition, Half Moon Bay bootleggers filled their customized shallow-hulled boats with cases of Canadian-made scotch, rum, gin, and champagne, darted through the surf at night, and made their prearranged drops in the shadowy coves south of Pillar Point. Most of the liquor was rushed up the coast to San Francisco speakeasies, though some went straight into the hollowed-out walls of nearby roadhouse/dance hall/bordellos like the Princeton Hotel and the Ocean Beach Tavern. Federal authorities were for the most part outgeneralled by the bootleggers, but in 1932, a midnight skirmish between a Coast Guard patrol boat and a local rumrunner in high seas off Moss Beach resulted in rifle fire, machine gun fire, *cannon* fire, a kidnapped government agent, some hypothermic open-ocean swimming, two separate chases, and four hundred cases of high-quality booze being tossed overboard.

Big fines and the prospect of serious prison time may have forced bootleggers to run this kind of no-surrender gauntlet. But it must have been fantastic open-ocean sport, too. "You experience a thrill and fear at the same time," big-wave surfing pioneer Buzzy Trent wrote in 1965, in a passage that might apply equally to Prohibition bootleggers and Maverick's surfers. "You hear that crack and thunder, you feel the wet spray, [and] you just power through, hoping you won't get the ax. And then if you *do* make it, you get a wonderful feeling inside."

Jay Moriarity HAD A different feeling inside—

not so wonderful—as he lifted off the face of his giant wave, spread his arms, and hung like a marionette just ahead of the crest.

Ten minutes earlier, Moriarity had paddled without hesitation from the starboard side of *Lizzie-Lynn* to the Maverick's lineup, smiling and calling out "Hey" to three or four surfers. He offered a curious, irony-free greeting to Evan Slater, who'd returned from his awful wipeout just a few minutes earlier: "Evan! Fun out here, huh?"

Then another set lifted into view, prompting a few moments of lineup shuffling and repositioning, and by luck or design Moriarity was on the spot for the first wave. Nothing but reflex now as he spun his board and began paddling, eyes nearly shut against the wind, barely conscious of the shouts of nearby surfers—one voice yelled, "Go, Jay, go!" or "No, Jay, no!"; he later couldn't remember which—all of whom were freaking at the growing size of Moriarity's wave as he got to his feet.

Moriarity, thirty feet above the trough, levitated for a little more than a second. The wind then flipped his board back over the top of the wave, and the curl, distended and grossly thick, pitched forward and blotted Moriarity from view. For a half-beat the wave poured forward, untouched and unmarked. Then Moriarity's surfboard reappeared from the wave's back slope and was swiftly pulled forward "over the falls" into the growing thundercloud of whitewater—a bad sign. Moriarity's board was tethered to his ankle by a fifteen-foot, nearly half-inch-thick urethane leash, and the only way it could have been brought back into play was if Moriarity himself, deep and unseen inside the wave, had been dragged down into Maverick's aptly named Pit.

The wave was now a thirty-foot levee of whitewater, crowned by fifty feet of swirling mist and vapor. Below the surface, energy and mass burst downward, creating a field of vertical-flushing gyratory columns, and Moriarity, trapped inside one of these columns, spun end over end until his back and shoulders were fixed against the ocean floor. He clenched, and a bubble of oxygen rushed past his teeth. Maverick's was a deepwater break, he'd been told; nobody ever hit bottom. The next wave would be overhead in another ten or twelve seconds, and Moriarity wondered if, from this depth, he could get to the surface—to air—before it arrived. A two-wave hold-down put a surfer one big step closer to drowning, and Moriarity had used this grim fact to inspire his training, but never had he imagined himself pinned to the rocks like an entomological display, trying to figure out if the overhead Neptunian rumble was from the diminishing first wave or the oncoming second.

He at least had his bearings. The trip down was disorienting, the water now dark, but Moriarity didn't have to pause to figure out which way to swim. Navigation is often a problem during a big-wave wipeout. Underwater flips and turns can disable a surfer's internal compass to the point where he might begin swimming for the surface only to bang head-first into the reef.

Moriarity pushed off and took a huge, sweeping breaststroke. He opened his eyes to near-opaque blackness. Four more strokes, five, legs in a flutter kick, exhaling slowly, eyes staring upward, stroke, the light becoming a diffuse gray-green, stroke, throat clamped shut, then one last thrust to break the surface—and he threw his head back, mouth stretched open. He'd been down for just over twenty seconds, but he'd beat the second wave—barely. Two quick breaths, and he hunched over defensively as the whitewater roared over, sending him on another underwater loop, shorter but just as violent. Pinpoints of light were zipping across his field of vision by the time he resurfaced.

Moriarity's breath was deep and ragged. There was no third wave. His respiratory rate eased, and as his eyes refocused, he saw that his surfboard was broken in half: the smaller piece—the tail section—was still attached to his leash; the rest floated nearby. Evan Slater suddenly appeared, looking concerned. Did he need any help? Moriarity shook his head. No, he'd be okay. He swam over to the front half of his surfboard, hoisted himself on deck, and began slowly paddling back to *Lizzie-Lynn*.

In the LATE EIGHTIES, a surf magazine writer theorized that the essential requirement for big-wave riding is not courage, or daring, or fitness, but a nonarousable imagination. Where an ordinary surfer taking full measure of a wave like Maverick's will lose himself in one of a near-endless number of death-by-misadventure scenarios, the big-wave surfer, fantasy-free, paddles out with some degree of aplomb. And as the untroubled imagination reduces fear and anxiety beforehand, it may also smooth things out afterward. Jay Moriarity, a week later, couldn't do much more than sketch out in the most obvious terms the big-wave vignette—generally described as the worst wipeout, or at least the worst *looking* wipeout, in surfing history—that soon appeared on the cover of *Surfer* and the front section of the *New York Times Magazine*. "I started to stand up," he told *Surfer*, "and thought, 'This will be a cool wave.' Then the whole thing ledged out and I had time to think, 'Oh, shit. This is not good.'"

But maybe that's unfair. Moriarity's banal reaction may have had less to do with a deficient imagination than with the general inarticulateness of sixteen-year-olds. Or perhaps he was just following the form of big-wave protocol that says, play it down, play it *cool*.

Either way, there was nothing banal about what Moriarity did for an encore that morning. After tossing the pieces of his broken board onto the deck of *Lizzie-Lynn*, he took a short breather, grabbed his reserve board, ran a bar of sticky wax across the top for traction, and paddled back into the lineup.

Forty-five minutes later he caught another wave, nearly as big as the first one, and made it. In the next five hours he caught eight more waves—and made them all.

HOT CURLS AND BLUEBIRDS

big-wave surfing
circa 1900–1956

Big-wave riding as a distinct branch of the

sport of surfing—with its own science and design, its own ethos and code and self-awareness, its own written and photographic record—didn't take shape until after World War II. Before that, bigger waves were looked at and admired, usually from a safe distance, with a few surfers paddling out to the watery fringes and riding as best they could. By the time *Surfer* magazine was founded in 1960, however, big-wave riding had been virtually cordoned off from the rest of the sport. As presented, it was nothing like the fun and rambunctious form of surfing performed at Malibu, or in the near-shore waves at Waikiki; it was serious and daring and noble, and big-wave surfers were compared to bullfighters and astronauts.

About 250 years ago, *he'e nalu*—"wave sliding" on wooden surfboards—was the ecumenical sport of Hawaii, practiced by children and adults, males and females, royalty and commoners. Surfing chants and stories were passed on for centuries, and the sport often served as a pretext for wagering and a prelude to sex. Crusading Calvinist missionaries stationed in Polynesia during the nineteenth century then nagged, shamed, and legislated the sport to near extinction. "If they have amusement or pleasure, they conceal them," American historian Henry Adams wrote of native Hawaiians in 1891. "Neither dance nor game have I seen or heard of; nor surfing, swimming, nor anything but the stupid, mechanical hymn singing."

In the early decades of the twentieth century, Olympic swimming champion Duke Kahanamoku from Honolulu—also a graceful surfer and generous surf instructor—became the sport's great revivalist. He founded a series of surf colonies in California, New Jersey, New York, Australia, and New Zealand. When Kahanamoku's own enthusiasm for surfing flagged in the thirties, it was bigger waves that revived him. California pioneer surfer Tom Blake (the first person to ride Malibu, in 1926) made long visits to Hawaii, often surfing with Kahanamoku, and in Blake's 1935 book *Hawaiian Surfboard* he describes Kahanamoku taking a new sixteen-foot, 126-pound board out for a test run in some "bluebirds"—the rare, big, deepwater waves that once or twice a summer hump up across a graduated series of reefs off of Waikiki. Kahanamoku's first ride, Blake writes, "went to his head like wine. He yelled and shouted at the top of his voice as he rode in. He was happy. It put new life into him."

18

Kahanamoku and Blake and a few others were no doubt attracted to larger surf, but in 1935 there were few distinctions among types of surfers, and accounts of big-wave riding in *Hawaiian Surfboard* fit naturally alongside those of tandem surfing, canoe surfing, and paddleboard racing. More than anything else during the Kahanamoku/Blake era, it was the thick, heavy, torpid wooden surfboards that kept riders on the beach when the waves came up. Surfers in the thirties could use either a solid "plank" board or a "cigar-box" hollow board. The planks were about ten feet long, four inches thick, and templated more or less like an ironing board—square at the bottom, with gently flared rails moving up to a rounded nose. Some were made of laminated redwood and balsa, or redwood and pine, but most were solid redwood and weighed between fifty and seventy pounds, with oversize models topping one hundred pounds. The cigar-box—constructed usually of rib-supported balsa or plywood, dowels, waterproof glue, and varnish—was longer, lighter, and more streamlined. Plank and cigar-box boards were both finless and lumbering, and virtually uncontrollable in waves over six feet. Even in smaller surf the idea usually was to chart a straight and undeviating course to shore, which explains why the original high-performance repertoire included headstands, chest- and bicep-flexing poses, and tandem riding, all of which were performed while riding on a plumb line to the sand.

Because the plank was nominally easier to manage than the overly buoyant cigar-box, it was preferred by most of the good Waikiki surfers. From this group of plank-riders, somewhere between a dozen and two dozen were interested in riding the larger waves—six- or eight-footers—at places like Castle, First Break Canoes, Cunha Break, and Browns, all located within sight of Diamond Head on Oahu. From this antecedent big-wave group, just four or five riders wanted to push out to even bigger surf. To do so, they'd have to build new boards.

John Kelly, Wally Froiseth, and Fran Heath, all of them teenage Hawaiian *haoles* (whites) who liked to angle across the wave instead of riding straight off like the older surfers, paddled out together at Browns one summer morning in 1937. The surf was running high, and their wide-tailed planks, as usual, were "sliding ass"—meaning the tail section would fall out of its diagonal-cutting line and swing around, like the skidding rear end of a car. Slide ass and you either lost your board and made a long retrieving swim (leashes wouldn't be in use for another thirty-five years), or you went prone, gripped the sides of the board, and bounced inelegantly shoreward until the wave fizzled out.

At Browns, all morning, wave after wave, it was one slide ass casualty after another. Kelly, Froiseth, and Heath paddled to the shore, disgusted, and walked to Kelly's house at nearby Black Point, where Kelly took Heath's board and set it atop two sawhorses. Then he laid out a small pine-handled ax, a drawknife, some sandpaper, and a can of varnish. Kelly had an idea: reduce the tail area and the board might cleave better to the wave face. How big a reduction, though, he had no idea.

Big-wave surfing's nativity moment was as sharp and rough as Kelly arcing his wrist around and burying the ax into one side of Heath's board, near the tail. Then the same thing to the opposite side. After a few more digs with the ax, Kelly picked up the drawknife and began shearing out two symmetrical parabolic curves along the aft rails, until the back end, originally fourteen inches wide, was down to five inches. Kelly also sculpted a longitudinal V-shaped area down the rear hull, which he hoped would add even more wave-holding traction. By two o'clock that afternoon, with the newly applied varnish sticky beneath his feet, Kelly was back out at Browns leaning into his first wave on the redesigned board and feeling it bite the face—just as planned. One day in the water a few weeks later, after several of the boards had been made, distributed, and raved over, and surfers were riding at sharper angles than ever before, Froiseth shouted out, "Hey! These things really get you into the hot curl!" Everyone agreed, and everyone liked Froiseth's jazzy phrase, too, so from that point on the new narrow-tail, V-hulled boards were called hot curls.

Summer and early fall produce the biggest and best waves for the south-facing Waikiki and Diamond Head reefs, while the north and west sides of Oahu come up from late fall to spring. The hot curl surfers knew they were living on an island of boundless good surf, but since they didn't often go wanting for waves of one size or another in their little Elysian corner, they didn't often stray from Honolulu. Only a few breaks outside of Waikiki/Diamond Head had been identified and named. Other islands in the Hawaiian chain might as well have been in outer space.

The new boards, though, inspired a new sense of adventure. One autumn afternoon, just a few months after the

invention of the hot curl, Kelly, Froiseth, and a few others loaded up Kelly's Model T and set out to the arid and barely inhabited west side for an overnight surf reconnaissance/fishing trip. No boards this time. Thirty-five miles northwest of Honolulu they pulled over near a sandy hook of coastline, just in front of the towering lava-ribbed walls of Makaha Valley. The ocean stretched away from shore like a blanket, completely still. After exploring the rocky point to the north, they walked back, set out lobster nets, ate a brown-bag dinner, and went to sleep on the beach. At 3 A.M., as Kelly recalls, they woke to a "huge roaring sound." Everybody stood and stared out to the point, now wreathed in pale white lines of surf. Someone pointed out that the lobster nets were probably getting mangled, but the concern was lost. The hot curlers had just discovered Makaha, the new big-wave El Dorado.

It was Makaha, in fact, more than any particular surfer, or group of surfers, or new board design, that inspired a dedicated approach to big-wave surfing. Ten-foot-and-under surf at Makaha wasn't much different from the soft, rolling surf at Waikiki. But Point Surf Makaha, as Kelly, Froiseth, and the rest soon discovered, was another matter entirely. Here was a wave big, strong, and fast enough to push the surfers and their new boards to the limit and beyond. Point Surf, located another seventy-five yards past the everyday Makaha surf line, starts to break at ten or twelve feet, but doesn't really open up until fifteen feet or bigger—which usually happens just four or five times a year. Maybe three times a decade the Makaha surf hits a glorious and terrible twenty-foot-plus, each wave moving down from Kaena Point, folding over in vast sections like buildings collapsing one after another, until it reaches the transformative underwater topography of Makaha and gets spun into a long and tapered blue-green wall. The curl arcs down at the top of the point and spirals evenly for two hundred yards, finishing in a deepwater channel.

No flat spots. No direction changes. Easy to catch, but once in, it's a blood oath; the wave goes from fast to faster, steep to steeper, inescapable, then pours into the concluding Bowl section, where it suddenly flares up and out like a cobra hood before folding in on itself. Most riders at Point Surf Makaha, even today, are derailed in the Bowl section—often with violent, underwater, lung-testing results. Big-wave icon Greg Noll—who remembers staring out to sea during the mid-sixties and raging to the unknown, "Come on, goddamnit! Give me something I can't ride!"—says that huge Point Surf left him in a state of wide-eyed humility. "It doesn't get that big that often," Noll says today. "But, man, when it does it's really something. I remember being out there on a huge day and just going into a mental freeze-up. A haze settled over my brain, like I was in a dream. No place put the fear of God in me like big Makaha."

Not long after Makaha and hot curl surfboards rearranged the tiny but spirited domain of big-wave surfing, World War II rearranged nearly everything else. John Kelly, decorated Boatswain Mate First Class, Navy Reserve, spent the first two weeks after Pearl Harbor trawling above the sunken boats and pulling corpses out of the water, occasionally loading a Japanese pilot and a U.S. Navy sailor side by side into the same wooden storage box. The experience affected him profoundly, and after the war Kelly became a unionist, a peace activist, and a Communist Party member.

Surfing, though, remained a constant in Kelly's life, and in the postwar years he and Wally Froiseth (who would become the Pearl Harbor fire chief) and a few others developed a rudimentary big-wave circuit on Oahu, with Browns and Makaha as the two primary breaks. Hot curl design was improved, mostly through subtle changes to the hull and by trimming the weight down. Original hot curler Fran Heath left the big-wave fold to work for his father's insurance company and raise a family, but new faces began appearing in the lineup when the surf was up, including Russ Takaki, Woody Brown (a pacifist and conscientious objector who spent the war years peddling a single-speed bike around Oahu), and west-sider Henry Lum. Then, in the midforties, a wiry, dark-eyed, semitruant teenager named George Downing joined the group.

Downing was a paddleboard racer, as were most surfers of the time, and he made local headlines in 1949 when he beat Waikiki's reigning paddleboard champion, an older pug-shaped man known as Big Jimmy, in the annual Fourth of July sprint from the Outrigger Canoe Club to the Waikiki Surf Club and Tavern. When Big Jimmy complained that Downing took the race only because he had the faster board, the seventeen-year-old swapped boards for an instant rematch and won again.

Wally Froiseth was Downing's guardian and mentor and helped him shape his first hot curl board in 1945. Big-wave surfing then opened up to Downing like a new and uncharted branch of science—something to be researched, studied, and practiced. When the swell was up he timed the interval between waves, the number of waves in a set, and the minutes between sets of waves. He noted carefully the rate of swell-size increase and decrease over a given period. When the ocean was calm he snorkeled over the reefs to investigate their wave-shaping profiles. He reviewed weather maps, watched ocean currents and wind patterns, and learned everything about big-wave surfboard design, theory, and construction. Over time, as the gathered information began to combine and cross-reference, Downing would regularly turn up on the best waves on the best days. It was nothing more nor less than self-directed study and diligence—but Downing began to meld with the ocean in such a way as to earn a reputation as a kind of surf-world mystic.

In 1948, Downing, Froiseth, and Russ Takaki visited Malibu—already established as California's great crucible of waves, surfers, and board designers—and Downing spent a lot of time comparing his redwood hot curl to the new Malibu balsa model, which had a fuller silhouette, a scooped-out prow, and a rear-anchored stabilizing fin, or "skeg." California board makers—including Matt Kivlin, Bob Simmons, and Joe Quigg—were also using some new aerospace-developed construction materials, and were now covering their boards in a thin protective shell of resin-saturated fiberglass. The Hawaiians were still finishing their boards in varnish.

Downing recognized that some of the California templates, and probably all of the new building materials, would have application in big-wave board design and construction. But he also knew the Malibu balsa boards themselves wouldn't cut it back at Makaha. "Sliding ass" had become a surf lingo anachronism, but that's just what these wide-hipped West Coast boards were going to do in any kind of serious surf. Then again, the hot curl design had limitations as well—it was all but unidirectional in bigger waves, the idea being to set a sharp angle across the face and go like hell—and some big-wave surfers, Downing and Woody Brown in particular, were now looking for a board that would run up and down the wave at Makaha in a larger-writ version of what the California guys were doing at Malibu. The hot curl, moreover, while a huge improvement over the old plank board, had never offered anything like infallible tracking and bite. The finless tail section could drop from its track and "side-slip" (a stem-to-stern drop down the face; a variation of sliding ass), and it did so more often as the surf got bigger.

When Downing returned to Hawaii, he got together with Brown and talked further about big-wave board design. Matt Kivlin and Joe Quigg, back in California, did the same thing. Quigg had, in fact,

already built and ridden (at home and in Hawaii) a gorgeous, streamlined, all-balsa, finned "speed board" for big surf—but it hadn't caught on. Kivlin then made a similar board, also with a fin. So did Brown. But it was Downing, in 1951, who produced what would soon be regarded, fairly or not, as the first post–hot curl big-wave surfboard. Downing's board was ten feet long, just over twenty inches wide, and weighed forty pounds; it was shaped from a laminated balsa-redwood "blank" and wrapped in fiberglass, like the Malibu boards. A blunt fin, about the size of a croquet wicket, slightly raked back, was slotted

above
California surfers Les Williams and Buzzy Trent, Makaha, 1952.

left
California surfers at Makaha in 1953, including Flippy Hoffman (center, in white pants), Buzzy Trent (second from right), and Walter Hoffman (far right).

far left
George Downing (in white shorts) shows off his new big-wave "elephant gun" to Walter Hoffman (center) and Buzzy Trent, Makaha, 1952.

into the tail section. The fin had more sur-face area than those used on the Malibu boards, and according to Brown, who was there when Downing test rode the new board, the fin made all the difference. "He came back in," Brown remembers, "and said, 'Hey, Woody, it's much better with a skeg.' I asked, 'How is it bet-ter?' He said, 'Well, it's not any faster, but it's more solid and you can turn it real easy.'"

By "solid" Downing meant there was no side-slipping. That was the important thing. Just as the hot curl provided traction in eight- or ten-foot surf, Downing's new board would hold fast in surf fifteen feet or bigger. Thus equipped, he was now ready to paddle out at Point Surf Makaha and steal his way up the big-wave ziggu-rat—not quite unrivaled, but nearly so.

Downing was riding the same

board in late 1953 when Honolulu photographer Skip Tsuzuki drove to the west side one afternoon and took a shot of Downing, Brown, and a California surfer named Buzzy Trent riding in loose formation on a sparkling fifteen-footer at Makaha. The Associated Press bought Tsuzuki's shot and put it on the wire. Newspapers across the nation picked it up over the next few days, and big-wave surfing was put on public display for the first time.

If, by 1953, surfing remained an obscure little recreational subspecies, it was nonetheless identifiable to nearly all Americans. *Life, National Geographic, Collier's, Popular Science,* and *Popular Mechanics* had all by then done fea-ture articles on the sport. Big waves were often described within these stories—usually as "tow-ering billows" or "rolling mountains of water"—but none of the accompanying photographs ever showed a rider on anything over six feet high.

As such, Skip Tsuzuki's widely published image of a fifteen-footer at Makaha caused a mild sen-sation among the public at large—and it was a

life-changing siren's call to some of mainland America's five thousand or so surfers. Fred Van Dyke, a twenty-two-year-old Santa Cruz schoolteacher, and a regular among the shivering, blue-lipped surfers at Steamer Lane, was having lunch in the faculty lounge when his superin-tendent handed over a copy of the local paper featuring Tsu-zuki's shot. "And that was it," Van Dyke says, remembering his first look at Makaha. "I quit my job and headed for Hawaii." So did a dozen more thrill-seeking Cali-fornia surfers, who would in the years ahead be collectively known and revered as the "big-wave pioneers."

This sunburned group was, in a sense, cutting back against the surf culture's general drift. After World War II, south-ern California had in many ways replaced Hawaii as the world's surfing capital. West Coast board builders had left their garages for rented beach-community store-fronts and invented a cottage industry. Retail prices were high (sixty-five dollars for a new ten-foot Hobie balsa in 1954), but the boards were better designed and built than those from Hawaii. California surfers were better, too—or at least they were doing snappier turns and riding closer to the curl.

Southern California was in fact monopolizing the merging forces of surf industry and entertainment, and the entire

right
Nineteen-year-old Dewey Weber, the original Malibu hot dogger, takes on Point Surf Makaha, 1958.

sport was being remade to an image more teenage-suburban than Polynesian. California surfers in the midfifties not only outnumbered Hawaiian surfers by about three to one, they were living at youth culture Ground Zero. In 1956, just after Hollywood's opening fusillade of teen-rebel movies *(The Wild One, Blackboard Jungle, Rebel Without a Cause, Rock Around the Clock)*, a Viennese-educated scholar named Fredrick Kohner mailed off the finished manuscript of his first novel, cryptically titled *Gidget.* By 1962, with the Beach Boys and Dick Dale both topping the charts in California, the iconic-surfer mantle had already been lifted from the broad, dark-complexioned shoulders of Duke Kahanamoku, riding in stately fashion toward shore at Waikiki, and laid upon the grinning and habitually obnoxious "bushy-bushy blonde" Malibu hot dogger. California surfers appropriated Hawaiian surf culture as needed. They had summer luaus, painted tiki heads on their boards, strummed ukuleles, and wore palm-frond hats. But when Bel-Air's own Jan and Dean harmonized in falsetto about "Surf City" and its incredible promise of "two swingin' honeys for every guy," the setting, although never named, was West Coast all the way.

This all happened despite the fact that Hawaii had the bigger, stronger, bluer, warmer waves. Surf traffic flowed steadily up and down California's Pacific Coast Highway, but it was West Coasters only circulating between California and Hawaii. Surfers from Hawaii had little or no interest in trying the California waves. When George Downing, Wally Froiseth, and Russ Takaki turned up at Malibu, it was a rarity of the highest sort.

While 1953 has long been noted as the beginning of big-wave surfing's California-to-Hawaii pioneer movement, a few mainlanders had actually been doing reconnaissance work on Oahu's beaches for years.

In the summer of 1948, Walter Hoffman sailed into Honolulu after a five-day cabin-class trip on the SS *Lureline,* a Matson Line steamer. Hoffman, a heavy-set, good-natured Malibu surfer, had just graduated from Hollywood High. He'd met George Downing earlier that year on the beach at Malibu, and a few hours after Hoffman's arrival in Hawaii, Downing had him out in some thumping ten-footers off Diamond Head. Hoffman soon returned to the mainland, but Navy enlistment brought him back in 1951, and that winter he became the first Californian to regularly surf Makaha, driving from Pearl Harbor to the west side three or four times a week. "I'd heard about Makaha," he recalls, "and then I got there and found out, man, the place got really big." Hoffman mailed a roll of 8-mm film to his older brother, Flippy, and Buzzy Trent, both Malibu surfers, to show the guys back home what the Makaha surf was like. "We went wild," Trent said later, describing the moment they saw the big Hawaiian surf for the first time. "We started screaming and slapping each other on the back. We ran that two hundred feet of film backward and forward for what seemed like a thousand times." Trent moved to Hawaii immediately and permanently. Flippy arrived for his first visit one year later, along with another half dozen California surfers, all friends and acquaintances.

The visitors pooled their money and took out month-to-month leases during the summer on ramshackle houses just a few blocks from Waikiki beach for thirty-five dollars a month. Beginning in the fall of 1952, Trent, the Hoffman brothers, and the rest of the California surfers also began driving to the west side and staying for days, weeks, even months at a time at Makaha—first in makeshift wood-and-canvas shelters, then in tents, then in rented frame houses and army-built Quonset huts. Walter Hoffman's pine-walled bungalow, located a few hundred yards up Makaha Valley and not far from a watermelon field, became a kind of West Coast expatriate headquarters, where shirtless dungaree-wearing surfers could patch their boards, drink beer, eat peanut butter sandwiches, and doze through the midafternoon heat.

A few weeks after Skip Tsuzuki's AP-distributed Makaha photo prompted another dozen mainland surfers to cast off for Hawaii, a features editor for the *Honolulu Star-Bulletin* learned about the Makaha surfer encampment and its growing roster of college-age suburbanites. It sounded interesting and eccentric and gently subversive, and a reporter was quickly dispatched to the west side. The article ran on January 7, 1954, and it began:

A small band of Californians have found Makaha. They are content to go without the usual luxuries of modern day living, just so they can surf there. Three Californians arrived about ten days ago to join a hardy band of some fifteen ascetics living in a shack about two blocks from the surf. The new arrivals have taken a cottage across the street—for about ten dollars a month each—and have scattered swim fins, spears and surfboards around their new house—the kitchen being a Coleman stove.

In a sense, a kind of default political stance was being taken. The visiting surfers, by dedicating themselves to big waves, were also dedicating themselves—some for a few months, others for good—to a pleasurable, passionate, nonproductive, nonmonied existence. As a group, they were aggressively apolitical. They didn't vote (or at least not with any kind of group predictability), agitate, expound, or crusade. They rode waves, and in most cases did so with numbing single-mindedness. But they were nonetheless aligned opposite the forces of postwar American convention and protocol just as surely (if less self-consciously) as were Jack Kerouac, Jackson Pollock, and Elvis Presley. The Makaha surfers lived anonymously and virtually unnoticed compared to the famous society-changing painters, writers, and rock-and-rollers. But to look at the snapshots of the crew lined up in front of Walter Hoffman's shack—with their grinning faces, everyone stripped to the waist amid the clutter of balsa surfboards, wine jugs, and peanut butter jars—is to see a happier and more contented band of revolutionaries.

Some surfers, to be sure, were happier than others. "I spent three months at Makaha, and it was awful," Flippy Hoffman remembers

overleaf
Unidentified surfer, Point Surf Makaha, 1959.

of the winter of 1952–53. "I was sick. I had boils and carbuncles all over. Dysentery—we were all really fucked up because we were living in tents, camping out on the beach the whole time. I had to get out."

Boredom was a more common affliction. Even during the winter season at Makaha there are long periods, days or even weeks at a time, where the surf murmurs in at a sedate two or three feet, or goes flat altogether. Wave forecasting in the pre–weather satellite era was about as sophisticated as "Red skies at night, sailor's delight/Red skies at morning, sailors take warning." Surfboards were often burned in big-wave sacrificial rites, which produced nothing more than a toxic column of black smoke. Spearfishing and skin-diving took up some time on these hot, slow days, and Buffalo Keaulana and a few other local surfers would often arrive to hang out with the visiting *haoles*. They might lounge on the beach for hours phlegmatically working their way through several cases of Primo beer, then head for Waikiki at night, just forty-five minutes away. Buzzy Trent alone worked to stay in shape: running, skipping rope, and shadow boxing.

Makaha wasn't the only place on the island with big surf, however. The waves on the north side—just a few miles away, on the far side of Kaena Point—were bigger, maybe twice the size of Makaha on average. After two or three flat days at Makaha, someone would invariably offer a speculative remark about trying one of the surf breaks on the north side—like Sunset Beach—but the response was usually mixed. Walter Hoffman, Wally Froiseth, and a few others, even before the war, had explored the area and ridden some good waves. Other surfers, though, had come back rattled and spooked, and the whole area, as late as 1957, was, as one Makaha surfer recalls, "the big taboo land."

As a result, only a few surfers ventured to the north side from 1953 to 1956. And, of course, when the big winter swells finally lumbered down past Kaena Point, the north side was forgotten altogether, as Makaha then met and exceeded the needs of the entire big-wave community. By the mid-fifties, the sport's evolution could be charted from swell to swell. Big-wave riders were all using elongated Downing-style boards, and long, carefully executed turns were sometimes carved into the big, sloping Makaha faces. Walter Hoffman and Buzzy Trent, furthermore, were able to match Downing foot-for-foot on those days when the big surf chased nearly everybody else back to the beach.

Downing's big-wave knowledge and panache, though, remained of another, higher order. This was never more apparent than on January 12 and 13, 1958, when Point Surf Makaha hit twenty-five feet— larger, more immaculate, and better-formed than anything Downing had seen in more than ten years of big-wave riding. He and Trent and a few others shot themselves like arrows across the blue-sapphire walls, contrails peeling back from the tail sections of their boards like exhaust. Most waves were too fast to make from the point all the way through the Bowl section, and as riders were absorbed into the huge blossoms of whitewater, their missile-shaped boards whirled and spun toward shore like twigs.

Downing caught and completed more waves than anybody. And this has a lot to do with why he's often regarded as the original big-wave surfer, and why his 1951-built balsa-and-redwood ten-footer is often regarded as the original modern-era big-wave surfboard. California designer Joe Quigg may have been the first to make a finned big-wave board, but he never threw himself and his equipment into the Makaha crucible—or at least not the way Downing did. Quigg has quietly defended the primacy of his big-wave board design. In the midnineties he sketched out some of his early surfboard ideas on a sheet of graph paper and wrote "firsts" in the lower left corner, next to a handwritten note: "George Downing hadn't built any boards yet." But Quigg doesn't hesitate in naming the prototypical big-wave surfer. "Downing," he said in 1994, "pioneered the riding of really big, nasty waves."

By the late fifties, things were only getting bigger and nastier. Near the end of the wondrous two-day run of surf at Makaha in January 1958, Downing was trapped under a big breaking wave, and his sinuses ruptured from the sudden change in pressure. Blood poured from his nose as he surfaced.

And that was fine. Big-wave surfing had entered its grinning, bare-knuckled adolescence. Beauty, joy, comrade-ship, even self-knowledge could still be found in riding and preparing for the heavy surf, but size and danger had become the things that really mattered. By the late fifties, big-wave disciples were viewing their sport in nothing but the hairiest terms. The big-wave surfboard was now called a "rhino-chaser" or "gun," which was short for "elephant gun." As steely-eyed Buzzy Trent famously put it, "You can't shoot elephants"—ride big waves—"with a BB rifle. You need an elephant gun."

The developing machismo was an obvious, maybe even necessary, psyche-up tool for the nerve-stretching challenge of riding huge waves, and sometimes it made for great theater. Trent would later pose for a magazine ad, coolly surveying his new big-wave board, bare-chested, jaw set, muscles like foothills across his chest and arms, with a one-word all-caps inspirational message taped to the wall behind him: "GUTS."

It was all thrilling and exciting and deeply self-involved; not quite disrespectful of the past, but not much interested in it either. The new big-wave burliness, in fact, would almost completely obscure the sport's rather gentlemanly opening phase—when avowed pacifists led the charge, wooden boards were coated Stradivarius-like in varnish, and surfers rode hot curls, billows, and bluebirds.

h₃ o₃ (heavy water)

december 20 1994

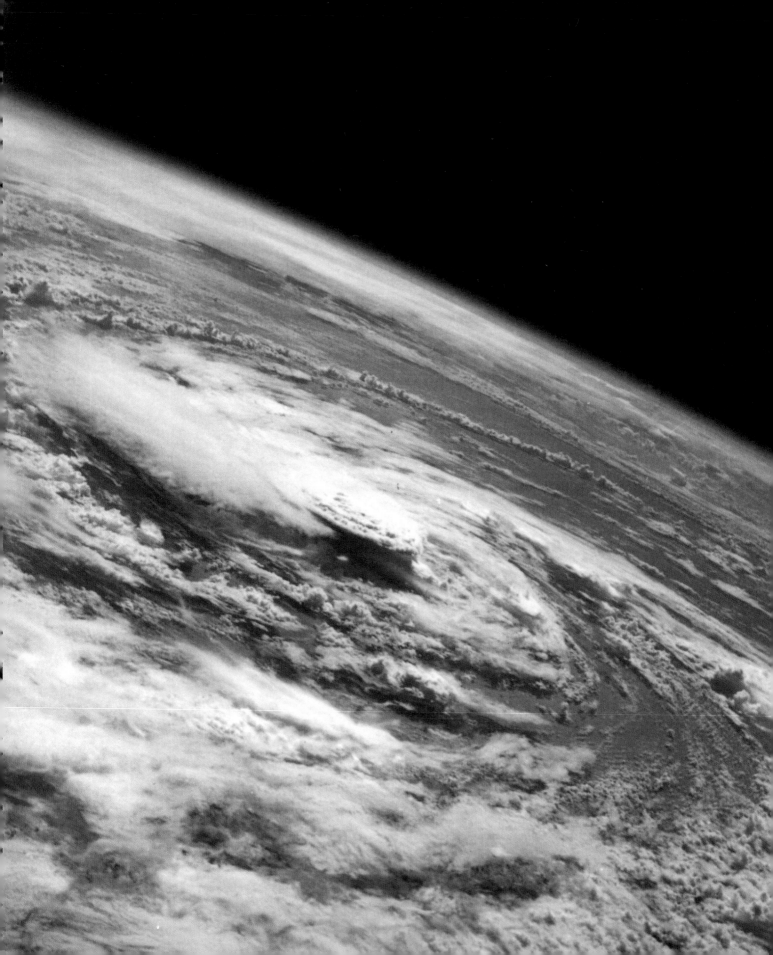

good

big WAVES ARE HARD TO COME BY. Worldwide, only about two dozen charted locations produce well-shaped fifteen-foot-plus surf with any kind of regularity. Weeks and months pass without a single over-size wave rising up in either hemisphere, and when an open-ocean storm of appropriate mass, vigor, and duration does broadcast a heavy sea, the resulting good surf might last for just a few hours. Or it might be huge and inspired at one break and wind-chopped, badly angled, or otherwise misfiring at another.

All by way of emphasizing that Tuesday, December 20, 1994, while abbreviated by the upcoming winter solstice, was a day of rare Pacific Ocean big-wave riches.

On the Hawaiian island of Maui, at a break called Jaws, Pete Cabrinha manned the WaveRunner jet ski and towed Dave Kalama into a thirty-foot colossus of a wave, then did it again, and again, before the two surfers traded places and Kalama guided Cabrinha into a similar round of giant swells.

On the North Shore of Oahu, Ken Bradshaw and Mark Foo rode eighteen-footers by themselves at Outside Alligator Rock, an "outer-reef" break that had only recently been surfed. Foo often talked about how obscenely crowded the North Shore's Waimea Bay, the center of the big-wave universe for the last thirty years, had become, and he knew fresh big-wave thrills could be found among Hawaii's distantly positioned outer reefs—each one a conduit to what Foo liked to call "the unridden realm." Bradshaw felt the same way, and in fact had been scouting the outer reef waves, and riding them on occasion, for almost ten years. While both surfers had hoped the current winter season would bring twenty-five-foot, even thirty-five-foot, swells to the outer reefs, they happily accepted the sun-sparkled eighteen-foot surf at Outside Alligator Rock on its own merits.

Meanwhile, twenty-six hundred miles to the northeast, Hawaiian surfer Brock Little was gliding through a lustrous afternoon of twenty-footers at Todos Santos island, in northern Baja California. Little, like Bradshaw and Foo, was a full-time professional surfer, and well traveled because of it. Even as he was enjoying Todos Santos, Little had it in mind that, if the surf held for another day, he'd go straight from a meeting with his sponsor in Costa Mesa, California (his seventy-thousand-dollar annual salary from Gotcha sportswear was up for renewal), to San Francisco and then Half Moon Bay—to see about this new break called Maverick's. By doing so, he could write himself into a big-wave surfing historical footnote as the first person to make a two-for-one West Coast big-wave run. Three years earlier, Little and Foo had pursued a swell across the Pacific from Hawaii to Todos Santos. Nobody had yet gone straight from Todos to Maverick's.

Not that it was any big deal. It would be fun, though, and Little, unlike nearly all of his solemn-voiced peers, took a lighter view of the sport—particularly the business aspect, as he made clear in a 1991 *Interview* magazine profile.

> *INTERVIEW:* How come you won't tell people how much money you get from your sponsors?
> *LITTLE:* It's unfair, how much I get. It's way more than other guys who ride big waves get, and I feel sort of guilty about it. It's not right. I shouldn't get so much.
> *INTERVIEW:* Do you ever think about how unusual your life must seem to the average person?
> *LITTLE:* Oh, yeah. It's comedy, what I do for a living. People ask me what I do for a living, and I do *nothing.* I pick up a check in the mail and go surfing. And when the waves aren't up in Hawaii, somebody pays me to surf somewhere else.
> *INTERVIEW:* Is riding big waves a kind of spiritual quest?
> *LITTLE:* Nah, nothing like that. It's just the funnest thing ever.

And it really did look like the funnest thing ever on this exquisite late-autumn afternoon at Todos Santos, with Little gliding like a pelican across one bottle-green twenty-footer after another. On Gotcha's dime, too.

At Maverick's, SAN FRANCISCO surfers Grant

Washburn and Evan Slater arrived just after daybreak, hoping to be first in the water. They changed into wetsuits and waxed their boards, then jogged onto a gently winding, scrub-scented, half-mile dirt trail, passing along the way the border of a salt marsh wetland preserve and the mudflat-covered northwest edge of Pillar Point harbor—where four hundred small commercial and recreational boats were quietly and safely moored behind the breakwater—until they arrived at the thin, barren, rock-studded strip of beach in front of Maverick's. The beach adjoined the Pillar Point headland's western face: a seventy-five-foot cliff that angled down along its southern edge into a small alluvial fan next to where Slater and Washburn now stood. An eight-foot-high chain-link fence ran along the plateau ridge. Two hundred yards back from the fence was the sprawling and foreboding Pillar Point Air Force Tracking Station, the great engineering eyesore of Half Moon Bay. Hangar-size military buildings, windowless, clustered at the center of the headland's broad crown, where three tracking dishes were positioned at various skyward-facing angles—the biggest a real Cold War brute, eighty-five feet in diameter and raised 135 feet above ground. The

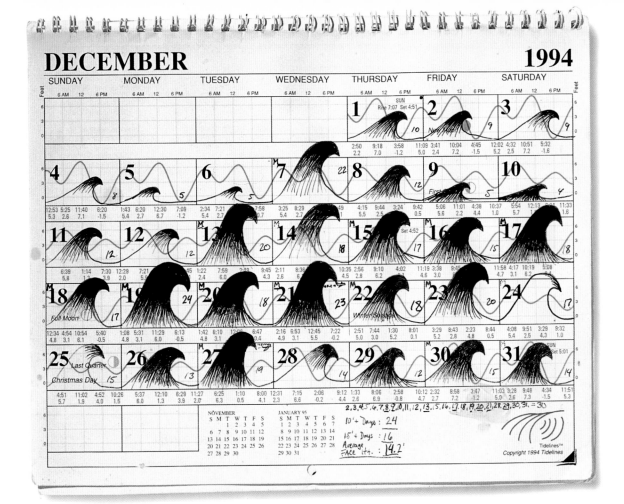

Grant Washburn's annotated December 1994 calendar.

dishes, once of military strategic import, were now idle for the most part, used occasionally to follow the progress of test missiles shot from Vandenburg Air Force Base, north of Santa Barbara.

    Slater and Washburn climbed up the headland's rutted dirt shoulder for an elevated look at the surf. Halfway to the fence they paused and stared through the wintry morning light at the Maverick's lineup, a half mile to the west. No action. Both surfers stood, waiting, watching, breathing audibly from the climb. The Pacific swell's bulging midsection had shifted down the coast to southern California and Baja, and across the ocean to Hawaii. Slater, disappointed, wondered aloud if maybe the surf had vanished completely. Then here it came, a two-wave set, twelve feet, maybe even fifteen, each wave becoming a small white banner over the distant reef, the noise floating through the air softly, like thunder from another county. Not giant surf, but smooth and refined. Washburn and Slater hustled back down to the beach, picked up their boards, and trotted three hundred yards along the base of the cliff to a launch point just north of the break. The air was brisk, but both surfers were warm, even sticky, in their wetsuits. As they pushed into the ocean, the cold water trickling past their nylon-stitched seams came as a relief.

    Fifteen minutes later they were in position. Slater opened with an unremarkable ride, and Washburn followed, then they were back in the lineup and

41

waiting out what felt like an interminable lull. To pass the time, they talked about yesterday's surf and when the next big swell might hit. Washburn was a devout weather-band radio listener, giving extra attention to the data-loaded buoy reports, and the new numbers, he told Slater, were good. High-grade, medium-big-to-massive waves had already been thumping into California's beaches for eight straight days—not for years had the coast been so inundated with surf—and two more heavily freighted wave trains were now rolling across the north Pacific. The first was due that night; the second on the twenty-third, two days before Christmas. Washburn and Slater both grimaced and shook their heads, pleased and worried about the repercussions of this freakish open-ended run of good big surf. Work, chores, family, girlfriends—the nonsurfing parts of their lives had already been relentlessly shuffled, stalled, finessed. And now the holidays . . .

Overnight, Maverick's had become the liveliest topic in Bay Area surfing circles. Filmmaker Steve Spaulding was describing the previous day's wind-whipped session at Maverick's as "total carnage," and his 16-mm film footage showed riders skipping and rolling down the huge spume-flecked walls like so many neoprene-wearing crash-test dummies. Jay Moriarity's dramatic air-to-surface wreck was in a class alone, but a dozen other wipeouts weren't far off the mark. Zack Wormhoudt from Santa Cruz came up coughing blood after a long hold-down. Two surfers taking off side-by-side were bucked off their boards simultaneously, about fifteen feet below the ledge, and hit the water locked together like wrestlers. Dozens of big waves were successfully ridden later in the morning and that afternoon, but early on it was, as Evan Slater phrased it, "countless horrendous wipeouts and primal screams."

But for all the gruesome moments—well cataloged in photos, film, and videotape and passed along surfer-to-surfer in lurid anecdotal form—nobody, save Wormhoudt, was injured. Washburn and Slater talked about this, too. Either Maverick's wasn't as dangerous as it looked, they figured, or a lot of people had been lucking out.

The Maverick's SURF SEASON generally

begins in October, peaks in December and January, and tails off in early spring. Off-season waves roll through on occasion, but almost never with winter-quality size and form. Members of a three-person Maverick's faction have—by installing themselves in the lineup even when the waves are storm-lashed, or barely trickling onto the reef, or otherwise not worth the effort—squeezed in as many as eighty days of Maverick's surfing per season. Most regulars, though, average about twenty days a year.

Understanding in detail the meteorological specifics behind any one of those twenty days is a complicated and often enigmatic business, involving tide measurements, open-ocean wave height, wind speed, current speed, isobar charts, atmospheric weather maps, tide charts, nonograms, wave trains, wave period, wave refraction, wave fetch, capillary waves, wave vectors, wave group velocity, and wave phase speed. The full climatic cast of characters ranges from the water molecule up to the cosmos-illuminating solar magnetic flare.

On the other hand, good big surf can also be understood as the result of a pretty simple two-part weather process: first, a large, distant, well-anchored open-ocean storm, and second, a benign—or at least nonstormy—near-shore climate.

Light local wind is a big-wave surfing prerequisite. Zero wind is best, although some surfers, mostly for aesthetic reasons, prefer a mild offshore (land to sea) breeze. Light onshore or sideshore winds are tolerable, but once they have any force at all—over, say, 10 knots—they create small hollows, bumps, and "chops" on the ocean surface; shooting across a wind-chopped big wave is roughly equivalent to skiing through moguls without turning. Probably ninth-tenths of the big waves that roll into Maverick's (and half those at Hawaii's Waimea Bay) are either compromised or made unridable due to poor wind. Local tides and tide-produced currents can also have a bad effect on wave quality.

Regional conditions, while important, are meaningless without those dynamic, turbinate, charted, named, tracked, and often celebrated ocean-spanning storms. Most surfers take a mildly perverse associative pride in these gnarly open-sea blows, since, for pure destructive power, they square up pretty well against earthquakes, volcanic eruptions, landslides, and twisters. Surfers, of course, benefit from the gnarliness. The deadly Atlantic Ocean nor'easter of October 1991, as described in Sebastian Junger's *The Perfect Storm*, gave Florida wave riders, as *Surfer* magazine cheerfully reported, "the biggest Halloween treat of their lives."

A storm big enough to produce waves at Maverick's begins as an atmospheric dimple in the North Pacific, which grows into a "low-pressure system"—the corkscrewing union between an arctic air mass and a warmer ocean-heated air mass. The maturing system is drawn along the malleable one-way, west-to-east atmospheric highway known as the jet stream. A storm that moves slowly along the jet stream will produce larger waves than a faster-moving storm of equal size and strength. Ripples are created by the initial friction between wind and water, and as wind speeds increase, the ripples merge into small waves, which combine and recombine into bigger waves. Counterclockwise winds along the perimeter of a North Pacific big-wave storm might hit up to 60 to 70 knots, and the wave-producing "front"—the side of the storm facing down toward Hawaii and California—might measure up to fifteen hundred miles. In satellite photos, these storms look like vast, soft, cottony Van Gogh swirls.

As energy-carrying swells detach from the storm front and radiate across the ocean, they begin to organize, refine, and separate themselves; this grooming process continues (barring a second, cross-hatching swell met on the way) until the resultant waves spill over whatever reef, point, or sandbar they're destined for. "Swell" usually refers to the aggregate and corrugated mass of waves produced by a single storm, but it can also mean an isolated oceangoing wave. A well-struck, unalloyed North Pacific storm should produce two days of Maverick's-size surf.

This is a nautical chart (NOAA-style) of the Pillar Point / Pillars Point Harbor area near Princeton and El Granada. Soundings and navigational features are marked throughout. Notable labels include:

Land / shore features:
- Seman Hbr (upper left)
- TOWER
- Princeton
- El Grana (El Granada)
- RADIO TELESCOPE
- RA TRS
- Pillar Point
- Dennison Cr.
- San Agustin
- Deep C

Harbor and navigation:
- *Pillars Point Harbor*
- Fl R 2.5s 17ft "2" Priv PA
- Fl G 2.5s 17ft "1" PA
- Fl 3s 17ft "A" Priv PA
- Fl R 6s 30ft 4M "6"
- COLREGS DEMARCATION LINE 80.1140 (see note A)
- Fl 5s 50ft 14M HORN
- LT OBSC
- G "1" Fl G 2.5s GONG
- G "3" Fl G 4s BELL
- R "2"
- Sail Rock (32)
- Outer breaker
- Rk 2
- Rks
- Kelp
- Breaks
- Bares 4 ft
- G Sh

Abbreviations on chart: rky, rks, hrd, gy S, S, M

(Numerous depth soundings in feet are printed across the chart, e.g. 22, 15, 7, 11, 32, 24, 48, 37, 27, 9, 55, 66, 46, 34, 43, 78, 72, 84, 90, 96, 98, 102, 108, 114, etc.)

Five separate storms contributed to the dramatic two-week run of big waves in mid-to-late December 1994, the storms overlapping and sometimes working in combination—although such distinctions were lost almost at once. Great swells are remembered not by source, but by duration and size.

Nearly all Maverick's-affecting storms can be staked out along a 40-degree, west-to-northwest arc—stretching more or less from Japan to the Alaskan mainland. Waves behave differently at Maverick's depending on their point of origin. "West swell" waves are shorter, steeper, and more dangerous; those from farther north are longer and easier to ride.

Big-wave surfers monitor swell direction and height, but they pay special attention to "interval," measured as the average number of seconds it takes for back-to-back open-ocean waves to pass a stationary point. Wave energy in "long-period" swells is mostly submerged and thus better preserved. If ten-foot open-ocean waves from the northwest are separated, for example, by a thirteen-second interval, the resultant Maverick's surf will be about fifteen feet. With a twenty-second interval, ten-foot waves will blow into Maverick's at twenty or twenty-five feet. This is why, in a 1998 interview, Grant Washburn talked about swell period, not swell height, when he said, "Some mornings I wake up and hear those twenty-second intervals booming in front of my house, and I lay there and think to myself, 'Why don't I like fly-fishing? Or sailing? Or something else—anything else.'"

A long-period big-wave swell, in one day, will travel about six hundred miles and lose about 25 percent of its height and energy. Shorter interval swells—produced from storms with a smaller or faster-moving front, or from storms originating at closer range—lose energy at a proportionally faster rate. Maverick's is a great big-wave break in part because it's far enough removed from the North Pacific storms to allow waves to smooth out and separate, but close enough to harvest the largest possible amount of the storm-system energy.

Maverick's is a great big-wave spot, too, because of its underwater topography. A northwest-facing underwater valley cuts into the sea floor, beginning about one and a half miles west of Pillar Point. An ocean wave will first pass through this energy-preserving canyon and then flare up along a submerged promontory about two hundred yards beyond the surf zone, expanding in size and portent as it moves across the reef like a balloon filling with air. Advancing at around 20 mph, the wave's peak rises to vertical, while its northern and southern flanks both taper down smoothly. Fringe appears along the crest—signifying that the wave is about to break—when the water depth between wave and reef is twenty to thirty feet, depending on tide and wave size. Because a wave will almost always break first from its tallest point, from high to low, the Maverick's curl drops from the summit, then winds off simultaneously to the south and the north—a vast organic smelting of precision and pandemonium.

Maverick's is by and large considered a "right"—meaning a surfer, after standing up, angles to his right. When the surf is running under twenty feet, riders also have the option of angling to the left—although these north-running waves are much shorter.

Outside the North Pacific, the essential components of big-wave production come together less often. Wave-generating storms move too fast, or peak at a lesser intensity, or the coastal reefs aren't angled properly, or the entire coastline (the Eastern Seaboard, for example) is fronted by a shoaling, wave-reducing underwater plateau. Big surf exists in other parts of the world, of course: Atlantic cyclones often produce fifteen-foot waves in Puerto Rico, storms from the Indian Ocean's infamous "Roaring Forties" send bruising surf out to Australia's west-facing beaches and up to Indonesia, and South Pacific weather systems tracking along the Humbolt current can send huge waves into Chile and Peru. But the North Pacific is the great big-wave mill. And while Maverick's doesn't turn out the *biggest* ridable surf in the North Pacific—Hawaii does—it has proven to be the world's most consistent producer of oversize waves.

Catchable oversize waves, that is. Required of any paddle-in big-wave break—tow-in breaks being another matter—is a relatively small and condensed takeoff area. Waves have to fold over, if not in the exact same spot, at least within an area that surfers can navigate by the relatively slow means of paddling. The lineup at Maverick's (the staging zone where surfers line themselves up with approaching waves) expands and contracts with tide, swell size, and swell direction, but an average day might find surfers plotted across a roughly rectangular area measuring twenty yards north to south and ten yards east to west. Smooth, ridable waves over twenty-five feet, rarely seen, break beyond the usual Maverick's lineup and along a wider north-south arc, and thus are all but impossible to paddle into.

Wave frequency ("surf beat" to oceanographers, "consistency" to surfers) at Maverick's can on occasion be relentless enough to bar surfers from the line-up altogether. It can also be low enough—with one or two breaking waves an hour, say—that surfers will paddle into position, languish for a time, and paddle back in without so much as moistening their hair. On an average day, sets of waves, each set consisting usually of two to five bigger-than-average waves, roll through every ten or fifteen minutes.

Few days at Maverick's, though, seem average. Flux and change are the break's defining characteristics, almost as much as great size and power. "You're dealing with a lot of elements, a lot of factors," says Jeff Clark, a Half Moon Bay native with twenty-five years' experience at Maverick's. "Some things are knowable, or at least predictable. But a lot of it is still kind of mysterious. Conditions change just like that. Some guys for sure have Maverick's more figured out than other guys, but nobody knows the place completely. Nobody ever will."

Maverick's SURFERS all have at least a working knowledge of midocean wind patterns, swell speed, barometric charts, and the rest of the ambient factors of big-wave production. Some are meteorological-data junkies. Others get by on just the cardinal numbers—buoy readings and tide charts—and intuition.

But if there's variance among Maverick's surfers' interest in big-wave science, there is also a group-wide fascination with the character and nature of the wave itself. The blasé Maverick's rider doesn't exist. Maverick's has been surfed for a relatively short time, and there remains a sense of pioneering discovery, which has only brought added emotional texture to an experience—big-wave surfing—that has never wanted for sentiment or feeling. This is why Mark Renneker's observation that riding Maverick's is "a real Nietzschean experience" plays in a curious sort of harmony with Darryl "Flea" Virostko's remark that surfacing from a Maverick's wipeout is "like trying to do a sit-up with a fat chick on my face." Both surfers were interviewed on the same afternoon after a day of twenty-foot, El Niño–inflated surf in January 1998. One surfer's description might be considered pretentious, and the other's patently crude, but in those aprés-surf hours, Renneker and Virostko were sharing the same rare state of mind—absolutely sure of what they were doing and of their place in the world. Each beamed with conviction as he spoke to the camera. Each, in his own way, wanted to channel a blood-deep passion for Maverick's into thought and language.

The basic Maverick's cartographic work was done in the late seventies and eighties by Jeff Clark. Surfers in the nineties then mapped out in finer detail the germane few acres of above- and below-water topography, meticulously describing the facets, moods, and quirks of the wave itself.

Everybody's attention, then as now, focuses on the Maverick's Bowl—the term for the wave at its crowning height and steepness, just before it breaks, where the curl gathers and begins throwing out into a cantilevered arc. The wave at this moment is shaped like a cupped hand, or a shallow-bottomed bowl on its side. Lesser Maverick's waves have a soft, virtually nonexistent Bowl section. Other waves are so inwardly flexed and bent with condensed power—totally unridable, more like a black hole than a breaking wave—that first-timers at Maverick's, upon seeing such a wave, have turned their boards around and paddled back to shore. Nearly all Maverick's action photographs show a surfer (or surfers) arranged in one of three classic positions in the Bowl: charging down the face in a controlled low-slung attack, paddling like mad up and over the apex (or having failed to paddle fast enough, abandoning ship and burrowing gopherlike toward the ocean floor), or wiping out. This is the meat of any Maverick's wave. A surfer can do no better than to pull one out from deep in the Bowl.

The Pit—as in pit of despair, gladiator pit, or pit of the stomach—describes either the looping Bowl-created tube section or the flat area adjacent to the base of the Bowl. The Cauldron is a ring-shaped vortex, twenty feet in diameter, that begins to seethe and bubble on the surface two or three seconds after the Bowl dumps into the Pit. "There's a large hole in the reef that causes this particular area to be extra nasty," Evan Slater wrote in a 1995 issue of *Surfing* magazine. "Water comes spurting out of the Cauldron and into the air, like a blowhole. It's a spot you want to avoid. After falling on a wave right over the area, I popped up from the initial wipeout, only to be sucked underwater three more times after the wave had passed."

Once past the opening Bowl section, the Maverick's wave either flattens out for good (slow spots correspond to deep areas in the split-leveled and wildly asymmetric reef) or it pauses for a few moments before tilting back up into another, smaller bowl-shaped section, sometimes identified as Train Wreck, but usually called Second Bowl. A third section—Third Bowl—sometimes follows. It takes a surfer eight seconds to go from takeoff, through the Pit, and into the channel side of the Bowl. A ride lasting all the way past Third Bowl, and on toward a minor navigational hazard known as Mushroom Rock, might last as long as fifty seconds and cover six hundred yards.

If Point Surf Makaha is big-wave surfing performed at full gallop, start to finish, Maverick's is a kind of steeplechase. Because fast waves are better than slow waves, Makaha by definition should be regarded as the better break. It *looks* better—polished and smooth-running. But there's something to be said for changes in rhythm. The terraced sections at Maverick's open up performance opportunities. Knowing the wave is about to soften up, a rider might pitch his bottom turn so as to gain a higher angle of ascension, then hook into a long opposite-rail turn along the cornice. Or in the flat spot itself, he might double back to the north for a few yards, then round off and steer into a Second Bowl tube-ride. Where the big-wave tension at Makaha is drawn out and sustained, at Maverick's it often comes in serial form, with as many as three tension/release episodes per ride. Maverick's, as the expression goes, rides better than it looks.

Maverick's has its badlands, too. A shallow area known as the Boneyard fans out from the Pit toward shore (sub-ten-foot waves pass unbroken through the lineup and unload over the Boneyard with sickening power), which in turn spills into an above-surface stand of rocks and rock-lined rapids—a jagged, triangular field about three hundred yards along its wave-facing west side. Mushroom Rock, to the south, forms the pointy tip of the triangle. Sail Rock, the biggest formation in the chain, is about thirty feet tall and sixty feet across; it marks the rock field's northernmost corner and rests at the centerpoint of an imaginary half-mile line between the Bowl and the shore.

About thirty seconds after a wave breaks at the Bowl, the whitewater leavings will surge over and around the rocks—with terrible pressure and force in some places. During a west swell, surfers caught on the shoreward side of a long set of waves can be transported from the Bowl into the jutting shoals of the rocks in less than ninety seconds. With or without a surfboard (surfers break leashes at Maverick's the way lead guitarists break strings), it's possible to maneuver into the calmer deepwater areas to the north and south and avoid the rocks. There are, furthermore, known safe routes through the rocks. Even without knowing these routes, surfers will more often than not be unceremoniously flushed past the rocks into the still-water lagoon, scratched and bruised but otherwise fine.

But not always. In 1998, Darryl Virostko tumbled into a roiled-water pass in the rocks, and his ankle leash caught on an outcropping and held fast. Six waves poured through, with Virostko literally and figuratively at the end of his

leash, underwater and struggling, unable to double over to unhook his Velcro ankle strap. Virostko would pop up for a few seconds between waves, buoylike, then disappear. "I'm dead," Virostko remembers thinking. "These waves are pushing me around so hard, pushing me against the bottom, and it's like, 'OK, fuck it. Just give up right now.'" After about two minutes of flailing, Virostko was able to reach down and undo the strap—at which point he was immediately sluiced to the lagoon. "Take the leash off before you get to the rocks," Virostko said later, in a rare moment of quiet. "You just never, ever want to get stuck like that."

On an overcast morning in 1993, Jeff Clark unhooked his leash as he was being washed through the rocks and instinctively pulled himself out of the water, climbing to the summit of a room-size crag just south of Sail Rock. Breathing heavily, he got to his feet, put his hands on his knees, and then quickly flattened down into the mussels and barnacles as the next wave washed over. Clark vanished under the spume, then reappeared, still prone. Again he was on his feet, head swiveling this time as he looked first to the lagoon, about twenty yards distant, and then for an exit route. Then back down just before the next wave hit. Clark was pinned for nearly an hour. There were pauses in the surf beat when he was able to take a few exploratory steps to the edges of his rock, but even then he couldn't see where to go in the surge and drain of the water below. Not until a friend climbed a nearby rock with a better view and gave the go-ahead did Clark jump clear and traverse through to the lagoon, crawling and swimming as required.

The experience BROUGHT WITH IT a kind of justification, as Clark had been saying for years that Maverick's was a heavy and dangerous surf break. Certainly it was his place to describe. By 1993, the first wave of Maverick's recruits were still trying to take in and accept the huge shaggy girth of the place. Not Clark. With his added fifteen years of experience, he viewed the interplay of waves, tide, current, and rock the way a med student views the mesh of skin, nerves, muscle, and bone.

If Clark already had something like a cubit-by-cubit understanding of Maverick's, his knowledge has only grown with the passing years. It wouldn't have been so obvious on that particular morning in 1993, with Clark pressing himself mollusklike into the rocks, but in 1998 he neatly expressed the idea that Maverick's domain extends not from the lagoon to the Bowl but from the lagoon all the way to the Aleutians.

"You turn around and paddle and catch the whole ocean," he said, coolly loading a few hundred thousand square nautical miles into the Maverick's lineup and making it sound like plain fact.

right
Jeff Clark, Maverick's, 1993: "Luckily, there were cracks that I could wedge my arms and knees into. I just held on for wave after wave."

BULL MARKET

big-wave surfing

1957–1969

"Someone asked me recently what I think of

the nickname 'The Bull,'" Greg Noll said in 1989 at his home in Crescent City, California. Brawny, thick-necked, and stubborn, he'd been known as the Bull for most of his life. "I told 'em, 'I don't know. Better than "Shithead," I guess.'"

Noll was and remains an outsize surfing character. In the late fifties, it was Noll, more than anybody else, who helped shift big-wave surfing from Makaha to Oahu's rugged and intimidating North Shore. He led the charge at the North Shore's then-unridden Waimea Bay, which became the break that defined big-wave surfing for more than three decades. He was also an entrepreneur and an industrialist: he opened a surf shop, published a surf magazine, and made surf films. "If I could have made a buck waxing guys' boards," Noll says, "I'd have done that, too."

Fitting perfectly inside his six-foot, two-inch, 230-pound frame, Noll embodied the rowdy, straight-talking, big-wave rider of the late fifties and sixties. He brawled spontaneously and often, drank hard, and joked harder. When Noll's friend and employee Ricky James sawed off his thumb while working at Noll's surfboard factory, Noll rushed him to the hospital. When the doctor said the thumb couldn't be reattached, Noll quietly asked for the graying digit, took it back

to the factory, dropped it into a Dixie cup full of clear resin, and turned it into a paperweight. Noll could be charming, civil, and politic, or he could be a gargoyle—whatever suited his mood. "There was a time," Noll says today, "where I had all the goddamned confidence in the world. I'd be getting my butt kicked good on a big wave, really whipped around underwater, like my arms were being torn out of their sockets, and I'd start giggling. 'Cause I just knew I was in control. For a few years there, I was invincible."

Noll was seventeen when he flew to Hawaii for the first time in the fall of 1954, living for seven months in a Quonset hut at Makaha and irregularly attending classes at nearby Waipahu High. He surfed for hours at a time, nearly every day, and didn't back down from many waves. He listened carefully to stories about the North Shore—how the surf there, particularly at a place called Sunset Beach, was bigger and wilder than anything on the west side—and in mid-December, Noll and three other visiting California surfers loaded their boards in Noll's decaying '37 Plymouth pickup and set out to discover the North Shore for themselves. They arrived at Sunset Beach, near the far end of the North Shore, an hour later. The waves were medium-size, about eight feet, but burly and hard-breaking. Noll and the others charged down the short, steeply canted beach, paddled out, and rode in complete solitude. Just four of them in the water—no one else was on the beach or even passing along the highway.

Noll quickly discovered that the seven-mile-long North Shore wasn't "the dark side of

previous page
Makaha International Championships contestants, midsixties.

left
Greg Noll waits for a lull at Pipeline on the North Shore of Oahu, Hawaii, in 1964.

57

the moon," as it had been described. Haleiwa, the North Shore's only town, had all the necessities—general store, bank, gas station, restaurants—which mostly served the local sugarcane and pineapple field workers. Houses were scattered along the entire Kam Highway from Haleiwa to Sunset and beyond, some with yards full of pigs and chickens and others owned by the Honolulu bourgeoisie as country retreats.

The North Shore, compared to Oahu's arid west side, was also lushly, almost luridly, tropical, full of sprawling, glossy-leafed trees, thickly perfumed flowers, and pyrotechnic sunsets. It had terraced, sun-warmed beaches and fields of sparkling ocean that were by turns navy and turquoise, teal and sapphire. Afternoon squalls often produced rainbows and double rainbows. Sea turtles made lazy submarine arcs beneath the waves.

If Greg Noll was initially scared of the North Shore, like everybody else, it was easy enough to see that it was a hothouse of well-formed waves. "We drove by all these places that weren't even named yet," Noll said in his 1989 autobiography, *Da Bull: Life Over the Edge*, "and I remember every couple of minutes someone would point out to some empty breaking wave and yell, 'Wow, look at that!' It was just such a beautiful day. We felt like we'd emerged into Shangri-La."

From certain angles, the North Shore looks the same today as it did to Noll and his friends in 1954. The surf, of course, is unchanged. "For size, power, consistency and variety," *Surfer* magazine wrote in 1989, "there just isn't anything in the surfing world that compares." *Surfer* identified forty-four distinct North Shore breaks, eight denoted as big-wave spots. "It is big-wave surfing's geographical and spiritual anchor. It is Mecca, and more."

By late 1957 resident and visiting surfers—double the number from two years earlier—were gathered in Oahu, ready to ride big waves. Kealoha Kaio, Joey Cabell, Sammy Lee, and Kimo Hollinger were some of the best young Hawaiians. Fred Van Dyke, Peter Cole, Jim Fisher, Warren Harlow, Pat Curren, and Jose Angel were standouts among the Californians. Makaha aces Buzzy Trent and George Downing were at the front of the pack, and Noll was somewhere in the middle, impatient and excitable—and always pushing.

The big-wave theater had split in two, with surfers now circulating between Makaha and the North Shore. Makaha was a glorious and variegated big-wave break—but it was just *one* break, and by 1957 it was known inside and out. The North Shore was expansive and cryptic, full of small, medium, and large surf, and it lay before big-wave riders like a half-solved puzzle. Of course, it wasn't Shangri-La. The northerly tradewinds often ruined the surf. Occasionally it went dead flat, like any other stretch of coast. Sometimes it was too big, and sometimes it rained so hard that you could barely keep your eyes open in the lineup. The North Shore was nearly as erratic as it was exciting—but it made Makaha seem tame.

Still, a few times each year, when the waves were big enough to shut Sunset Beach down—at about eighteen feet or bigger—everyone raced for Makaha, where it was sure to be somewhere between ten and twenty feet. Indeed, most surfers were relieved when Sunset overloaded because the Makaha waves would be smaller, smoother, and easier.

The run for the west side had begun on the morning of November 7, 1957. All the familiar North Shore breaks were washed out, and Mike Stange and Greg Noll were ready to drive to Makaha. Then Noll, at the wheel, suddenly downshifted onto the muddy shoulder at Waimea Bay and called for a quick surf check. Stange—hot for Makaha—frowned and swore, reluctantly following as Noll got out of the car. Two more cars pulled up, and they were joined by Pat Curren, Mickey Muñoz, Fred Van Dyke, Harry Church, and five or six others. The group came together almost magnetically, chattering and gesturing along the Kam Highway guardrail and watching the big, empty Waimea waves. Two or three times before, Noll had gone so far as to puff up and recommend a go-out—but no one had ever seconded, and the idea had always died without any real protest from Noll.

Waimea Bay, located in the middle of the North Shore, had already become big-wave surfing's main repository for fear and dread. This had to do,

in part, with its setting. The gouging Waimea valley, with its flinty black volcanic-rock cliffs, knifes through the tree-covered North Shore coastal terrace until the valley river spreads into a lagoon, which in turn gives way to Waimea's great U-shaped bay and its vast, softly curved beach. Noll and his friends, in their big-wave vigil, were miniaturized by the surroundings. In addition, one of the local houses was supposedly haunted, and the nearby St. Peter and Paul Catholic church, with its fifty-foot, square-sided, windowless campanile—easily the tallest structure on the North Shore—didn't quite saturate the bay in gothic gloom, but it introduced nonetheless a touch of apostolic severity.

But these were trifling concerns compared to the Brown-Cross legend, big-wave surfing's original true-life horror story, which had come to such an awful denouement right here at Waimea Bay.

On December 22, 1943, with a
majority of the country's surfers away at war, Woody Brown and Dickie Cross drove from Honolulu to the North Shore to try a recently mapped break called Sunset Beach. Others had ridden Sunset, but not many, about a half dozen, and none more than two or three times.

Cross was a seventeen-year-old high school senior. Brown, a pacifist and conscientious objector, was thirty-one. Fifteen years earlier Brown had dropped out of school and left the cocoon of his wealthy, Mayflower-descendant New York family. He had reinvented himself along the way but maintained a society-learned graciousness and civility, and here in Hawaii, he'd become the warmest of big-wave surfers.

Brown and Cross arrived at Sunset in the middle of the afternoon. The waves were big, maybe twelve feet, but smooth, with a safe deepwater channel adjacent to the surf. They

overleaf
Greg Noll (left) and unidentified surfers, Waimea Bay, Hawaii, 1966.

paddled out two hundred yards from shore and waited for something to ride. Then they paddled out farther to clear what seemed to be a bigger-than-average set of waves. Ten minutes later, the next set, bigger still, again forced them to reposition. Then another graduated set, and another adjustment, and they found themselves in the deepest section of the channel.

That morning, though Brown and Cross didn't know it, the surf had been dead flat. In the half hour since they'd paddled out, the twelve-foot waves had grown to eighteen feet, and the first twenty-footers were starting to hiss and spill into the channel. Neither surfer had seen or even heard of a swell coming up this fast. During a break between sets, Brown turned to Cross, gestured toward shore, and said, "Let's go." They wheeled their long wooden boards around and began paddling for the now-distant beach, but an outgoing riptide held them in place. The next set of waves forced them to turn around again and bolt for open sea—the idea of getting caught before a breaking wave and pushed underwater was terrifying for them both. Better to stay on the far side of the surf zone and wait for another lull. Out past the waves, though, Brown and Cross could see that there was no way they'd ever get through the completely impenetrable field of roiling water between them and the shore.

Breathing heavily from exertion and anxiety, Brown told Cross they should paddle three miles down the coast to Waimea Bay and come in through Waimea's much deeper channel. Cross nodded. Forty-five minutes later they arrived to find Waimea just as washed out as Sunset. Worse, the surf had grown. Sets were now thirty feet, or more, and Kam Highway near Sunset had already washed out. "It was the biggest surf they'd had in years," Brown recalled in 1996. "And I'm stuck out there. And this guy who's with me, a young kid, one of those guys— all guts and nothing upstairs."

Suddenly, Dickie Cross snapped and bolted for shore— and was predictably rolled under by a wave. He surfaced, but his board was gone. Brown moved to pick Cross up, then saw another, enormous group of waves slouching through. "So I turned around," Brown said, "and started paddling back out to sea for all I'm worth, because I figured if I lose my board, too, then what chance do we got? Two guys swimming, eh?" Still, the first wave caught Brown and stripped his board away. More waves followed, four or five altogether, and Brown dove thirty feet beneath each one. When the set ended, as Brown recalls, "I hollered and called and looked, swam around, and there was no more Dickie anywhere." Brown treaded water, rising slowly up and down on the backs of unbroken waves, suspended almost without effort in the salty amniotic warmth. The sun was setting behind Kaena Point. The beach was empty; the highway was empty. Nobody even knew they had gone surfing that day.

Exhausted and despairing, Brown's only option was to do what Cross had tried—swim for shore. He slipped off his trunks to reduce drag and began swimming. For a few minutes the ocean was calm, and when the inevitable set of waves arrived, the leading wave toppled over about two hundred yards out from Brown, and he received "a terrible

62

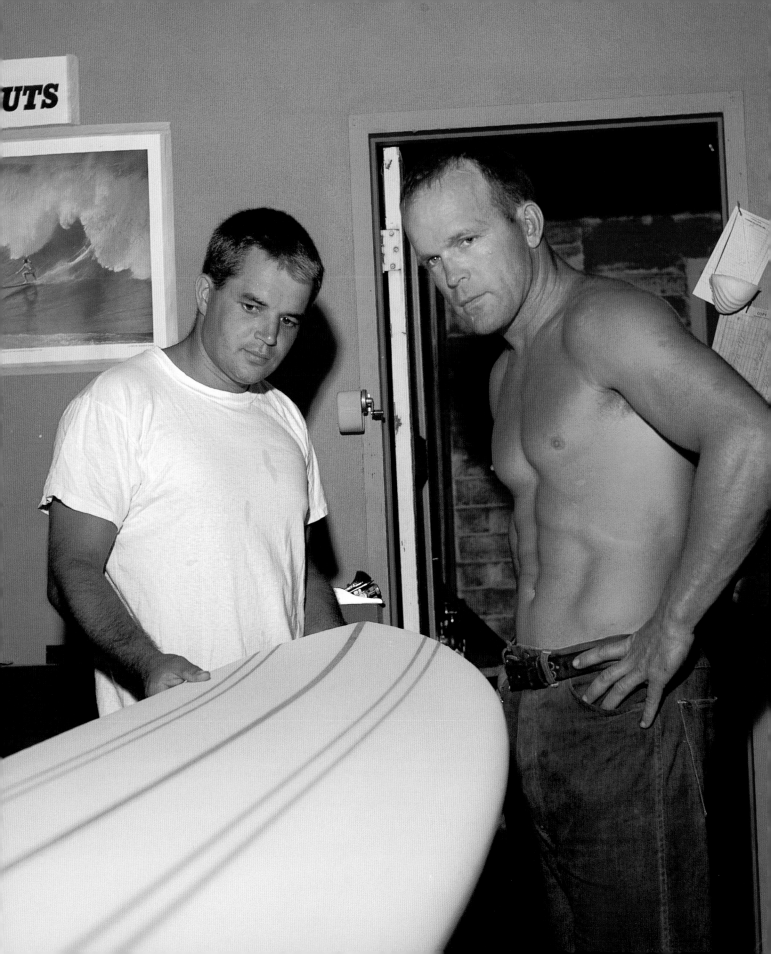

underwater beating; I didn't know what was up or down; black dots coming up in front of my eyes." Fighting to stay conscious, he surfaced, took a gasping breath, then ducked as the next wave rolled over.

Two minutes later, naked and barely sentient, Brown washed through the shorebreak. As it turned out, a group of soldiers from nearby Schoffield barracks had been watching. Three of them ran down and dragged Brown from the water.

Cross's body was never found. Brown eventually worked his way back into riding big waves at Makaha, but it took time. "After that thing with Dickie," he said, "I couldn't even go out at Waikiki in little two-footers."

Perched along the Kam Highway

guardrail, Greg Noll and the others leaned forward to watch as a three-wave set took shape just beyond the Waimea reef.

The first wave reared up, burst into a misting cumulus of whitewater, then quickly and obediently lost energy as it hit the deepwater channel. The second and third waves did exactly the same thing. Noll stood and bounced a few times on his toes. *Okay, good.* The takeoff area, he understood, would be easy to find and stick to. The wave itself looked pretty straightforward. Ten-second rides, not much more. Nothing like the long, shifting, hard-to-read peaks and walls at Sunset. From this distance, Noll thought the surf was probably twelve- to fifteen-feet. But thick, *massively* thick. The back slopes barely tapered off at all, and each curl dumped over as if it were coming through a floodgate. The water boiled and churned, and a gauzy saltwater haze hung over the surf zone.

Noll did a quick drum roll on his belly, turned, and walked to his car, saying, "Fuck, I'm paddling out." Mike Stange rolled his eyes and followed.

Twenty minutes later, the two surfers were floating on their boards, safe in the channel adjacent to the break, watching from close range. Another half dozen surfers soon followed, and everyone watched together. Then, as a group, a few yards at a time, they all cautiously moved into position.

An exquisite tension settled over the lineup: heads up and straining, eyes fixed seaward, shoulders and arms almost twitching with the desire to paddle somewhere, away, back to the beach. Then the taboo-breaking wave rolled in, expanding as it refracted off the Waimea reef, steep and deep blue—and here the story shifts abruptly from one of big-wave conquest to something close to big-wave burlesque.

Somebody rode that first wave.

Fred Van Dyke says it was Mickey Muñoz.

Muñoz says it was Harry Church.

Stange says Pat Curren and Greg Noll rode the first wave together.

Curren says it doesn't matter because they had lousy surfboards, and it was one wipeout after another, all morning long.

Noll says he rode the first wave alone.

Well, of *course* Noll would say that, friends and rivals alike pointed out later, because Noll was a bone-bred PR hound, and he knew that as the Waimea groundbreaker he'd sell a few more Greg Noll surfboards to the zinc-nosed kids back in Hermosa Beach.

So Waimea Bay has no Neil Armstrong moment. Then again, if nobody can say for sure who rode the first wave, everyone agrees that Noll was first on the scene, and that he was the instigator that morning. Noll moved while the others hesitated, and for that alone he deserves—and has been granted—first-wave credit.

Meanwhile, the first Waimea surfers were drawing a crowd. They were being filmed for a soon-to-be-released commercial movie, and cars were pulling over one after the other until both sides of the bay were lined with spectators—as Noll recalls, it was like surfing in an enormous open-air theater.

In fact, the big-wave show that opened at Waimea Bay on November 7, 1957, would run for more than thirty years without any real change. The sport revolved around the North Shore, the North Shore revolved around Waimea, and the newly introduced spores of big-wave business and entertainment would grow and divide, grow and divide.

As reported in the October 28, 1957, issue of *Life*, author Fredrick Kohner had just sold the *Gidget* movie rights to Columbia for fifty thousand dollars, plus 5 percent of the gross. The book itself was a best-seller—an underwhelming, even offensive, fact to most surfers. "If I had a couple of bucks to buy a book," said one *Life*-quoted Malibu local, "I wouldn't. I'd buy some beer."

For *three* bucks, however, a surfer could buy some beer and a one-dollar ticket to Bud Browne's new seventy-five-minute, all-action, no-plot movie *The Big Surf* (featuring Waimea's big-screen debut), which Browne barnstormed from San Diego to Santa Cruz in the summer of 1958. Greg Noll's *Search for Surf* also toured that summer, usually playing to the same rowdy audiences in the same Elks Lodges and junior high school auditoriums.

In 1960, John Severson, another surf-movie maker, published a thirty-six-page booklet titled *The Surfer* (soon shortened to just *Surfer*), while Noll produced *The Surfer's Annual*, and the pages of these prototype surf magazines were filled with black-and-white photos of big surf.

Surfing itself, meanwhile, was jumping viruslike from coast to coast, nation to nation. By the early sixties, Australia, New Zealand, the East Coast of the United States, England, Brazil, Peru, France, and South Africa were all supporting surfing colonies of one size or another. The expanding surf media (twelve films and six magazines in America in 1964) watched and reported on the sport's growth, but returned unerringly, even relentlessly, to the big waves on the North Shore. Big surf, in fact, was being oversold—too many photos, too much exposed film, and too many expository first-person articles. "It was an unusually restless night," Ron Church wrote in a 1964 article for *Surfer*. "Old man Waimea had awakened from an eight-month sleep. My little house trembled and quaked as the rampaging waves licked their watery fingers out, trying desperately to grasp it."

Such gallantry and drama played well with surf publishers and the entire surf industry, whose common goal in the early to midsixties was to present the sport as grown-up and responsible. It was a big, maybe impossible, job. Teenagers were rolling Panzer-like across America's cultural landscape. Concerned beachfront communities had for the most part kept out the bikers, but rock-and-roll was unstoppable, and now these *surfers*—hundreds of them, loud and coarse, bare-chested and peroxide blonde—seemed to turn up overnight. Surfers, *Time* magazine told its readers in 1963, were "fond of nudity and occasional ransacking of beach homes," and at night they could be found "throbbing to guitars at midnight twist parties." A few years later, when surfers began wearing the German Iron Cross as a fashion accessory, the media again portrayed the group as not just insensitive but slightly criminal. "We just don't have the feeling about this Nazi thing that our parents do," a Los Angeles teenage surfer told *Time*.

Real violence and mayhem on the beaches was rare, and surfing-related sex and drinking were probably just slightly higher than average, but it didn't matter. Some beach cities passed municipal ordinances prohibiting surfing between the hours of nine and five, and surf movies were occasionally banned. The surf industry was concerned. Personal freedoms were at stake. So was the sport's economic viability. The surf press launched a counteroffensive, scolding the bad element ("the ugly surfer" and the "surf hooligan" as identified in one *Surfer* editorial) and championing the vast majority ("the serious surfers; the real sportsmen") as good and upstanding young people.

The big-wave rider, better yet, was presented as good, upstanding, *and* heroic. Greg Noll, Buzzy Trent, Pat Curren, and the others were treated with great respect and reverence by the surf press and its audience. Hot doggers and world champions might be loved or loathed, like movie stars, depending on trend and fashion, but the big-wave coterie was surfing's own Marine Corps, whose tan-faced members were brave beyond measure, slightly and attractively crazy, and above criticism. "These men are in a league private unto themselves," surf journalist Leonard Brady wrote, prefacing a round-table exchange among big-wave surfers. "They are the purest wave riders, the elite. We have been privileged to collect and share with you their thoughts and feelings."

When Bruce Brown's surf film *The Endless Summer* made its magnificent and improbable jump from beach-city auditoriums to mainstream movie theaters in 1966, audiences across the country were given a full dose of big-wave drama. "A surfboard hurled with the force of one of these waves can cut you in half," Brown says in a voice-over during the Waimea sequence, as the music shifts to a minor key. "Watch how long his surfboard stays held down," Brown instructs a few minutes later, after Dick Brewer wipes out onscreen. "You'll finally see it pop up in the upper right-hand corner of your picture. Imagine what his *body's* been doing under there all that time!" Moviegoers searched for Brewer's board, cringing in their seats at the awful time-consuming wipeout—and didn't notice the film had been shot in slow motion.

Big-wave surfers themselves generally played along. They looked either brave and solemn or brave and rakish when posing for surfboard or surfwear ads. When interviewed, they compared the sport to mountain climbing, big-game hunting, skydiving, and auto racing. They attended award dinners. When Greg Noll was voted the top Big Wave Surfer in *Surfing Illustrated*'s 1965 readers' poll, he walked to the podium dressed in a beige crested blazer, charcoal worsted vest, and silk tie, humbly said a few words, and accepted his prizes—a clock-trophy, a matching trunks and windbreaker set, and a transistor radio.

Noll's skilled and relentless use of the surf media, in fact, allowed him to tower over his big-wave peers. He and Pat Curren both walked off the beach that first day at Waimea with a new sense of vocational calling, but where Curren set out to design and build the perfect big-wave surfboard (and more or less succeeded, giving himself a five-year run as Waimea's dominant surfer), Noll set out to design and build the perfect big-wave persona. His custom-made surf trunks with the wide horizontal black-and-white stripes were as recognizable to surfers as

Superman's cape. He was "the Bull" the way George Herman Ruth was "the Babe." He posed in print ads for surf companies, stunt-doubled in Columbia Picture's *Ride the Wild Surf*, and blanketed surfing magazines with ads for Greg Noll Surfboards—which produced up to two hundred boards a week in the midsixties. He wrote big-wave surfing articles, made plenty of guest appearances on Los Angeles' three surfing TV shows, and worked the aisles with back-slapping professionalism at the annual Surf-O-Rama trade show.

Whether image- and money-conscious surfers like Noll were honoring or degrading the sport was a lively topic even in the early sixties. The commercialization that buoyed Noll's career was anathema to Pat Curren, who quit Waimea and the North Shore for good in 1964.

"I hated the business aspect, too," Noll says today, in a voice that isn't entirely convincing. "But I wanted to surf all the time, you know, and early on I had this vision of making a living from surfing—and I decided to do it any way I could."

Noll was the star Waimea surfer in *The Endless Summer*, but big-wave characters of all kinds were turning up with some regularity in the entertainment world. In 1964's *Ride the Wild Surf*, Hollywood heartthrobs Fabian and Tab Hunter are high-spirited, all-American surfers who both come to see big-wave riding as incompatible with love and marriage, school and work. California surfer Michael Freesmith, the irredeemable lead character in Eugene Burdick's 1954 novel *The Ninth Wave*, quits surfing to become a corrupt and murderous California political power broker, then returns to the beach during a huge swell and dies a slow, horrible, and well-deserved underwater death.

Jonas Vandermeer, the second lead in James Houston's 1971 novel *A Native Son of*

overleaf
The surf press offered steady big-wave coverage in the early and midsixties.

SURF GUIDE
MAY/JUNE 1964 FIFTY CENTS
The Surf Enthusiast's Magazine

SURFER
A John Severson Production
VOL. 3 NO 2
75¢
MAY - JUNE
THE INTERNATIONAL SURFING MAGAZINE
PAUL GEBAUER • SUNSET BEACH HAWAII
IN THIS ISSUE
PERU • AUSTRALIA / MAUI • SOUTH BAY / SOUTH AFRICA • GIRLS / MURPHY • MALIBU / NEW CARTOON CONTEST

surfing MAGAZINE
SAND SHOES BEACH AUSTRALIA
THE BIG PICTURE OF INTERNATIONAL SURFING
SURFING FUNDAMENTALS: PART II

surfing MAGAZINE
SURFING MAGAZINE SPECIAL FEATURES
BUILD YOUR OWN SKIM-BOARD
SPECIAL INTERVIEW WITH TOP ISLAND SURFERS
AUSSIE ROUNDUP FROM DOWN UNDER
EXCITING FULL COLOR CENTERSPREAD
THE BIG SECRETS OF MAKAHA POINT
THE BIG PICTURE OF INTERNATIONAL SURFING

...FER
THE INTERNATIONAL SURFING MAGAZINE
JOHN SEVERSON PUBLICATIONS
VOLUME FIVE NUMBER TWO
APRIL-MAY
75 CENTS
...FING BEHIND BOATS • THE BIG SURF

THE SURFER QUARTERLY
A John Severson Production
75¢
VOL. 2, NO. 3 - FALL
IN THIS ISSUE:
- THE AUSTRALIAN SURF
- MURPHY and the SURFING CONTEST
- SOUTH SWELL PICTORIAL
- BIG SURF PREVIEW . . . Be Prepared

THE SURFER QUARTERLY
A John Severson Production
75¢
VOL. 2, NO. 1 - SPRING

surf guide
JANUARY 1965 / SIXTY CENTS
THE SURF ENTHUSIAST'S MONTHLY

CAMERA ON THE SURF/internation...
FIJI, SOUTH AFRICA, FRANCE, AUSTRALIA, HAWAII, EAST COAST - USA, CALIFORNIA AND NEW ZE...
The Unbeatable Blacks Pipelin...
RAPID SEQUENCE PHOTOGRAPHY FEATURING - RICK GRIGG, JOHN PECK AND MIKE H...

PETERSEN'S surfing MAGAZINE
MAY 1964 50¢
...TING FULL COLOR PINUPS!

SNOW SURFING TIPS • SURFING AT MALIBU, TRESTLES, TORRANCE, MANHATTAN, HAWAII • OVERSEAS BIG-WATER ROUNDUP • 8-PAGE SPECIAL: INTERNATIONAL SURFING CHAMPIONSHIPS

SURF GUIDE
AUGUST 1964 FIFTY CENTS
The Surf Enthusiast's Monthly
'WAY DOWN SOUTH:
Windansea Surf Club • Kemp
Aaberg: Mazatlan • Ron Church:
Little Point • John Peck: Trestles
Surfing on Sand • Sunset and Alamoana . . . . in France!!!
Rusty Miller

INTERNATIONAL SURFING
JUNE 1966 - 75 cents

SURFING AT IT'S BEST

INTERNATIONAL SURFING
OCTOBER 19.. 75 c...
TODOS SANTOS ISLE
BRITISH CONTEST
TOP YOUNG SURFERS

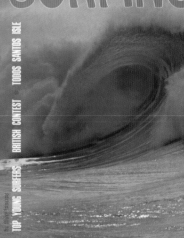

...FER
...our • September • 75 Cents

PETERSEN'S surfing MAGAZINE
JUNE 1964 • 50¢

PETERSEN'S surfing MAGAZINE
FEBRUARY 1964 • 50¢

surf guide magazine
The Surf Enthusiast's Bi-Monthly/March 1966 60cents
SURFING & SKIING the sliding game / BIGR...
TWENTY-FIVE=TWENTY by peter cole / HOLLYWOOD BY THE SEA IN COLOR / BODY SU...

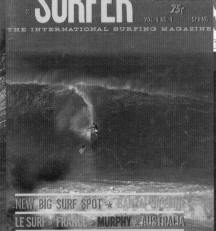

A John Severson Production
Vol. 3 No. 1 · 75¢ · SPRING

SURFER
THE INTERNATIONAL SURFING MAGAZINE

NEW BIG SURF SPOT ★ BANZAI PIPELINE
LE SURF ★ FRANCE ★ MURPHY ★ AUSTRALIA

SURFIN
TOP SURFERS REPORT ON HAWAII'S WIN

Results: International Championships
A Look At New Zealand
Australian Point Surf
Makaha's fantastic wipeouts

SURFER
THE INTERNATIONAL SURFING MAGAZINE

INSIDE WAIMEA BAY
WAR AT MALIBU
BIG WATER AT HUNTINGTON
THE MOST BEAUTIFUL
    SURF IN THE WORLD
BIG WAVE DANGER—A HOAX!

SI
SURFING ILLUSTRATED

SURF GUIDE
Vol. 1, No. 3
Published Monthly—August, 1963
50 cents

BUTCH VAN ARTSDALEN   "Mr. Pipeline"

SI
SURFING ILLUSTRATED

SURFER
JANUARY / 75 CENTS / 100 PAGES
THE INTERNATIONAL SURFING MAGAZINE

IN COLOR / EXPLOSIVE S
HEMMINGS–NEXT WINNER AT MAKAHA? / U.S. CHAMPIONSHIPS / EAST COAS

PETERSEN'S
surfing
MAGAZINE
DECEMBER 1963   50¢

Mike Doyle Reports: MAKAHA CONTEST '63
ington...Like Haleiwa! □ Makaha Point Surf by Buzzy Trent

SURF GUIDE
DECEMBER 1963 · No. 6
FIFTY CENTS

SURF GUIDE'S 1ST ANNUAL
ALL AMERICAN
SURFING TEAM

★ ★ ★ RICK GRIGG — MAN AND THE SEA ★ ★ ★

INTERNATIONAL
SURFING
FEBRUARY 1965
75 cents

SPECIAL REPORT: CALIFORNIA'S SOUTH BAY

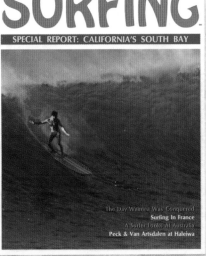

The Day Waimea Was Conquered
Surfing In France
A Surfer Looks At Australia
Peck & Van Artsdalen at Haleiwa

SI
SURFING ILLUSTRATED

SURF GUIDE
MARCH 1964   FIFTY CENTS
The Surf Enthusiast's Magazine

AN INTERVIEW WITH CORKY CARROLL
Mike Doyle—Australian World Surfing Championships

SURF GUIDE
SEPTEMBER 1964   FIFTY CENTS
The Surf Enthusiast's Monthly

SURFING/ILLUSTRATED
DECEMBER 1966 · SEVENTY-FIVE CENTS

INTERNATIONAL
SURFIN

FILMED
IN THE
WILD WATERS
OF HAWAII'S
WAIMEA
BAY!

RIDE
THE
WILD
SURF
IN COLOR

STARRING
FABIAN · SHELLEY FABARES · TAB HUNTER · BARBARA EDEN · PETER BROWN · ANTHONY HAYES · SUSAN HART
and JAMES MITCHUM as Eskimo · Written & Produced by JO and ART NAPOLEON · Directed by DON TAYLOR · A Jana Film Enterprises Picture
A COLUMBIA PICTURES Release

the Golden West, is big-wave surfing's best-drawn and most authentic character: unstable, self-absorbed, misogynistic, entertaining, flush with energy, and ambitionless except that he "wants to catch a bigger wave than any other man has ridden."

One day Vandermeer's friend Hopper Dunlap arrives in Honolulu. They meet in Vandermeer's dingy hotel room. Dunlap says he'd like to go surfing, and asks a favor.

"Can you get me a board?"

"Where's yours?"

"I sold it."

Jonas jumps up and stands over him, grimacing and blinking. "Jesus Christ, Hooper, why'd ya do that?"

"I needed the money."

Joe shouts, "That was a great board! A fantastic board!"

"I said I needed the money."

"What're you gonna do without a board?"

"Rent one, or borrow one, I guess."

"Shit, you can't rent a board. Soldiers rent boards. Summer coeds rent boards."

Joe paces, [then] slaps a fist into his palm and observes the action of his triceps in the long mirror on the closet door across the room. "I really feel good this morning. I feel like getting wet. You know how it feels after you take a good, quick, heavy dump?"

"Sure."

"Well, let's get going then. You can use my extra board."

Genuine big-wave surfers browsed these pop culture portrayals with mild interest or mild disaffection. None of it really caught their attention until Fred Van Dyke wrote a *Life* magazine cover story in 1968. The blurb beneath the Waimea cover shot signaled something different: "Peril of the Surf—a Veteran Surfer Asks: Are Surfers Really Sick?"

A breakout quote from Van Dyke, in large type on page forty-four, seemed to answer the question plainly enough: "Many [big-wave surfers] are escaping their jobs and families, many others are latent homosexuals."

Van Dyke, a big-wave vet with fourteen years' experience at Makaha, Sunset, and Waimea, explained himself carefully. Big-wave surfers weren't necessarily attracted to each other sexually, but emotionally they'd been stranded at a male-dominated preadolescent stage, "like 10-year-olds . . . like the kids down the street with the gang and the clubhouse." Big-wave riders were heroes in the small, confined world of surfing, Van Dyke said, but they were developmentally unqualified for any kind of mature relationship—particularly with women. Surfers themselves weren't so much at fault, he continued, as was an American culture that revered competition, celebrated violence, frowned on male sensitivity, and objectified women. Van Dyke tacitly blamed surfing, too, for its

JOHN SEVERSON PRESENTS
BIG WEDNESDAY!
1961 SURF MOVIE

FILMED IN **HAWAII · CALIFORNIA** and for the 1ST TIME **PERU** SOUTH AMERICA
· NARRATION BY JOHN SEVERSON ·

FIRST LOS ANGELES-SANTA MONICA SHOWING
SANTA MONICA
CIVIC AUDITORIUM
TUES. & THURS. 8 P.M. APRIL 25 & 27
TICKETS $1.50
TWO **FREE** DEWEY WEBER SURFBOARDS

addictive properties. "On a red-hot glassy day of surf, I don't care who stands in my way. I will surf. Responsibility, society—it can all get lost. The surf's up and that's where you'll find me." Van Dyke was almost forty, married, and teaching English at the best private school in Hawaii. But he wasn't too far removed from the big-wave clubhouse himself, and he knew it.

Van Dyke paid dearly for such psychologically nuanced thought. Most surfers went bug-eyed at "latent homosexual" and quit reading. Some of Van Dyke's big-wave colleagues screamed out "faggot" the first time Van Dyke went surfing after the *Life* article was published; one or two even kicked their boards at him as they rode by.

far left
Columbia's 1964 movie *Ride the Wild Surf* ends with a big-wave showdown at Waimea Bay between Fabian and James Mitchum.

left
John Severson's surf movie *Big Wednesday* toured California and Hawaii in 1961.

overleaf
1963 *Surfer* Reader Poll banquet. Honorees included several top big-wave riders. *Top row:* Joey Cabell (far left), Greg Noll (second from left), Ricky Grigg (third from left), and Mike Doyle (third from right); *bottom row:* Butch Van Artsdalen (far left), Mickey Muñoz (third from left), and Pat Curren (third from right). Later that evening, Noll says, "about thirty people got shoved into the swimming pool, wallets, suits, and everything."

Asked about his famous quote in 1992, Van Dyke simply broadened the indictment. "Status among your male friends—that was everything for us. There are still an awful lot of men, all ages, single and married, who can relate only to other men. Most *Monday Night Football* guys are like that."

Greg Noll woke before dawn on

the morning of December 4, 1969, with the breaking surf coming through his Haleiwa bedroom windows like white noise, and at first light he left for Waimea Bay. Rays of sun were just creeping over the edge of Waimea valley when Noll pulled over and watched a set of forty-foot close-out waves. It was the biggest surf he'd seen in fifteen years of wintering in Hawaii, and it was attached to the biggest *swell* he'd ever seen—now in its fourth day. Plainly this was a Makaha swell, but for half an hour, Noll remained transfixed, as he hadn't been for a long time, by the raw basal force of big surf.

This run of giant waves would come to be known as the Swell of the Century, or the Swell of '69, and it remains the standard against which all other big swells are compared. Surfers link '69 to enormous, destructive surf just as the rest of the country links war to '41, or financial ruin to '29. At 8:30 A.M. on December 1, the National Weather Service issued a high surf warning for the north and west shores of Hawaii. Twelve hundred North Shore residents were evacuated over the next five days. Sixty North Shore homes were destroyed or damaged, some completely lifted off their foundations. Boats were flushed from their berths at Haleiwa Harbor and deposited like bathtub toys on the inland side of Kam Highway.

Noll arrived at Makaha just after 10 A.M., and it was a revelation. The atmosphere was sunny, cloudless, and still, with a steamy mist hanging over the point. The biggest waves were twenty-five or thirty feet, and the outer edge of the surf zone was a quarter mile or more beyond its normal position—which had the peculiar side-effect of neutralizing the dreaded wave-ending Bowl section. Rather than being a comfort, the Bowl's absence only made things stranger. Noll lifted a pale-yellow, eleven-foot, four-inch gun from the back of the station wagon and felt sick to his stomach. The Makaha setting was so familiar, but the circumstances were so bizarre.

Big-wave pioneer Wally Froiseth was already in the water, along with 1968 world champion Fred Hemmings and five or six others. Fifty or so spectators were on the beach. The surf appeared to be getting incrementally bigger and more erratic. Many waves peeled off smoothly, but at least half were malformed to one degree or another, some dumping over in huge, scything fragments.

Noll paddled out and joined the tight-jawed cluster of surfers already in the water. One of them darted in and picked up a fifteen-footer, riding safely to the beach. Froiseth left also. The rest mostly sat and watched.

After forty-five minutes, Noll still hadn't taken a wave. He was used to setting a mood in the lineup, but the radiant tension and stress of the group was bothering him to no end. After one surfer wondered aloud if maybe they should signal for a helicopter rescue, Noll broke away and paddled farther out, well past the surf line, to get some time and space to himself.

Years later, Noll would say that he woke up that morning, December 4, 1969, "totally stoked on surfing, and totally stoked on the idea that I'd be doing just what I was doing for the rest of my life." As he pulled up about fifty yards beyond the other Makaha surfers, though, engrossed in the moment, Noll was in fact wrapped in concentric bands of doubt and worry. His girlfriend was with him in Hawaii, but his estranged wife and their two kids were in Southern California. Greg Noll Surfboards was failing. Noll, furthermore, at age thirty-two, after chasing and riding big waves for half his life, knew that he'd plateaued—that they'd *all* plateaued. Pat Curren and two or three others had ridden twenty-five-foot waves at Waimea in 1959, and Noll had soon followed, but nobody had gone much past that point in ten years. Thirty-footers seemed off-limits—too much water rushing from trough to crest. In addition, big waves were still being ridden the same way: charge down the face, angle, and draw a straight line for deep water. Big-wave performance limitations were all the more obvious following the 1967-launched "shortboard revolution," when boards for

small- and medium-size waves were chopped and streamlined, and surfers began doing sharp, radical turns and riding inside the tube. Pipeline, another famous North Shore break, had the biggest, widest tubes, and immediately became the focal point for the North Shore and the entire surfing world—just as Waimea had been a few years earlier.

Surfing in general, meanwhile, had been catapulted deeply into the late-sixties counterculture. The Waimea-free surf movie *Cosmic Children* was 1969's hot ticket. *Surfer* magazine hired *Zap* cartoonist R. Crumb to do a subscription ad, while *Surfing* published "A Vegetarian Surfer's Guide to Good Grazing." Two of Hawaii's hottest young surfers, both whippet-thin from macrobiotic dieting, spent their off-hours mastering yoga positions. Jug wine and beer weren't entirely out of fashion, but surfers looking to change their heads—as most surfers were—liked to get started with a lid of Sensimilla or a tab of Purple Owsley.

Greg Noll grew a wicked Fu Manchu mustache in 1969, but was otherwise the same rough-talking, Primo-drinking, cheeseburger-eating, big-wave leatherneck he'd always been—and nothing but bullheaded determination had kept him on the scene when the hurricane-force winds of change should have swept him away.

But it was the rest of the world that began to vanish, not Noll, during his half-hour retreat at Makaha. The last few surfers paddled or rode in, joining the three dozen people still watching. Now alone, Noll sculled back toward the line-up as a wave began to break more than a half mile up the coast, collapsing in huge slabbing divisions, each section curling over in indolent slow motion. That wave right there, Noll thought, would kill you. And with that, his invincibility was gone—for the first time, and for good.

Noll began to concentrate, realizing first that the *possibility* of drowning didn't make it a sure thing, then reminding himself that this was, in fact, where he'd always hoped to be—in line for the biggest wave. He'd been trying for it, and thinking about it, for more than ten years. Not *one* of the biggest. *The* biggest. And this was, almost certainly, his one chance. Makaha probably wouldn't get this big for another fifteen or twenty years.

"Then all of sudden," Noll says, recalling the moment, "it felt like I didn't even have a choice."

He had a plan of sorts. Any wave he selected was going to close out, or fold over in sections, without a tapering shoulder—all the waves by that point were shapeless. The huge Makaha surf, however, was still pitched to allow a surfer entry, and the idea was to get to the base of the wave in one piece, eject off the back of the board, then curl into a ball, sink, and try to avoid getting pulled back up the face and thrown over the falls.

And that's exactly how it went. Noll propelled himself off the cornice of a thirty-footer, locked into his brute, boxcar stance, made a long and slanting descent to the flats, then kicked his board away and vanished in a whitewater deluge. He corkscrewed into the depths and felt the pressure settling like bricks into his eardrums. All was violence—the noise, the rushing blackness in front of his now-opened eyes, and especially the bucking, gravity-free tumble. Twenty seconds after Noll hit the water, as the turbulence began to ease, just as the edges of his vision were going black, he surfaced and caught a breath. Then back down for the next wave. Three or four more waves passed in this way, then Noll churned out a one-hundred-yard crosscurrent swim to the beach, where he crawled up to dry sand, dug his hands into the ground, and lay there gasping.

Greg Noll, for one last time, vaulted to the top. His thirty-foot Makaha wave was, indeed, the biggest ever ridden. The *Honolulu Star-Bulletin* ran a six-column article on Noll's achievement, and the story was picked up by the wire services. *Surfer* and *Surfing* magazines ran Noll feature articles, and both magazines continued to revisit the story every few years. In 1996, Noll was asked to describe the ride for a TV documentary, and it's depicted on the back cover of Noll's 1989 autobiography in a serigraph painting by Ken Auster, with a miniature Noll racing along at the base of a gigantic, fringing wall of water.

Yet, at the center of this great, hugely conspicuous surf story there is a big, wonderful empty space. No photographs of the ride exist. Three or four photographers had been at Makaha, but after Noll paddled out past the surf and all the other riders came in, they put away their cameras and left.

Noll's great wave, then, was witnessed but not documented—much to the benefit of the big-wave canon. Surf photographs, even great ones, are static and fixed. Greg Noll's wild ride at Makaha, especially as described by Noll himself, has a life of its own; it's grown and flourished with time. The story serves Noll, of course. But Noll serves the story, too, and the entire sport, by fitting the ride itself into a real narrative, full of content, plot, subplot, and digression. "I remember sitting out there by myself," Noll says, "looking way up the point and seeing this tremendous goddamn wave rolling through, *barreling* through, and by the time it got down to near where I was sitting, the water on my board, the water drops, were just *dancing* there, just shaking and dancing around. Man, I'd never seen anything like that before."

Noll picked himself off

the sand, found his board, and drove from Makaha back to Haleiwa. That afternoon he sat in his room and decided not to go to a friend's party that night—an event he'd been looking forward to all week. The sound of breaking surf continued to filter through the house. "You can't top that," he remembers telling himself. "So now what?"

He quit surfing, liquidated Greg Noll Surfboards, lived in a motorhome in Alaska, then worked for twenty years as a commercial fisherman in Crescent City. Then when a wave of surf-nostalgia humped up in the early 1990s, Noll picked it up just as surely as he'd picked up his thirty-footer at Makaha, licensing his image and name to a new clothing line, making ten-thousand-dollar wooden surfboards for collectors, repackaging his old surf movies, and writing his autobiography.

Big-wave surfing itself, meanwhile, didn't follow Noll into the void in 1970, but it did enter a long period of quiescence—until 1984, when *Surfer* published an article titled "Whatever Happened to Big-Wave Riding?" and the genre began to revive.

As Noll could have predicted. As he more or less *did* predict, in mid-December 1969, just a few days after the Makaha wave, when responding to a *Surfing* interviewer who had both the gall and foresight to tell Noll, "Many people just don't give a damn about big-wave riding, and don't even consider it a valid test of contemporary, 'now' surfing."

Noll, neither angry nor defeated, said: "Everyone can get into the small-wave high-performance thing, whatever it may be at the time—hanging ten, exploding off the lip, smooth turning, whatever. But big-wave surfing is sort of like the final challenge. You feel close to small-wave surfing, and that's great. What's left, though, is a big, damn, terrorizing wave. People criticize big-wave riding now. But later on they may end up digging it."

They did end up digging it. And they were digging it at places Noll never would have imagined, and riding in ways he never would have dreamed of. By the mid-1990s, nothing in surfing was more valid or "now" than big-wave surfing.

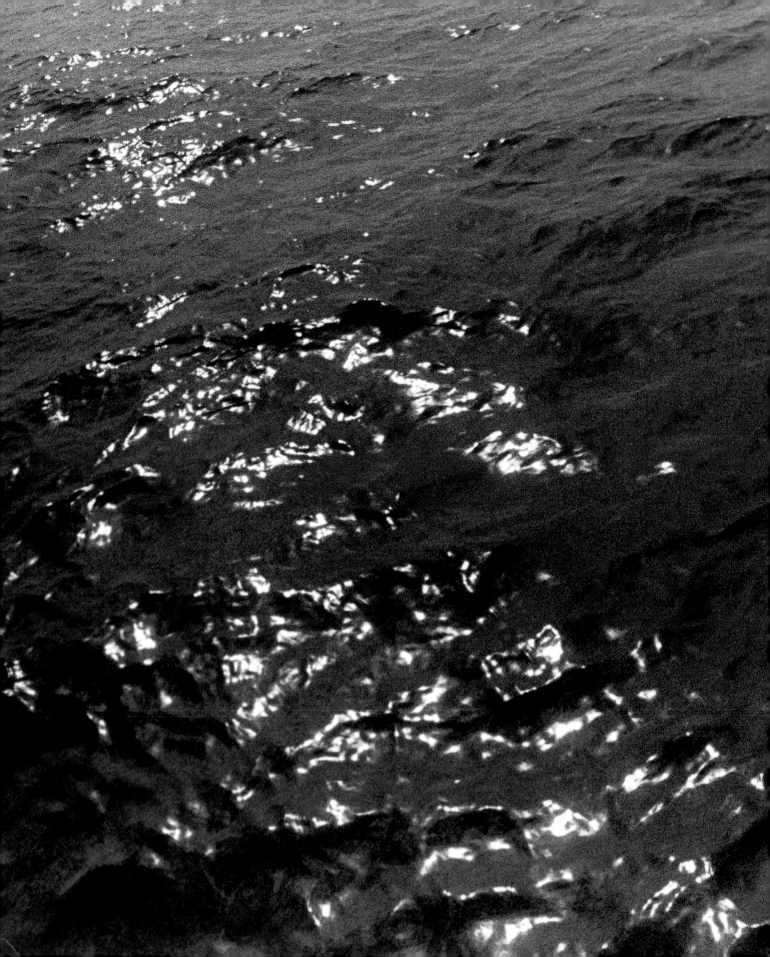

singular **achievement**

december 21 1994

5

grant

washburn OPENED the rusted front gate of his San Francisco beachfront apartment, guiding the key in by twilight, and entered his warm and unruly surfer's nest, a clutter of surfboards, wetsuits, leashes, and all manner of surf-related gear and paraphernalia spreading unmethodically across the garage and the vestibule, up the stairwell, into the two bedrooms, the bathroom, the living room, even the kitchen—where Washburn cleared some table space and began his daily surfing journal entry for December 21, 1994.

He printed "Big Wednesday" in block letters across the top of the page and followed with the day's buoy readings: a momentous fifteen feet at twenty-second intervals. "Unbelievable," Washburn wrote. "The ninth straight day of hugeness. Unparalleled, unprecedented, unreal." The surf was the same size as on Monday—twenty feet or more on some sets—but without the diabolically strong offshore wind. Also, the swell angle had shifted a few degrees north, adding some slope to the bottom half of the Bowl section. Some of the wipeouts, though, were "insane . . . brutal." Jay Moriarity, Washburn noted, did it again. "I witness him flying down the face of a BIG ONE; his first wave of the morning. Then he over-rotates and gets obliterated. Déjà vu—but not as gruesome as his wipeout two days ago."

Overall, though, the number of completed rides was higher than during "the Monday Massacre," as Washburn called it. Evan Slater flat out got the largest, thickest, heaviest wave of his life. Local boy Ion Banner looked sharp. Big-wave surfer Paul Moreno had flown over from Hawaii three days earlier to ride Maverick's for the first time and had adjusted well to the long, shifting waves and the 25-degree difference in water temperature. Peter Mel from Santa Cruz was the day's standout rider—faultless in his wave selection and charging across the big faces like a gazelle, loose, fast, and rangy. The entire Cruz contingent, in fact, lit it up: Darryl Virostko, Josh Loya, Moriarity, and the Wormhoudt brothers, Zack

right
Grant Washburn,
San Francisco, 1999.

and Jake. More photographers were perched on the cliff than Washburn had ever seen, and probably twenty surfers altogether rode between dawn and dusk.

Washburn ended his afternoon with a mildly masochistic flourish. "Here comes a fine one," he wrote, reliving the moment. "I'm late, but spin and go anyway: two strokes and up on my feet as the bottom drops out and I'm thrown into the Pit. A healthy wipeout, satisfying my need for a spill. I'd been feeling like a cheater after four sessions without any kind of serious fall."

Washburn, born and raised in Connecticut, learned to surf in the small and generally woeful breakers of central New Jersey. In 1990, at twenty-two, he moved to San Francisco to work as a carpenter, and threw himself into the powerful ebb and flow of Ocean Beach, quickly discovering an aptitude and enthusiasm for bigger waves. He first rode Maverick's in 1992, and his big-wave interest blossomed into a multidisciplinary devotion. When he wasn't surfing, he was filming other surfers, working on an outline for a Maverick's documentary, filing local oceanic data into his computer, or writing long passages in his surfing journal.

Midway through Washburn's five-page entry for December 21, he mentioned his friend and informal Maverick's mentor Jeff Clark, and his habitually effusive tone dropped to one of plain-spoken empathy. "Screwed royally once again," Washburn wrote of Clark, who'd knocked his fin loose on his first ride, forcing him to turn for shore. "Jeff just hasn't been able to get in a solid session these days."

Clark, thirty-eight, the original and dominant Maverick's surfer, was moonlighting as a Federal Express dock loader, and had been given a rotten December schedule—mostly night shifts. Also, a loose surfboard had ricocheted off his right ankle earlier in the month, and the joint was still painful and stiff. He was able to surf, but not with his usual drive and efficiency.

Washburn, earlier in the week, had even defended his friend's reputation to a Maverick's newcomer who, in passing, wondered aloud if maybe Clark had lost a step or two. "It felt weird having to vouch for him," Washburn noted in his journal. "I've caught more epic waves over the past few days than I can count, but I'm certain Jeff would have surpassed my efforts had he been feeling well. I've been hoping to help get him back into it."

Washburn did what he could that morning after Clark broke his fin, paddling over and exchanging surfboards, so that Clark might try again. An hour later, though, Clark was on the beach. He'd aced one wave, and snuffed it on another—and that was it. Better than nothing, but still below par.

Maverick's had for years been known as Clark's spot. It still was. It just wasn't his week.

Jeff Clark's CLAIM TO MAVERICK'S has nothing to do with the fact that he has registered the word "Maverick's" with the U.S. Department of Commerce Patent and Trademark Office, and everything to do with the dizzying notion that Clark rode this fearful and beautiful big-wave break *completely alone* for fifteen years.

In 1966, Clark's father, a San Mateo County deputy sheriff, built a house for his six-member family on an oceanfront lot in Miramar, just south of Pillar Point, that had a view of the waves off the headland, two miles distant. Jeff was nine years old. That summer he began surfing, and by junior high school, after having attached himself to an older, car-driving group of surfers, he had developed a near-encyclopedic knowledge of the breaks from Santa Cruz to San Francisco. Clark learned early that the freakish big-wave reef north of his house was called Maverick's, and that it was too gnarly to ride.

Clark was a devoted young surfer but not a great natural talent, even by the provincial standards of Half Moon Bay. He had guts, though. As a high school freshman, he was known as the kid who would paddle calmly into big waves and take his knocks like a prizefighter. Stoicism is an odd trait in a teenager, and while Clark had friends, he also made people a little nervous. "There weren't many people around here who wanted any part of big waves," he recalls in a drawling, bemused voice. "I'd go to the surfshops and say to guys there, 'Come on, let's go ride the biggest waves we can find.' But nobody wanted any part of it. So I was pushing guys past their threshold just on the beachbreaks and other [non-Maverick's] reefs around here." Clark set himself apart, too, as a seventies teenager with no interest in pot, whites, reds, or Quaaludes. "I wanted to surf. And that's pretty much all I wanted to do."

At age sixteen, he began watching Maverick's. During the winter he often surfed Ross's Cove, a break just north of Pillar Point, and when Ross's hit ten feet, he would sit on his board and cast a speculative eye toward the big, empty, shadowy peaks at Maverick's. Clark knew that kids his age in Hawaii were riding Waimea Bay and Sunset Beach; he thought he could do something like that right here, at Maverick's. It was almost as big as Waimea. Maybe as big. And just as well shaped, too. Nobody rode Maverick's, though, and Clark often wondered about that. When the *Surfing California* guidebook was published in 1973, the entry for Pillar Point said: "Huge winter walls outside Half Moon Bay harbor. Shallow reefs. Too dangerous for surfing." Plain enough. But Clark nonetheless began climbing the rim of the headland when the surf was up, evaluating, considering.

On a warm February afternoon in 1975, Clark and his friend Brian Pinoche were slouched into their familiar west-facing position atop Pillar Point. Clark was seventeen. Pinoche, a little older, had for the past two years been the one guy to match Clark, even push him, in bigger surf. Now Pinoche began to fidget as Clark watched impassively. A half mile distant, the wedge-shaped Maverick's waves were peaking at ten or twelve feet, no bigger. The sun was out and the ocean surface was titanium-smooth. The bigger waves, though, were detonating over the reef, each blue-green wall replaced by a mushroom cloud of whitewater. Maverick's broke harder than any other wave in the area, maybe harder than anywhere else on the coast. Clark knew this better than anyone. He also knew that conditions wouldn't get any better for an introductory go-out than they were on this particular day. He

overleaf
Jeff Clark (stretching) and Grant Washburn, about to paddle out through the north channel at Maverick's, 1994.

83

turned to Pinoche and said as much. Pinoche balked. "I tried for an hour to get him to come with me," Clark remembers, "and he said something like, 'Good luck, and I'll call the Coast Guard and tell 'em where I last saw you. But I'm not going in.'"

Clark approached from the north, paddling slowly and deliberately. Maverick's, as he saw it, was a left-breaking wave. The rights were long and intricate, maybe *too* intricate, and bordered by a long stand of rocks. The lefts were shorter and more predictable, spilling into what appeared to be a rock-free channel. That was the direction he intended to ride.

If he was going to ride. Clark was on his longest board—seven feet, three inches—and the closer he moved toward the breaking surf, the more obvious it became that he was underequipped. What would he need, though? An eight-footer? Nine? Bigger, maybe, Clark thought. Seven-three, in any event, was ridiculous; it would probably wiggle and spin down the face like soap on porcelain. Clark paused. He could stand down, right now, paddle in, tell Pinoche what Maverick's looked like close-up, and try again some other time. *But look how smooth it is,* Clark argued with himself. *For sure that's going to make the waves easier to ride. And it's just a seven-three, but it's a really GOOD seven-three.* He moved a few yards closer.

Clark dropped carefully, almost chastely, down the front of his first wave, a sensible ten-footer, and was nearly paralyzed by the speed and velocity. Seven seconds later, gliding into deep water, mouth agape, Clark went prone and felt his heart thumping like a speedbag into the deck of his board. The next two waves were the same: blurry with acceleration, but safe. Wave number four was a different story. Clark had unwittingly positioned himself too far to the south, on the wrong side of the apex, on a wave that was five feet bigger than the others. Paddling hard, just before standing up, he glanced to his left and felt dread wash through him like gasoline as a long, impossible section tilted up vertically in his path. Clark was beyond the point where he could rein in and let the wave roll by. Pushing to his feet, he made a risky choice: rather than descend to the bottom, he gently initiated an elliptical line of retreat along the building crest of the wave—knowing that if he pushed too hard, his board would slip out of its track, and he'd drop like a bridge-jumper into the void. But the seven-three held fast and Clark exited down the wave's trailing slope, just as it folded over upon itself with a hydrodynamic roar.

A half hour later, Clark caught his last wave and returned to the rock-lined beach north of Maverick's. He raved to Pinoche, who, to Clark's amazement, just shrugged and looked blank at the suggestion of a follow-up Maverick's session. Visiting the local surf shops in the weeks and months to come, it was the same thing. No takers. Clark was dumbstruck. He'd *done* it. Maverick's was *surfable*. Maverick's was like—Clark hesitated at first, then got used to saying it—it was like *Sunset.* Or *Waimea.* Still, no takers.

Clark rode Maverick's alone from 1975 to 1989. He may have skipped a few seasons (in an early interview he said he rode there "pretty much" every winter; later he filled in the blanks and it was every winter), and local surfers occasionally paddled out with him to watch from the safety of the channel. But for fifteen years Clark was the only person to ride the "too dangerous for surfing" waves off Pillar Point, and it doesn't much matter if that translates to 10 sessions or 110 sessions. His solitary period at Maverick's is a stunning, unmatchable big-wave achievement.

"He's a nut, really; he's psycho," says Santa Cruz's Josh Loya, one big-wave surfer bestowing upon another the highest possible compliment. "Riding that place by yourself for all those years. . . . God, I would *never* do that. I wouldn't surf out there even *once* by myself."

Clark RETURNED HOME after his first day at Maverick's and knew he had to solve his surfboard problem. The seven-three had gotten him off the mark, but he wasn't going to push his luck. Maverick's clearly required an out-and-out, fully loaded big-wave gun. Local manufacturers lacked either the interest or the expertise to produce such a board (which looks like a longer-version shortboard, but isn't; just as a cello isn't a scaled-up violin), so Clark finally bought materials and set up shop in his garage.

In this way, he apprenticed for the most venerated—maybe the *only* venerated—production job in surfing. Pat Curren, Mike Diffenderfer, Dick Brewer, Tom Parrish, Pat Rawson, and other big-wave board shapers had over the decades formed a composite mythical figure: part artist, part armament maker, part guru. These board makers each had a stable of top big-wave riders, and they often made their customers, famous and nonfamous, wait months before taking delivery on their personally designed boards. Some were autocratic and temperamental. "Brewer made me a beautiful new nine-foot, six-inch gun for Waimea in '73," North Shore master surfer Jeff Hakman remembers. "He says to me, 'Here it is, what do you think?' And I looked and said 'Nice, nice.' Then I said, 'The tail seems a little bit pulled in, don't you think?' 'A little pulled?' he asks. 'I can fix that.' And he got a saw and cut a foot off this perfect board, and the whole thing just dropped to the floor. 'How's that?' he asked me. 'Huh? Is that better for you?'"

Jeff Clark would never develop into a beatified big-wave surfboard shaper. By the mideighties, though, he was building efficient full-race guns for himself, and a decade later he was making boards for perhaps a third of the fifty-or-so regular Maverick's surfers.

Clark's boards were fundamentally the same as those built by George Downing in the early fifties: about ten feet long, twenty-one inches wide, three and a half inches thick, pointed on both ends, with the nose section fuller than the tail section, and slightly bowed. Because big waves are harder to catch than small waves (they move faster and displace more water), paddling speed was Clark's primary design concern, ahead of handling characteristics. All other design elements being equal, the longer a board is, the faster it will paddle. At about the eleven-foot mark, however, the board's weight and mass make it nearly impossible to steer once the wave is engaged. Ten feet was Downing's baseline size, and it was Clark's, too.

There were also obvious differences between Downing's and Clark's big-wave boards, too. Where Downing used a homemade laminated slab of balsa with vertical redwood strips as the core material, and did most of the shaping work with a draw-knife, Clark used factory-made closed-cell polyurethane foam blanks (standard since the early sixties) and a power planer. Downing's boards had a single stabilizing fin, and weighed about thirty-five pounds. Clark's boards had either one, three, or four fins, and weighed about fifteen pounds.

As much as Clark labored in the garage, he worked even harder in the surf, teaching himself how to ride switchstance in big waves—the surfing equivalent of switch-hitting in baseball. About two-thirds of all surfers ride in a left-foot-forward "regularfoot" stance, and the rest use a right-foot-forward "goofyfoot" stance. Riding frontside means you're facing the wave as you angle across. Riding backside means your back is to the wave. Frontside is easier than backside, just as a forehand tennis stroke is easier than a backhand one, and in big surf the advantage—having the wave in your line of vision—is even greater. Nonetheless, just a handful of surfers over the past fifty years have mastered switchfoot surfing, and only two—Jock Sutherland and Butch Van Artsdalen, both famous in the sixties—were able to switchstance in big waves. Clark, a Sutherland disciple as a preteen (and, like Sutherland, a born goofyfoot), practiced riding as a regularfoot for hours at a time in the Half Moon Bay shorebreak, and ten years later, when he decided to take on the long and complex right-breaking waves at Maverick's, he was able to do so in a frontside stance. Clark was the only ambidextrous big-wave surfer in the world at the time, and remains so today. Switchfooting is his great achievement within the achievement.

On the MORNING OF January 22, 1990, Clark drove to San Francisco's Ocean Beach—having by now given up on recruiting any local surfers, he decided to try to import a few guys from elsewhere in the Bay Area—and in the parking lot at Sloat Avenue, he began talking to Tom Powers and Dave Schmidt from Santa Cruz, and Mark Renneker from San Francisco, all of whom had some big-wave experience. Well-shaped fifteen-foot surf was pumping in steadily, but at Ocean Beach there was no paddling channel through the corrugated lines of foam. Renneker proposed that they suit up anyway and try to punch through. Clark counterproposed, saying he had a spot in mind, not too far away, that could handle the size. Schmidt and Powers were interested. Renneker waved them off.

One hour later Schmidt and Powers had joined Clark in the Maverick's lineup, and were gaping at the surf as if in the presence of an alien life form. Clark wore a little smile as he offered tips and instruction. Schmidt ended up riding six waves, and Powers got two. Clark put on a big-wave demonstration that seemed to be three-parts authoritative and one-part mad. "He just blew us away that day," Powers later said of Clark. "He was taking off super deep, charging into these big, black, hideous pits. We were worried about him. We were awestruck."

Eighteen months later, Maverick's made its feature-length debut in *Surfer*, and Clark became an instant big-wave sensation. He'd ridden those huge, cold, rock-smashing waves by himself, quietly, year after year, without photo, film, or video documentation. "Core"—short for hardcore—had long been a surf-world accolade, and Clark's solo run at Maverick's seemed to initiate a new, higher order of core.

Never before had anyone in the sport come to prominence in their midthirties, and Jeff Clark looked his years: handsome and trim, but weathered, with sun-damaged lips and thick, mannish black hair covering his workman's forearms. Everything about Clark—his soft, detached voice, the stony silences, the drill-bit blue eyes, the tight expression—suggested that this was a surfer with abundant, possibly unimaginable experience. It seemed like he'd been around for years.

In 1992 and '93, as the surfing press discovered new details about Clark, he only looked tougher, braver, cooler. He once piggybacked a drowning man to the beach, pumped water out of his stomach and lungs, waited for the ambulance to arrive, then paddled back into the surf. In 1991, he was aboard a friend's boat in the Maverick's channel after breaking two ribs during a wipeout. "I couldn't breathe too well," he told *Surfing*, "and I was really worried that I might have done some serious damage." A photographer on the boat happened to be carrying a bottle of prescription painkillers. Clark swallowed two, waited twenty minutes, then "paddled over and caught three more waves."

Clark plainly was nothing like the slick, young, media-raised, southern California surfers; for fifteen years he'd worked as a carpenter and general contractor. Though he was now also shaping surfboards professionally and earning a small monthly stipend as an industry-sponsored big-wave rider, he'd never be one to zigzag the trade show aisles, grinning professionally, slapping palms with people he didn't know and singing out "Hey bro!" But as an interview subject, he produced quotes and sound bites as easily as if he were cutting out sections of floor joist. "Maverick's is a spot that takes care of itself" was an early and oft-repeated favorite. "You have to be 100 percent committed to ride big waves," he told the *San Francisco Chronicle*. "When that set comes, your heart starts to pound, and when you take off every ounce of adrenaline in your body is pumping. It sounds like thunder when the wave crashes." When describing the hazardous aspects of Maverick's, Clark would level his icy blue-eyed gaze and lower his voice slightly. On record, he never joked about big-wave surfing.

With all of the attention, Clark soon found himself cutting a higher profile—Hawaii's Laird Hamilton excepted—than any other big-wave surfer. Intentionally or not, when Clark spoke he often did so for the entire sport, and no one blinked in 1994 when *Surfer* labeled him as one of the "world's best big-wave riders."

Clark, though, was the outlier among his big-wave peers, both geographically and experientially. His domain was proscribed and defined like nobody else's—he was the press-titled "Maverick Man." Where most other big-wave riders would resent being tied so closely to one break, it didn't seem to bother Clark. No doubt his long and unique relationship with Maverick's had created the strongest possible bond between surfer and surf break. But Clark must have recognized, too, that there

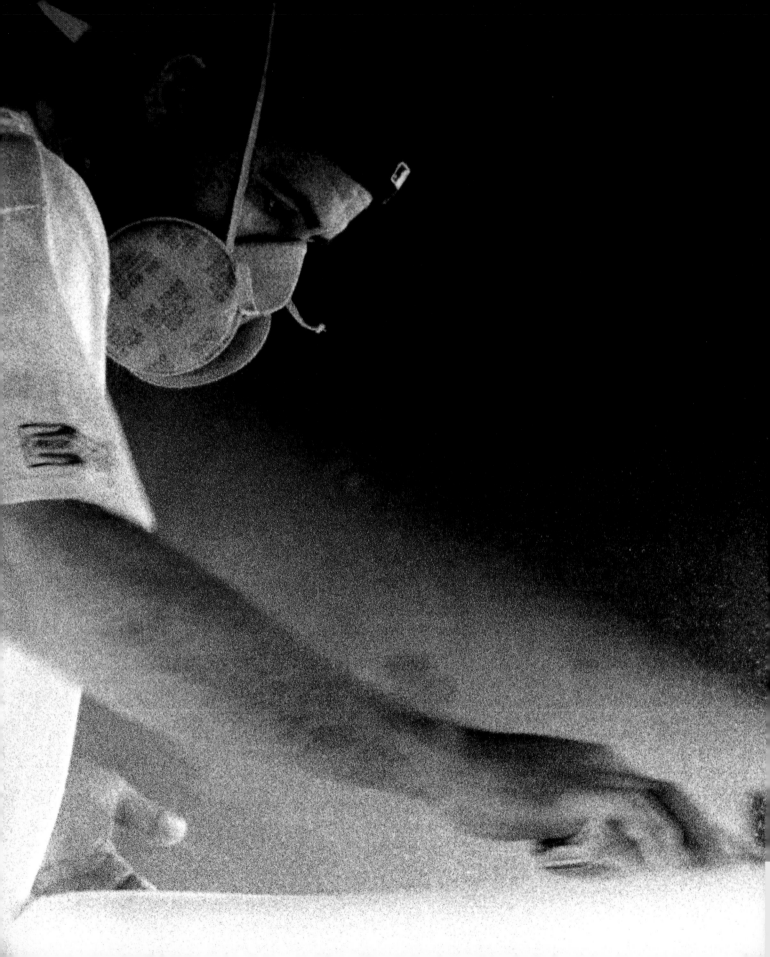

would be little or no career advantage in venturing from his Maverick's dominion. To become a more cosmopolitan big-wave rider, he'd only bump shoulders with a few dozen others just as hungry and guts-up as he was. Clark rose to big-wave prominence without having ever visited Hawaii, something that had never happened before. Uniqueness became a big part of his appeal. When he finally rode Waimea, in 1994, he performed well—but so did fifteen or twenty other surfers. Clark went unnoticed.

Jeff Clark is indeed the Maverick Man, and the designation doesn't appear to strike him as limiting, or as a laurel to rest upon, but as an expression of something very close to a monogamous big-wave marriage.

By 1994, THREE LOOSELY confederated, regionally defined blocs of Maverick's surfers had taken shape, with Jeff Clark standing more or less apart as his own one-man faction. Each group consisted of about a dozen surfers. The local assembly was led by Ion Banner of Half Moon Bay and Shaun Rhodes, Matt Ambrose, and Steve Dwyer of Pacifica. All were rock-solid big-wave bucks (the smooth-running Ambrose was regarded by some as Maverick's premier stylist), and all were restrained and unobtrusive. Or they seemed restrained and unobtrusive as compared to the noisy, jacked-up visitors from San Francisco and Santa Cruz. "I tend to be quiet out there," Banner said in 1994, "because I'm trying to focus. A lot of other guys are voicing their excitement; yelling a lot. I'm getting used to it. But it's kind of difficult to concentrate when the crowd gets loud. I like the quiet."

The San Francisco group was fronted by Mark Renneker—forty-one years old in 1994—a bright and garrulous USCF-trained oncologist who boiled over with polymathic enthusiasm for the sport of surfing. Renneker absorbed surfboard theory and design, surf history and surf trivia (he owned the world's most diverse collection of surfing magazines and books), and he often hosted informal surfing salons on the sidewalk in front of his beachfront house.

Grant Washburn, John Raymond, Bob Battalio, and another half dozen Maverick's surfers orbited around Renneker. None of them, Renneker included, were first-rate big-wave riders (although the superbly athletic Washburn was getting closer); all were college-educated, most had nonsurfing professional careers, some had families. As a group, they were giddy with excitement over this new big-wave break more or less in their backyard. They were the happiest of amateurs.

The Santa Cruz surfers, by comparison, often seemed crude, snide, rascally, and jaded. They were younger than the San Francisco crew, greater in number, mostly from working-class families, and they were all getting paid—some well, others nominally—to ride waves. Dave Schmidt and Tom Powers were the first two Santa Cruz surfers to ride Maverick's, but it was Richard Schmidt (Dave's younger brother), along with Vince Collier, who created and established a Santa Cruz big-wave style; Schmidt with his pure surfing talent, Collier with his loud and raunchy approach—the essence of which is neatly captured in a 1994 video clip from *Gravity Sucks,* as Collier, leering, arrives at the base of a big Maverick's wave, straightens up from a crouch, and with miming hands strokes an imaginary big-surf-inflated phallus. "Meet Vince Collier," a *Surfing* headline read. "The first man to actually *eat* a surfboard."

By the midnineties, the amiable Peter Mel had become not just the best Maverick's surfer from Santa Cruz, but the best Maverick's surfer, period. He rode in a stable, low-slung posture; arms, legs, head, and torso always moving in synchronization. "Peter impresses me more than anybody else," Evan Slater said in 1994. "He's smart. I tend to be overanxious; sometimes taking off on stupid waves. Peter just gets the good ones, and almost always makes them."

Twenty-three-year-old Darryl "Flea" Virostko, however, rough-edged and slightly manic, was in many ways Santa Cruz's real flag-bearer at Maverick's. Virostko got his nickname at age fifteen, when he shot his prepubescent, four-foot, two-inch frame across some eight-footers at Steamer Lane and Vince Collier nearly wet himself laughing at the fighting flea-size surfer. The teenage Virostko, cute from afar, was piranha-like up close, yelling in squeaky rage at anyone who got in his road. "You'd paddle up and dunk him," a Santa Cruz surfer remembers, "and he'd be screaming at you when he went down, then still screaming when he came back up. No matter how many times you dunked him, he'd still be snapping."

Virostko wasn't quite up to Mel's standard at Maverick's in 1994, but he charged like a Mad Max villain, selecting waves at the last possible second, and regularly launching off the precipice into a signature "air-drop," where surfer and board, as a unit, briefly take flight as the wave begins to hollow. A mind-blowing gambit if successful; punishing in the extreme if not. On land, Virostko was feisty, profane, and often funny. Asked by a surf magazine interviewer to describe his "dream girl," the unmarried Virostko began in typical surf-satyr fashion—"blond hair, green eyes, tan, big round breasts"—then went on to imagine her as "very spiteful . . . and living about four hours south of me."

Maverick's SURFERS hassle, argue, and back-bite on occasion, like any other group of athletes, but they ride well together for the most part, yelling encouragement during rides, exchanging pleasantries during lulls, and in general treating each other with casual beach-born civility. Whether or not the Maverick's surfers, along with the rest of their fellows worldwide, can be cast as a "big-wave fraternity"—as often described by surf journalists—is another matter. Collective and unifying traits are hard to find. By their language, dress, and mannerisms, big-wave riders are immediately marked as surfers, and they spend the vast majority of their surfing days, like the rest of the surfing population, in unremarkable small- to medium-size waves. Only on close inspection can big-wave riders be recognized as a surfing subphylum. They tend to be older—the average age of the twenty competing surfers in the 1999 Quiksilver "Men Who Ride

Mountains" contest at Maverick's was thirty-two, while the average age of 1999's world tour top twenty was twenty-four. Also, because there aren't many big-wave surfers, and because they make a point of looking out for each other during heavy conditions, the intergroup bonds tend to be stronger. (How deep the camaraderie goes is open to interpretation: "When somebody eats it out there," Darryl Virostko says, discussing the informal buddy system at Maverick's, "I'll be waiting to see if he comes up, or if he needs help, or whatever." Pause. "Even if it's just some kook.")

Similarities among big-wave surfers, though, are less interesting than the differences, beginning with body type. Greg Noll (6' 2", 230 pounds), Grant Washburn (6' 5", 215), and Laird Hamilton (6' 3", 220) seem to make the case that oversize waves are best matched with oversize riders. But a tradition of small and light big-wave surfers goes back at least as far as the fifties, when Henry Lum ("he couldn't have weighed much more than a hundred pounds," Woody Brown says) took anything that came his way at Makaha, and includes Hawaiians Noah Johnson (5' 6", 130), Mark Foo (5' 8", 135), and Darrick Doerner (5' 6", 140).

Roughly half of today's Maverick's surfers are employed, in one way or another, by the surf industry—Peter Mel gets about $75,000 a year as a fully sponsored pro; Steve Dwyer gets thirty cents a word to write for *Surfing* magazine—but carpenters, lawyers, and teachers fill out the lineup, along with a physician, an architect, a computer engineer, and a gaffer. (Lifeguards had a plurality at Waimea Bay in the mideighties, but regulars included a Republican state legislator, a Defense Department computer systems analyst, and a University of Hawaii professor.)

Sifting through all the big-wave surfing stoners and teetotalers, silver-spooners, down-and-outers, Democrats, Republicans, health-freaks, know-nothings, born-agains, cynics, scammers, straight-shooters, and drops-outs to try and come up with any kind of reliable political or social consensus, meanwhile, is a perfect exercise in futility.

If a big-wave fraternal bond exists, it has to do with the satisfaction and self-assuredness that rises off this wildly mixed group like ether. "Surfers are happy people," Mark Foo said in 1988, "because they always know what they want."

Surfers are romantics, too, of a kind, and big-wave riders perhaps even more so—because their preferred environment is beautifully dangerous and dramatic, and because the act itself is sustained for the most part by dreams and imagination.

"I have long feared this day," Grant Washburn wrote in his journal entry for December 21, 1994, sounding like a jilted lover, but really just bummed at having to fly out the next morning for a family visit in Connecticut. "I have no more options, and must depart."

Then the old enthusiasm returned as Washburn looked out of his San Francisco apartment kitchen window to a near-endless field of breaking surf. "Still huge—howling offshore barrels spitting and feathering everywhere. Unreal. The swell is supposed to hold for another two or three days. The Month of the Monsters can't go on forever. Or can it?"

ATHLETES, ARTISTS, PROFESSIONALS

big-wave surfing

1970–1990

Big-wave surfing didn't expire in December 1969

when Greg Noll quit the sport and flew back to California after his crash-and-burn thirty-footer at Makaha. But for the next fifteen years big waves were shaded—almost erased at times—by other surf-world developments. The shortboard revolution of the late sixties and early seventies, for instance, reconfigured small- and medium-wave surfing altogether. Riding inside the tube became the sport's new obsession, and because tube-riding required subtle edge-work and spontaneous midtrajectory adjustments, it was nearly impossible to perform in huge, blitzing surf.

Surfers themselves also changed. Hawaii's Larry Bertlemann, nicknamed "Rubberman" for his elastic, hyperkinetic small-wave technique—and hipped out in his bell-bottom wetsuit and globular Sly Stone afro—was the figurehead surfer of the early seventies. Bertlemann rode well at Sunset and Waimea, but he treated big surf as more of an auxiliary practice than a real calling. Most of Bertlemann's contemporaries in this dawning era of professional surfing felt the same way.

Professionalism, as much as anything, drew attention away from big waves. Surf contest promoters, hoping to attract the largest possible beach-going audience, often scheduled their events to finish on the weekend. Contestants, organizers, and spectators kept their fingers crossed for good surf, but with a fixed timetable they took what they got—and what they got was rarely big. Then there were the adventure surfers, who fanned out to ride gorgeous and relatively uncrowded ten-foot-and-under waves in Australia and Indonesia and beyond. Hawaii remained the great proving ground. But as the surfing map was redrawn, expanded, and diversified, Hawaii's preeminence was adjusted down accordingly—and so too was the focus on big-wave surfing.

Fred Hemmings from Hawaii, a superb big-wave rider in the sixties and a competition surfer of Teutonic will and discipline, advanced through this era of change as both observer and participant. He liked the shorter surfboards, but the newly strobe-lit and patchouli-scented cultural landscape bothered him. He was supposed to, as he understood the phrase, "go with the flow." But what if the flow was moving in the wrong direction? Hemmings resisted. When the rest of the contestants turned out for the 1968 world contest opening ceremonies dressed in beads, Jesus sandals, denim hip-huggers, and leather-fringe vests, Hemmings arrived in a navy blue blazer,

102

loafers, and a rep tie, looking more like a narco agent than a surfer—then rode smoothly and intelligently to win the championship. Hemmings would, in years to come, delight in calling himself surfing's biggest rebel in '68, and he's got a point.

Hemmings flew back to Honolulu with his world title trophy, retired from competition, joined the Junior Chamber of Commerce, and evangelically set out to promote, market, and organize professional surf contests. "Surfing needs professionalism!" he said. "Pro surfing will identify our sport, improve all facets of competition, and vastly improve and regulate the advancement of surfing techniques." Never mind that surfers themselves were ambivalent about professionalism and the creation of a new, monied class of surfer-sportsmen. The top guys were real athletes, Hemmings maintained, whether they knew it or not, and they should be paid to perform, hopefully on network TV, like baseball or football players.

Hemmings had some early, limited success. In 1971 he created the Pipeline Masters competition, and the following year he convinced ABC to run the Masters on *Wide World of Sports*. But a couple of things had to happen, Hemmings thought, looking ahead, before pro surfing could *really* break it big. Surfers had to straighten up. No drugs or unprofessional behavior of any type. Surfing had "a detrimental image," Hemmings said, and not unjustly, and the new breed of pro surfer would have to be "clean and healthy" to counter that image. He wished the guys would cut all that shaggy blond hair back to a respectable length—Hemmings's own Johnny Unitas haircut was about an inch longer than it had been in 1964, when he was an All-League high school football player—but it was a free country, after all, and he wasn't going to push it.

The other important pro surfing requisite, Hemmings believed, was that the sport had to look as exciting as possible for a national network audience. And this meant shifting the emphasis back to the big Hawaiian surf.

On this point, **Hemmings,** the newly hired Meet Director for the Smirnoff Pro-Am competition, reckoned he was in fat city as he pulled into the Waimea Bay parking lot on Thanksgiving morning, 1974. The Smirnoff competition was scheduled to run that day somewhere on the North Shore, and Waimea was the only possibility; the surf was enormous, and every other break was washed out. Waimea itself looked as if it were on the verge of washing out, and Hemmings had no choice but to put the contest on hold. An hour passed. Hemmings kept watching. Christ, was it getting bigger? One official said the waves should be tapering down, but at exactly 10:40 A.M., Hemmings, the eighteen Smirnoff competitors, and the three or four hundred onlookers clustered on either side of the bay were staring, whistling, howling, wiggling in place, or looking on dumbly as a blue-black mutant wave, thirty-five feet at least, rose up, collapsed all at once, and rolled toward shore in a huge smoking broadside of whitewater—a definitive close-out, no more open to athletic play than a landslide.

On a patch of grass near the Waimea parking lot, the contest judges and competitors all turned toward Hemmings, who lit a Kent cigarette and thought about what he'd just seen and what it meant for his contest. Okay, so that *particular* wave was off the chart. But there were plenty of other huge, ridable, photogenic twenty-five-footers. The sun was out. The TV news cameras were ready to roll. The *Sports Illustrated* writer was around somewhere. Hemmings flicked an ash onto the grass, rolled his head back and forth on his shoulders a few times, and once again looked out to the surf. Man, the Smirnoff guys would *kill* for the media coverage. There hadn't been a contest in waves like this—ever. Not even close. And didn't the surfers all sign release forms? Hell yes, they did.

Hemmings glanced over at the competitors, most of whom stood, arms crossed, a few yards away. They looked fidgety and stressed, possibly even mutinous—or at least ready to give up their shot at the five-thousand-dollar first-place prize. *Five* of the Smirnoff surfers, Hemmings would find out later, had in fact never surfed Waimea at any size, forget twenty-five or thirty feet. Most of them, Hemmings glumly admitted to himself, just weren't ready. But they *should* be, dammit! That's what being a professional is all about! And what a show it would be! Waimea Bay! *Huge!*

Hemmings took a long drag on his Kent and had an idea.

"Fred knew there were a lot of guys that morning who just flat-out didn't want anything to do with that huge surf," remembers four-time world champion Mark Richards from Australia, who was a seventeen-year-old rookie pro in 1974, jelly-kneed at the thought of putting on a colored Smirnoff competition jersey and entering the water. "But he also knew we were a bunch of egomaniacal surfers. So he called this little meeting there on the beach and said if we thought it was too big, then he'd paddle out and ride one, just to prove that it could be done. 'I'll go first,' he said. Just *challenging* us! And we all folded. We just gave up, no protest, the contest was on. Because we knew Fred would do it. And we'd all end up looking like a bunch of pussies."

Heat number one marched into the water. Traffic on Kam Highway was now completely jammed, and five thousand spectators were arranged across the beach and rocks. Richards speared down the face of his first Waimea wave and made it—and for the next four hours the drama rolled steadily on. Three contestants snapped their boards, one wrenched his back, and four or five others were pulled under for career-worst wipeouts. But nobody left in the ambulance that was standing by, the successful rides were nearly as spectacular as the wipeouts, and Hawaiian favorite Reno Abellira beat his neighbor Jeff Hakman in the day's final match by a microscopic half point.

The Smirnoff, as *Surfing* magazine raved, was "the greatest in the history of [surfing] competition." Maybe so. But not everybody was thrilled at Waimea's transformation, temporary as it was, from natural wonder to tournament-ready playing field. Hawaiian big-wave rider and noncompetitor Kimo Hollinger hoped to ride a few waves before the contest got underway. "I paddled out in total confusion," he wrote in *Surfer.* "I was about to communicate with nature, my God, in the most intimate way I knew how, by riding big waves. [Then the] powerboats and helicopters

overleaf
Hawaiian surfer
Reno Abellira, Sunset
Beach, early seventies.

appeared, and Fred started warming up the loudspeaker. The squares had invaded one of our last sanctuaries—big surf at the Bay. I began crying to myself."

Sell-out or showcase, either way, the 1974 Smirnoff turned out to be the only really conspicuous big-wave event of the decade. Cash prizes and ratings points—these became the going concerns of surfing in the seventies. In 1976, the international pro contests were brought together under a single organizational body, and at the end of the year Peter Townend from Australia was announced as the first professional world champion. Each year the circuit would finish with a series of contests on the North Shore, but the emphasis for the most part, as Mark Richards put it, was on the aggressive, sharp-turning, "rip, tear, and lacerate" style of wave riding. Teenage rippers now all wanted to be jet-setting, product-endorsing, check-winning *pros*—some liked big surf, too, but there didn't seem to be a teenager in all of surfdom who invested himself in big-wave riding the way Greg Noll had in the fifties and sixties. And it was hard to blame them. Waimea seemed to be a bygone surf break—it didn't make the cover of *Surfer* from 1967 to 1983—visited for the most part by surfers in their thirties and forties, even fifties. Giant waves were still ridden, year after year, but they were addressed in the classic big-wave style, the *only* big-wave style, with long, piercing, well-tempered arcs and lines. No ripping, tearing, or lacerating.

The big-wave revival began in 1983, and it was at least in part a collective act of surf-world self-purification. Pro surfing events were by now fighting for attention (and usually losing) with adjunct bikini contests and sponsor-product giveaways. Beach fashion had turned to muscle shirts and tight-fitting shorts in cornea-burning neon colors. Zinc oxide,

the original sun block, once chalk-white, was now available in green, yellow, blue, and hot pink. When the 1982–83 winter season produced the biggest North Pacific surf since 1969, with one prodigious swell following another, it was almost as if a terrestrial statement were being made against the new commercial vulgarity. Surfers once again got a long draught of what Greg Noll had called "the big, damn terrorizing wave," and many of them realized that this was something worthy of more attention. Indeed, it all looked so dramatic and exciting that it was hard to figure out why big waves had gone out of vogue in the first place.

Surfer magazine helped things along with a mildly bellicose article titled, "Whatever Happened to Big-Wave Riding?" As noted by author Leonard Brady in the introduction, just a dozen or so surfers in the early eighties were interested in riding waves twenty-five feet and bigger. And these "gladiators of the sea," these "fighter jocks who went surfing," were, in Brady's estimation, the sport's only true heroes. Pretty much everyone else was suspect. "What happened?" Brady asked. "Have surfers turned into candyasses?"

Professionalism, according to most of the big-wave surfers queried for Brady's article, was the main reason for the general disinterest in big surf. Furthermore, one of the interviewed surfers argued, the younger generation didn't have "the moral character" to ride big waves. Another panelist noted the long run of smaller-than-average winter surf seasons, and without the "monster stuff" as seen in earlier decades, it was natural that big-wave riding should have withered.

Although "Whatever Happened to Big-Wave Surfing?" was presented as a reassessment and critique, it seemed to have no real agenda beyond deifying the big-wave brotherhood, and this was done in part through rough-and-tumble phrasing. "The whitewater rips and tears at your body," one surfer said, "threatening dismemberment." Waimea, another offered, "is survival—just a straight-line death-drop." It was hairy, jaw-jutting man's talk. Which surprised nobody, as big-wave riding was a man's sport. Women in 1983 were bodybuilding, drag-racing, taking their karate blackbelts, and breaking bones just like the men on downhill ski runs. Only on rare occasion, though, were they paddling out and riding big waves. Reasons for this might extend beyond surfing's hoary legacy of sexism—although no such reasons suggest themselves. The gender-balanced surfing world as depicted in ancient Hawaiian chants and nineteenth-century wood carvings and lithographs gave way in the twenti-

eth century to something close to a male-only closed shop. Ten-to-one has long been cited as modern surfing's male-female ratio, but until the midnineties that count was too generous to women by far.

Female surfers weren't chased out of the water. *Gidget* had set a precedent, and women could expect some measure of encouragement and (usually condescending) cheerfulness from the fellows. But for the most part, as Makaha leatherneck Buzzy Trent pointed out in his 1963 *Surf Guide* article "Big Waves Are Masculine, Women Feminine," surfers—guy surfers—generally thought it best if the "girls" didn't try any fancy riding.

Girls do fine when it comes to housework, raising children, doing office work, doing the twist and riding the small surf at Malibu. More and more girls are surfing, and I'm glad to see it. There's nothing more beautiful than a well-shaped girl riding a six-foot wave with the wind blowing through her hair. But one thing I can't stand is girls riding (or attempting to ride) big waves. Why? Well, you see, girls are much more emotional than men and therefore have a greater tendency to panic. And panic can be extremely dangerous in big surf. There is nothing in the world more ridiculous than a girl who dares to show off and then panics out. Girls are weaker than men and have a lesser chance for survival in giant wipeouts. Girls are better off and look more feminine riding average size waves.

Some girls went out in the big surf anyway. Fifteen-year-old goofyfooter Linda Benson rode Waimea Bay in 1959, and Phyllis Dameron, a sunny-natured Waikiki nightclub stripper, did the same in the late seventies.

But women's big-wave surfing was more or less invented and refined in the seventies and early eighties by Hawaii's Margo Oberg. Oberg didn't ride the biggest big surf, but she rode with confidence and fluidity in waves up to eighteen feet, and was a master in the shifting,

variegated, open-field waves at Sunset Beach, becoming, as the women's surf magazine *Wahine* put it, "the all-time great big-wave dominatrix." Oberg used both practical and ethereal language to describe the sensation of paddling into a big Sunset peak. "There's no turning back once I've seen it. There's nothing else. All I care about is that the nose of my board doesn't pearl [dig under the water]. It's a mindless surrender; I feel completely in God's hands; a complete letting go—like I'm bargaining with God. Angels are holding my arms up. It's a miracle."

Some male big-wave riders felt that same piquant religiosity in heavy surf. The majority, though, put their faith in testosterone, not God. "That was good, Brock," big-wave surfer Roger Erickson growled out to Brock Little in 1985, after one of Little's first giant waves at Waimea. "*Real* good! All *balls!*"

The opening phase of the big-wave

comeback was summarized by the 1986 Quiksilver/Eddie Aikau Memorial, the first surf contest designed specifically for Waimea Bay. Quiksilver had picked a surfer worthy of a commemorative event: Aikau, a pure-blood Hawaiian, appeared as a natural big-wave-riding man-child in the late sixties, cantering down huge walls at Waimea as a teenager, atop a fire-engine red board, in a perfectly slouched posture. He died in a 1978 boating accident at age thirty-two. Darrick Doerner, a Waimea cub in the midseventies, rode with Aikau a few times, and remembers him as the embodiment of big-wave cool. "He surfed bowlegged," Doerner says. "Take off and drop in, lay out the big bottom turn, disappear into a mountain of whitewater, pop out, throw his hair back. That was Eddie. So cool. Just *bully* style."

Quiksilver's 1986 contest in Aikau's honor was attended by every name big-wave surfer—a few of whom teared up when it was

announced that Clyde Aikau, Eddie's younger brother, won the event.

New big-wave riders, most of them from Hawaii, were by that time regularly stalking the Waimea lineup. Hyper-social teenager Brock Little was introduced in the mideighties as the great all-in-one surfer: fizzy and quick in two-foot waves and stone-cold steady in twenty-five-footers. Darrick Doerner, stoic by comparison and not much interested in smaller waves, was the insider's choice when Waimea hit maximum size. They made an interesting contrast. Little was the surf media's big-wave darling, while Doerner's unsettling thousand-yard-stare pretty much chased the surf reporters away. Little lived with his family and had a rack of bright, color-coordinated green and yellow surfboards festooned with sponsor's logos. Doerner lived alone in a tiny plank-floor house few people had ever seen, and he rode clean, plain white boards.

Then there was Roger Erickson, the serene yet knife-edge-balanced Vietnam vet; Texas-born Ken Bradshaw, neatly captured in a *Surfer* portrait spoon-feeding himself a bowl of nails; Keone Downing, George's son, who not surprisingly did most of his big-wave surfing at Makaha; and Richard Schmidt from Santa Cruz, who startled people with his mismatched irises (one blue, one green), but was in fact, personality-wise, the least startling and most even-keeled big-wave rider.

Mark Foo, the acknowledged master of surf media, finished the Quiksilver contest in second place, behind Clyde Aikau. And, predictably, it was Foo's photograph, not Aikau's, that turned up on the cover of *Surfer*—with Foo shown in close-up wearing a white contest jersey with a block-print number "1" printed across the back, next to a cover blurb that read "Winning Moves!"

Mark Foo rode Waimea Bay for the first time in 1983, almost simultaneous to the publication of "Whatever Happened to Big-Wave Riding?" and it's easy to imagine the twenty-five-year-old Foo staring at the *Surfer* article pages the way a teenager from the early forties might have stared at an "Uncle Sam Wants You" recruiting poster. Foo was in a rut. He was surfing well, but not well enough to put his name anywhere near the top of the year-end pro circuit rankings—in four seasons he hadn't finished higher than sixty-sixth. He was a big believer in the power of positive thinking, but self-doubt was creeping in, he was nearly broke, and his mother and father were both unhappy (and vocally so) with Mark's occupational choice. "Good Chinese boys don't surf for a living," as Mark's sister SharLyn would say, using a gently mocking tone to convey

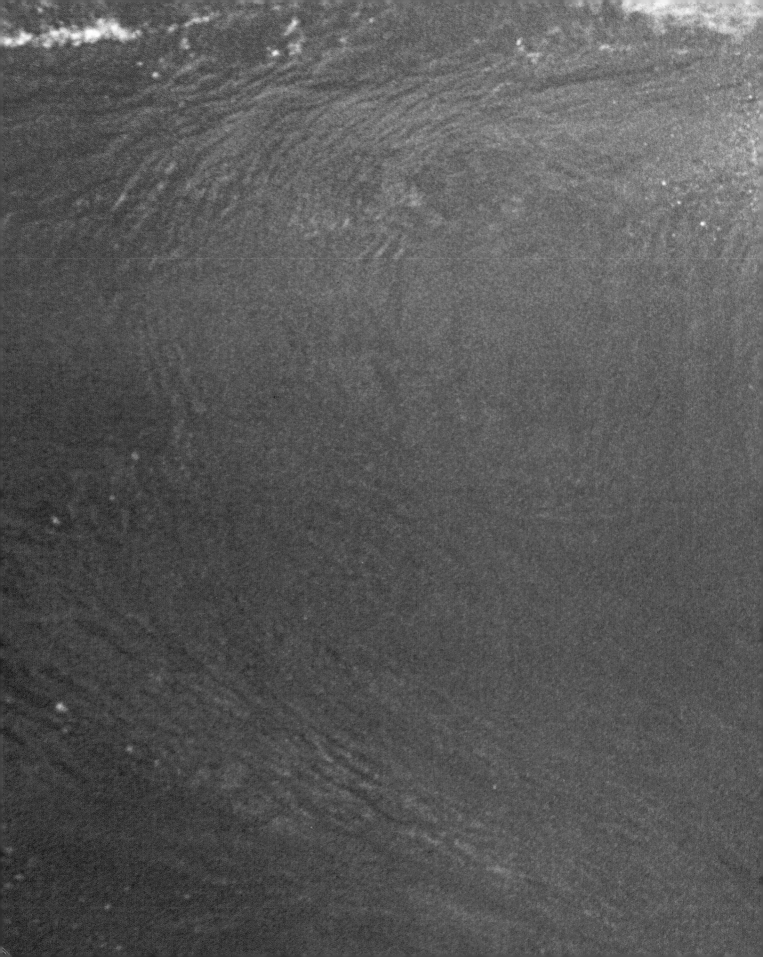

their parent's disappointment. Foo's mother had flat-out called him a "surf bum."

Big waves hadn't been much of a consideration for Foo up to that point. In early 1982, he'd talked eagerly about another go-round on the pro circuit, but at season's end he finished sixty-seventh. Now, looking ahead to 1983, he was warming to the idea that real opportunities might be found in big surf. Money and fame, yes, but more importantly a prolonged career in the sport he loved.

Foo had been surfing since 1969, when, as an eleven year old, he bought a second-hand surfboard with money saved from his paper route. One year later Foo's father, a midlevel employee with the U.S. Foreign Service, was reassigned to Washington, D.C., and the family moved from Hawaii to Rockville, Maryland. SharLyn Foo says her surf-touched brother was miserable. "He'd have tantrums and fits," she remembers. "He'd lay on the floor and kick and scream. Everyone knows how intense he was about surfing as an adult. Well, he was intense about it as a kid, too." At age fourteen, Foo left for Pensacola, a Florida beach town, to live with the family of a friend. Two years later the Foo family, Mark included, moved back to Honolulu. Nobody was surprised when Mark graduated from Roosevelt High School in 1975, one year ahead of his class; he was ambitious and smart. Nobody was surprised, either, when he blew off the commencement ceremony to jump on an early season south swell.

Foo moved to the North Shore that fall. He wanted to compete with the pros in the contests, and to immerse himself in the endless pre- and post-contest surf sessions at Haleiwa, Pipeline, and Sunset. And he hoped to get his picture in the magazines.

Foo surfed well, but not as well as the pros, and he invariably lost early in the competitions. But if the contest judges didn't love him, the camera did, and before the end of the decade

Foo was on the cover of *Surfer* and *Surfing* as often as the world champions. He drafted across the beautiful pellucid-blue North Shore waves in a compact, aerodynamic stance, and accoutered himself in the brightest colors possible—in a famous 1978 Pipeline photo, he's riding a pink-and-yellow surfboard and wearing scarlet-red trunks. Leveraging as best he could, Foo made small-money sponsorship deals with three or four surf companies. The goal all along, for Foo and the rest of the pros, was to make a living in surfing. Not by making or selling surfboards, or other surf-related items, or working surf-retail, but from riding waves. Prize-money contests were a means to that end. So were sponsorship deals, whereby surfers, in exchange for placing a company logo on their board, were paid in some combination of merchandise, salary, travel expenses, and "photo incentives" (a quarter-page black-and-white photo in *Surfer*, logo showing, might be worth fifty dollars; a cover shot could bring five hundred dollars). The pro surfing formula was simple. More magazine photos meant a higher surf-world "profile" (one of Foo's favorite words), which meant a higher personal market value. Sponsorship money plus contest winnings added up to an annual salary, and if it didn't add up to much for Foo, it didn't add up to much for anybody else, either. Peter Townend earned just over twenty-five thousand dollars when he won the world title in 1976. Three years later, Mark Richards, the new champion, made about forty thousand dollars. Surf company CEOs, a few of them, were making millions. Pro surfers were eating at Denny's and car-pooling from contest to contest.

Townend and Richards and the other top-rated pros, though, were at least respected by their peers. Mark Foo wasn't. The spectacular amount of media exposure he received was in fact out of proportion with his good-but-not-spectacular talent, and it didn't help matters when, after signing a contract with Anheuser-Busch brewery, he marched down the beach in the winter of 1981 with a lens-catching metalflake-gold surfboard bearing a gigantic red-and-white Michelob logo across the deck. Foo became known as a "photo slut," implying that he wouldn't bother paddling out until lighting conditions were of studio quality and the photographers were setting up their tripods along the beach.

The charge was both cruel and inadequate. Surfing was Foo's rapture and joy, and he rode constantly in gray, windblown, nonphotogenic conditions. Never for a moment, though, did he feel that it was anything but honorable to reap income and status from the sport, and to that end he was indeed tireless in work-ing with photographers. It would go far beyond that once Foo became a dedicated big-wave surfer. Foo hosted his own surfing radio show (and later a cable TV show), wrote articles for the surf magazines, did voice-overs for surf movies and color commentary for surf contests, and opened a surfer's bed-and-breakfast. He darted back and forth across the North Shore in a business-fueled blur, making appointments, showing up on time, and working the phones with great entrepreneurial flair. Local schools invited him to speak on professional surfing during Career Day assemblies. The money wasn't great, he would tell the kids, but the hours were flexible, and daily surf sessions were part of the business plan.

Foo was social, garrulous, and funny, always eager to connect with people emotionally and openly, but behind the steady line of business talk and social chatter, he kept a fundamental part of himself in watchful reserve. Detachment, in fact, proved to be Foo's greatest big-wave asset. When he rode Waimea Bay for the first time in 1983, he was alert and thrilled, but suffered none of the shrieking emotional feedback common to Waimea rookies. "Mark had this thing where he'd just get calmer and calmer as the conditions got gnarlier," says Bobby Owens, a former pro surfer and one of Foo's best friends. "He told me his breathing and heart rate actually slowed down on those giant days."

It was strange how Foo reacted in big surf, and Foo himself realized it. "I always drive really slow," he said in 1988. "I don't like heights. I'm afraid of roller-coasters. I pretty much don't like doing anything where I might get hurt." Yet riding big waves, as he pointed out, combined *all* of these things. Not long after his first Waimea experience, Foo seemed to order the disparate aspects of his character into a kind of big-wave Calvinism, where the prudent 55-mph driver, the diligent capitalist, and the swashbuckling surfer all merged in the name of a higher power.

"There has to be a bigger purpose to what I'm

doing," Foo said. "It's a plan God has. It's destiny."

Foo had a sensational big-wave coming-of-age moment on January 18, 1985, after a cloud-splitting fifty-foot closeout wave roared through Waimea, steamrolling Foo and three more surfers. The others lost their boards and began the long, rough swim toward shore. Foo's board popped up nearby, still attached to its leash, and he swung up onto the deck, realizing that he was now alone in some truly giant surf. From a relatively safe position just past the line-up, he watched the fire department helicopter move in, a rescue basket dangling thirty feet below the cockpit, to pluck one of the surfers out of the water and deposit him on the sand. Beach spectators stood and applauded, and cars parked along either side of the bay honked their horns. The other two swimming surfers were lifted to the beach in similar fashion, then the helicopter banked around to pick up Foo.

Thirty-footers were rolling through at a fairly steady rate, breaking in no discernible pattern twenty or thirty yards out past the normal Waimea lineup. A few of the waves, though, in Foo's estimation, looked ridable. The helicopter was now floating overhead, waiting. Foo ignored it.

After letting a few waves pass, he just missed catching a twenty-footer. Foo then wheeled his board around and saw that the following wave was bigger, maybe thirty feet, and that it was backed by a set of bigger-still waves. No choice: He'd have to catch the first one or get sequentially walloped by the next few. For ten seconds he paddled farther out, looking to intercept the wave at the exact right place, then he turned suddenly, pointed for shore, and dug in. He felt a rush along his board's keel, the aft section lifted up, and Foo snapped to his feet.

The ride came apart in stages. Foo and his board disconnected as a unit from the crest of the vertically pitched wave, then Foo disconnected from his board and fell like a statue thirty feet to the trough. The wave hit, and he actually heard his board splinter and snap in the underwater concussion. His watch was stripped from his wrist. Pinpoint specks of light were flickering across his eyelids by the time the turbulence began to ease, then Foo broke the surface and drew a shuddering breath. The rescue basket was dangling just to his right, and he climbed inside, sat on the nylon-mesh floor, steadied his breathing, and watched the tail section of his board twirl and spin at the end of its leash as he rode to the sand.

Ten minutes later, as Foo walked back to his Kam Highway home, he started blocking the event into prose. "I awoke early on January 18," his soon-to-be-published *Surfing* magazine article began, "unaware that I had a date with destiny."

Big-wave surfing lent ballast to Foo's life, personally and professionally. He was now respected and admired by the surfing world at large. His annual income was on the rise. His mother now saw him as a businessman, rather than a surf bum.

Foo's writing, too, seemed to benefit from his new big-wave career, becoming fluent, even eloquent. "How do you describe the feeling of looking into a thirty-foot tube?" he wrote in *Surfer*. "How do I convey the sights and sounds that only a handful of humans out of the billions of humans, past, present, and future will ever experience?"

Foo also developed a free-ranging interest in death. "It's not tragic to die doing something you love," he said in a 1986 interview. "It's like the [*Challenger*] astronauts. When they died, they were doing something they'd geared their whole lives to do. They were at the climax of that, and it's not a bad way to go." Foo's big-wave peers thought his death musings were a bit theatrical. Foo didn't mind. It *was* theater, in part. There was craftsmanship in quotes like "If you want the ultimate thrill, you have to be willing to pay the ultimate price." But that didn't mean that he was putting anyone on—himself included. Good surfers weren't dying in big waves. Foo knew this. Yet he accepted it as an article of faith that big-wave surfing was dangerous to the point of being deadly.

While most of Foo's peers rolled their eyes and smiled at his dramatically rendered versions of big-wave surfing, Ken Bradshaw grew to see in Foo everything that was wrong with the sport. The two surfers began feuding, and in 1988, the Foo-Bradshaw conflict was presented in an *Outside* magazine feature article titled

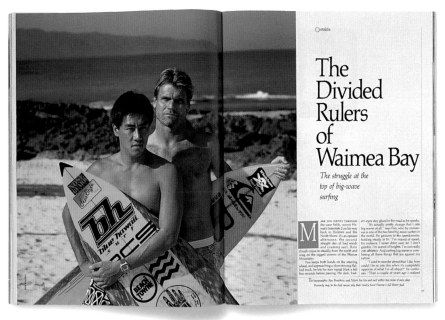

"The Divided Rulers of Waimea Bay." The article pointed out a huge, congenital difference between the two. Foo was an impatient big-wave surfer, a late-starter not overly concerned with big-wave legacy and patrimony. Bradshaw was a traditionalist—and in a sense had been since his 1967 surfing baptismal, in the placid mud-colored breakers of Galveston, where as a ninth-grader he rode his first wave on a rented Greg Noll surfboard. Bradshaw, a high school runaway, arrived on the North Shore at age nineteen, an artless but gutsy surfer, and brick-by-brick constructed a life and career for himself in big-wave surfing. He began to shape his own boards—the way Pat Curren and Greg Noll had. He scrupulously took care of his six-foot, 185-pound body; vegetarian diet, no drugs or drinking, plenty of nonsurfing exercise. He put the time in, made steady gains, and in 1982 he won the Duke Kahanamoku contest at Sunset Beach.

Bradshaw was deferential at all times to his big-wave elders. To most others, he was a brute. He'd paddle up to a surfer who had interfered with one of his waves, knock the surfer off his board, flip the board over, and with

Mark Foo and Ken Bradshaw, *Outside* magazine article, May 1988.

frowning Gestapo efficiency whack off a fin with the base of his hand. In a more emotional state—and to the horror of on-looking surfers—he would sometimes bite into the edge of the board and spit out a mouthful of foam and fiberglass.

Mark Foo, as far as Bradshaw was concerned, had been crossing the line as early as 1977, by grabbing too many waves at Sunset, and it was nearly a *pro forma* act when Bradshaw paddled up to Foo later that season and folded the smaller surfer down into an underwater headlock.

But the Foo-Bradshaw rivalry didn't really solidify until 1985, after Foo's first-person "date with destiny" Waimea account hit the newsstands. Bradshaw had aced a dozen huge waves on January 18 before Foo had even gotten to the beach, but that didn't get into print. Foo, on the other hand—and this was what really burned Bradshaw—had taken off on just *one* wave and hadn't even come *close* to making it. Then he'd gone home, written the article, and gotten famous! Bradshaw understood at some level that Foo had quickly and impressively made himself over into a big-wave rider. But that wasn't the point. He was acting like a punk. He was *pushing* it. Big-wave riding had tradition and custom, and Foo, as Bradshaw saw it, was just lifting a leg on the whole thing. It was a business hustle. Christ, he had *nine* sponsor's stickers on the deck of his board!

It got to the point where Bradshaw found fault with nearly everything Foo did. "Just the way he warms up before he surfs," Bradshaw told *Outside* in 1988. "He's down there at the edge of the water, this big public display, like 'Here I go, everyone! I'm getting warmed up now!'"

Foo responded with a smile and shrug. He was impatient. He admitted it. But he didn't consider himself a disrespectful person, and he got along pretty well with most other big-wave surfers. Bradshaw's animosity, he told *Outside*, had less to do with tradition and etiquette and more to do with jealousy. "Right when he's getting some real attention for what he's doing at Waimea, all of a sudden I'm out in the lineup with him. And making more money at it, too. I know what his sponsors pay."

But the gap between Bradshaw and Foo wasn't quite as chasm-like as they believed. Foo's impolite boasting aside, the sport was affording both surfers the exact same middle-class wages—about thirty thousand dollars in 1987. Bradshaw could be pushed into a grudging admission that he, too, like Foo, was a brightly accessorized (his trademark colors were orange and yellow) and attention-seeking big-wave rider. And Foo said that if he had to choose one person to surf with on a really huge day, he'd probably pick Bradshaw.

Animosity, though, was the rule. Bradshaw was incredulous when Foo told *Surfer* magazine that "good surfing is about making it look easy; Kenny's always had a make-it-look-hard approach." And Foo was embarrassed when, as reported in the *Outside* article, Bradshaw lumbered up one afternoon along Kam Highway and reached out with thumb and forefinger to tweeze one of Foo's sparsely grown chest hairs. "Hey, what's this?" Bradshaw boomed, squinting as he held up the lone black hair for inspection. "Foo-Foo! Check it out! You *are* becoming a man!"

Foo and Bradshaw were both top seeds for the 1990 Quiksilver/Eddie Aikau contest—and both of them bad-lucked their way to a low finish.

The Waimea waves for this second running of the Aikau were huge and smooth, and Keone Downing won the concomitantly huge fifty-five-thousand-dollar first-place prize with a steady, no-mistakes performance. Second-place finisher Brock Little, though, stole the afternoon by first smashing down like a meteorite on the day's only attempted thirty-footer, then, later in the afternoon, by riding inside the tube—a big-wave rarity—and nearly making it out.

In September of that year, Darrick Doerner made the cover of the "Huge Surf" edition of *Surfer,* which featured a Bradshaw-written "Expert Advice" column on how to get through a big-wave wipeout, a top ten list of big-wave surfers, a twenty-page article on Waimea, and some genuflecting big-wave commentary from the *Surfer* editors: "The rest of us can only wonder how it feels to respond to the challenge; to swing around and paddle for a twenty-five-foot wave, every nerve screaming; to launch over the ledge; to make the drop, hit max speed and feel the thunderclap at your heels."

Everything was in place. Waimea Bay, the top ten lists, the windy big-wave prose—it was 1964 redux. In just six years big-wave riding had gone from "Whatever Happened to . . . ?" to reclaiming a place at the top of the surfing hierarchy.

It was a rebirth. It was also, in some respects, a re-creation. Waimea was still the last word in big-wave surfing. Twenty-five feet, give or take a yard, was still the unbreakable size limit.

In his 1990 *Surfer* article titled "The Unridden Realm," Mark Foo talked about the size barrier, which, he said, began at about thirty feet. "The main limiting factor is board speed," Foo wrote, acknowledging the prohibitory up-surging current on thirty-foot-plus waves. "The break- through will come with either a faster bottom contour or possibly with some special kind of surface lubricant. Now, we could cheat our way in. For example, you could be towed in by a boat or jet-ski. But is that *surfing?*"

It was a question Foo and the rest of the big-wave riders, and indeed all of surfing, would soon revisit.

wheel of fear

december 22 1994

san

n francisco SURFER

Edwin Salem zipped up his wetsuit and again paddled out to Maverick's, his handsome face drawn into a mask of resolve. Three times over the past eighteen months he'd made a similar entry, although technically speaking he hadn't yet *surfed* Maverick's because—much to Salem's frustration and embarrassment—on all three occasions he'd paddled back to shore having failed to catch a wave. It wouldn't happen again, though. Salem knew this even before he'd arrived at Pillar Point, just after lunch, a brand-new eleven-foot, ten-inch Ken Bradshaw gun tied to the roof of his weathered Mercedes sedan. Something having to do with the weather, Salem thought; the atmosphere itself seemed to be ionized with uplift and encouragement. The coastline drive from San Francisco to Half Moon Bay had been a joy, the ocean and sky forming a razor-sharp horizon, sunlight flashing off the tops of incoming swells, and the sea-scented air hanging motionless and warm along the coast. Salem knew to expect a few warm Bay Area days in early winter, but this was nearly Mediterranean.

Arriving at Maverick's, Salem climbed the headland, shaded his eyes, and looked out at the surf. He was dressed in a clean white T-shirt, black V-neck sweater, cords, and espadrilles. His wealthy Argentinean family had lost a small fortune between the time he was born and the time he reached adulthood—Salem was now living in a ramshackle beachfront flat, working part-time as a bouncer and struggling to get a new surfboard-manufacturing business off the ground—but at age thirty-four, his demeanor and dress were still casually aristocratic.

Watching the surf for a half hour, he saw nothing but compliant twelve- to fifteen-foot waves. Two surfers to Salem's right mentioned that Josh Loya, Evan Slater, and Matt Ambrose had each picked off a twenty-footer earlier in the day, but Salem didn't see anything that big now, and was glad. Three days ago he'd begged off after standing on the same place on the cliff and watching twenty- to twenty-five-footers unload one after another. Too much. *Way* too much. Not that the surf today was mellow, exactly, but it was appealing to a degree he'd never before seen. Maverick's always looked so sinister. Beautiful but sinister—it attracted and repelled Salem at the same time, and the conflict seeped through his gut like vinegar.

Twenty minutes of steady paddling put Salem in the lineup. Five minutes later he drew a bead on an approaching wave, put his chin on the deck of his board, drove his arms through the water, felt the lift, pushed up into a crouch, and made a silky descent toward the base of his own gorgeous, fully expanded, blue-green Maverick's wall. Ten seconds and seventy-five yards later he taxied off and glided for another ten yards on the flat water behind the wave, a look of furrowed concentration giving way to a rapturous smile.

It was an arcing, perfect moment of joy, and for Salem such moments didn't come easily or often, at least not in big waves. He was an ambivalent big-wave surfer—if he was, in fact, a big-wave surfer at all. For the past decade he'd been riding ten-, twelve-, even fifteen-foot surf at Ocean Beach, but his big-wave enthusiasm rose and fell seismographically. Sometimes he charged right in. Other times he dithered on the beach for hours, watching, weighing the variables, trying to discern patterns and predictors in wave frequency and size. Huge surf often appeared as something not to be challenged or engaged, Salem thought, but rather looked upon with a kind of quiet, head-back reverence, the way you'd admire a grove of giant redwoods or an atmosphere-burning sunset.

Salem's big-wave ambiguity is noted in a scene from "Playing Doc's Games," William Finnigan's magisterial 1992 *New Yorker* article set among San Francisco surf society. Finnigan describes a late-winter afternoon at Ocean Beach, with a fifteen-foot swell running out of the northwest. "The kind of day," he writes, where most surfers "suddenly remember all the business they have in far-flung parts of the Greater Bay Area." Salem and another half dozen "nervous and jumpy" locals are concentrating on a group of surfers already in the water, and trying to decide if they themselves want to paddle out.

An unusual amount of profanity—unusual even for surfers—is being used to discuss the waves, the weather, the world. And then Edwin, who has been silently watching the ocean from behind mirrored sunglasses, erupts. "I have an idea," he announces. "Let's form a support group. I'm not going out there, because I'm scared to go out there. Why don't we all just say that? 'I'm not going out there because I'm scared to go out there.' Come on Domond, you say it."

Domond, a noisy tough who works in the local surf shop when he's not driving a taxicab, turns away in disgust. So Edwin addresses himself to another homebody, known as Beeper Dave, but he also turns away, grumbling and shaking his head. Everybody then ignores Edwin, who just laughs easily and shrugs.

"Set," somebody growls. All eyes swing to the horizon, where the blazing sheet of the sea is beginning to lift in sickeningly large gray lines. "Those guys are *dead*."

overleaf
Second Bowl
section at Maverick's.

127

Heavy LATE-AFTERNOON shadows angled down from the Pillar Point headland as Salem walked along the dirt road back toward the Maverick's parking lot. Salem's mood had darkened as well. He stopped and once again examined his new surfboard, where a fist-size piece of Maverick's reef had smashed through the fiberglass and foam, embedded itself nearly flush to the deck, and broken off. He'd never seen anything like it. Boards were dinged, fractured, gouged, splintered, flayed, or broken in two. But a broken-off chunk of rock jammed down flush like a meteorite? What the hell was *that*?

For ninety minutes things had been wonderful. Salem's first ride was followed by two more, both thrilling, and if he'd been just ten feet closer to shore he would have caught a fourth wave. But he missed it, barely, and turned around to see a full-blooded twenty-footer massing in the Bowl section, about to break. Salem cursed, hyperventilated for a few moments as the wave approached, then rolled off his board and pushed it away, closed his eyes, and tunneled for the depths. He heard a concessive roar and, in the same instant, felt his ankle leash tug sharply and then snap as his board was whipped shoreward.

Salem himself made it safely under the vortex and came up on the back slope, eyes searching wildly for a follow-up wave. Nothing. The set was over and Salem was momentarily headspun with relief. He began swimming, first to the southeast, parallel to the Boneyard rocks, then, after making a ninety-degree turn, into the lagoon. The beach was about seventy-five yards ahead. The water here was choppy but waveless, and Salem regained his composure. He began looking for his board. It had likely been pushed into the rocks, which meant he'd have to search the eddies and shallows—but no, there it was, floating in the lee of the rocks, fins up, about fifty yards to his left. Salem swam over, flipped the board right side up, and frowned when he saw the rock lodged in the deck.

Walking back to the parking lot, he tried and failed to get some perspective on the afternoon. The three waves he'd ridden dashed around in his head like living things, making the rest of his surfing life seem dull by comparison. But look at his board! He'd been so cautious—and look what happened! What if *he'd* been washed through the Boneyard? What if he'd smashed into the rocks the way his board had? The idea twisted his stomach like a tourniquet.

Again Salem considered his board. He could dig out the rock and patch the hole; it wouldn't be too big of a project. Meanwhile he could borrow a board, come back to Maverick's tomorrow, and try again. Maybe, in fact, today had been the best possible all-around experience. He'd ridden three waves, and he'd also pulled himself through a pretty gnarly situation.

Bullshit, he told himself. That wasn't even *close* to gnarly, not by Maverick's standards. Caught inside for one wave, broken leash, long swim in, dinged-but-fixable surfboard—it didn't get much *less* gnarly than that.

It was as if a light went out. Salem arrived at the parking lot and knew he wasn't coming back tomorrow—and he might not come back ever.

right
Helicopter rescue,
Waimea Bay, Hawaii,
1984.

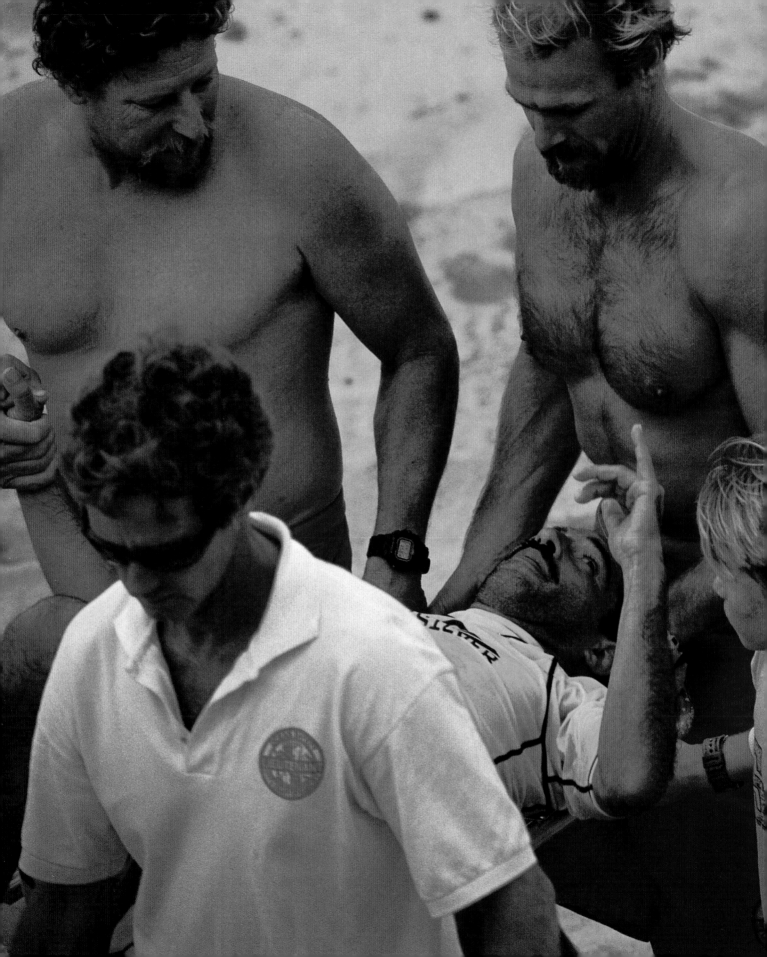

UCSF ONCOLOGIST Mark Renneker had been Edwin Salem's big-wave mentor in the eighties, and since they lived just four houses apart on the same street, the mentoring program consisted mainly of Renneker showing up at Salem's front door to wheedle his friend into the surf on days when Salem would otherwise pass. Occasionally Salem felt a little bullied by Renneker's chattering insistence. More often he was grateful. Eventually there were days at Ocean Beach in the ten-to-twelve-foot range where Salem rode as aggressively, and with as much ease, as Renneker.

But Renneker's surfing life was plainly different from Salem's. Renneker was virtually fearless. No dry-mouth surf checks, or chicken-out "support group" jokes, or gasping big-wave nightmares. Renneker, like Salem, played out extravagant big-wave scenarios in his mind, all the time, but as a kind of improvement drill—he wouldn't see himself mashed into the Boneyard rocks, as Salem feverishly did. He instead imagined himself picking out just the right seam through the crags and overhangs to arrive safely into the lagoon. Renneker acknowledged the risk of big-wave surfing. But the thrill of it, he felt, hugely outweighed the danger. He believed that completely, religiously. It was in his bones.

It was in his office files, too. In the late eighties, bringing science to bear on big-wave danger as best he could, Renneker gathered all available statistical information on surfing injury and death rates. There wasn't much, and none of it was big-wave specific. Still, Renneker worked on the numbers and eventually came up with an estimated surfing-related injury rate—an injury defined as being bad enough to keep a surfer out of the water, meaning deep cuts, sprains, fractures, and so on—of one per 250 days surfed. "The truth is," Renneker wrote in *Sick Surfers*, his 1993 book, "surfing is an extremely safe sport." Surfers and recreational fishermen, he noted, have a "roughly equivalent" injury rate. Cheerleaders were treated for injuries at a far higher rate than surfers.

Trying to figure out anything conditional to big-wave riding was harder. Big waves by themselves, Renneker knew, were of course more likely than small waves to hold a surfer underwater until he drowned. But in small waves, with the usual high-density crowd, a surfer had a far greater risk of being struck unconscious (by his board, or someone else's board, or from hitting the bottom) and *then* drowned. The unsupervised beginning surfer drifting into a strong riptide, furthermore, was at greater risk than the big-wave rider spiraling into the pit on a twenty-footer. And no big-wave surfer ever tested the odds as boldly as the untrained, pot-bellied, beer-staggered citizen bodysurfer.

Peter Van Dyke, who began surfing San Francisco in the early fifties and later moved to Oahu's North Shore as part of the original California big-wave invasion, was the first to try and peg back the danger involved with big-wave surfing. "It isn't perilous, dangerous or as hairy as it's cracked up to be," Van Dyke wrote in *Surfer* in 1966. Van Dyke listed a half-dozen Grand Prix racers recently killed on the track, pointed out that death in the bull-ring "is almost too obvious to mention," and

left
North Shore back injury, 1995.

noted that most big-wave surfers were so unconcerned about their fitness and stamina that they trained "on cake, Kool-Aid, ice cream and cigarettes." The last person to die at Waimea Bay, Van Dyke pointed out, was Dickie Cross in 1943.

By the numbers at least, the idea of death by big-wave misadventure should have been even further removed for Renneker, Jeff Clark, Jay Moriarity, and the rest of the serious big-wave riders in 1994. Cross was still the last surfer to die at Waimea. Nobody had died at Maverick's. Twenty or thirty surfers had died in medium-to-big surf over the decades, but none were validated big-wave riders. Drugs, bar fights, motorcycle wrecks, and suicidal depression had taken out a few good, hard-charging surfers. Not big waves.

John Raymond, a Pacifica bankruptcy lawyer, understood this. He and Renneker had paddled out at Maverick's for the first time in 1990, a few days after Clark introduced the break to Tom Powers and Dave Schmidt. Raymond surfed Maverick's consistently over the next four years and became almost inured to the idea of dying in big surf. "You might have a really bad wipeout," he said. "You might see God; you might swallow a bunch of water. But you're not going to die."

But you'd *think* you were. The water-choking, God-envisioning big-wave surfer (and nearly all of them get pushed that far at least once) feels ultimate mortal terror just as surely as the car driver skidding through a mountain road guardrail. Empirically, the two examples almost can't be compared. The driver's life hangs in the balance, while the big-wave rider invariably beats his way to the surface, makes a shaky retreat up the beach, and has a full appetite by dinner. But that isn't the point. For a few consummate moments, surfer and driver both feel as if they're rushing headlong toward death, and the spikes of terror are certainly equivalent. While the surfer can then process and rationalize the experience, it often comes back in a thousand shades of dread and anxiety. John Raymond, who in pragmatic moments believes that "you're not going to die" while riding big waves, also understands how big-wave fear can drift like smoke into the imagination. "The scariest moments I've had there," Raymond says in *Maverick's,* a 1998 documentary film, "I'm not even actually in the water. I start thinking about what could happen, about what it's like to drown, say, and I break out in a cold sweat. It just blows your mind sometimes. I've laid there in bed and thought, 'God, I'm never going to surf there again.'"

Most surfers never make a big-wave effort to begin with, at Maverick's or anywhere else. About one hundred surfers today out of two million worldwide make a regular practice of riding twenty-five-foot waves. Probably three hundred surfers total in the past fifty years have done so.

Maybe it's surprising the numbers are even that high. Humans are land animals, after all. Walking comes naturally, while swimming—terrifying enough to many—must be learned. We instinctively hold our breath underwater as a life-saving response, and we just as instinctively claw for the surface as soon as the oxygen begins its awful chest-constricting turn to carbon dioxide. At some atavistic level of self-preservation, stroking out to meet huge surf—and the guarantee, sooner or later, of an underwater struggle—is just barely more sensible than walking into fire.

Then again, humans are occasionally bold and forever inventive. Within reason, and with the right training and apparatus, you can walk into fire. Or fly, or traverse a cliff, or ride huge waves.

But the fear remains, and every big-wave surfer, to one degree or another, is in constant negotiation with his fear, and with the fact that his sport runs against safekeeping instincts millions of years in the making. And the terms of negotiation change constantly. Fear isn't always the enemy. It's also chased and courted. To examine fear in big-wave surfing—to identify, classify, and describe it, as both uplifting and crippling, as an agent of both joy and terror—is to examine just about everything unique and interesting in the sport.

San Francisco's Grant Washburn grins when he says, "We're waiting for those big days, and you *want* to be there when it's scary. That's what's fun. That's what you're after, to be scared, and be excited by the fear."

Josh Loya from Santa Cruz, on the same subject, looks sullen. "Why do we do it? I don't know. People just do stupid things. Why would you want to climb Everest? You get high enough up there and you can't even breathe; you have to wear an oxygen mask, you're exhausted. What's the fun in that? What's the fun in riding some giant wave and having it crash down on you?"

Washburn, beaming, gesturing, transported: "Some days you get to go out there at Mav's and see waves you can't even ride, waves that are just so far out of the realm of human comprehension. That's what's so cool about it. That's what's so exciting."

Loya: "The best thing about Maverick's, the best feeling you get out there, is when you come in."

When JOSH LOYA ASKS, "Why do we do it?" he's posing the immortal big-wave question. All big-wave surfers ask it of themselves. All of them field it from magazine writers, TV reporters, mothers, fathers, girlfriends, and wives. Surfers often couch their reply in interesting ways. "I do it because" regularly becomes "We do it because," or the second-person "You do it because," and occasionally the presumptuous "He does it because." Loya might be the only big-wave surfer, active or retired, to answer "I don't know." The rest know, or *think* they know, and their level of interest on this score usually begins at a point beyond curiosity and stops just short of desperation.

"It was a Freudian deal with me," Greg Noll says, "'cause when I was a little guy I got my ass kicked a lot. You get to the bottom of it, and that pretty much explains why I did what I did in big surf." Of course, just about *everything* was a Freudian deal in the sixties, and Fred Van Dyke, not surprisingly, offered some analysis. "One guy has a big-brother complex," he told *Life* magazine in 1968, "another guy has unresolved father problems. Is the big-wave surfer perhaps looking for a mother substitute? 'Look Mommy, look at the ride I just got.

overleaf
Caught inside at
Maverick's, 1994.

135

Look how much better it was than brother's.'"

Jeff Clark has said that Maverick's "appeals to the dark side of a surfer's psyche," but the Freudian take on big-wave motivation has mostly given way to the idea of behavioral genetics, whereby big-wave surfers do little more than march to chemically dispatched orders from their DNA. The D4DR gene, for example, located on chromosome eleven, has been linked to a personality trait scientists call "novelty seeking"—which includes thrill-seeking. A D4DR-made protein helps with the absorption of a pleasure-producing brain chemical called dopamine (the "liquor of fear," as surf journalist Ben Marcus puts it), which can be released during, or just after, dangerous experiences. A person with a balky D4DR gene might unknowingly try to compensate by pursuing a dopamine-rich life in bank robbery, bullfighting, or big-wave surfing.

Brock Little from Hawaii seems to be a living argument for the genetically predestined big-wave rider. At two years old, Brock was knocked over and dragged into the surf, vanishing without a trace, during a family walk on the beach. Stunned silence from both parents, then screaming panic, then Brock was tumbled ashore in the following wave and planted in the sand. As the water drained, he clapped his hands, laughing and bouncing. By 1994, he was a celebrated big-wave rider. He was also a street-fighting terror, a dirt biker, and ready at any time to jump from any high perch into any body of water. Bright, friendly, and dependable, but addicted to thrills. "I don't mind bleeding," he told *Interview* in 1991, "and I don't mind getting held underwater. If I get into a radical experience—getting into a fight, or driving fast, or riding a huge wave—and live through it, I'm totally stoked."

One final response to the question of why certain surfers thrive in big waves—not so much a separate rationale as an adjunct to nature/nurture theories of big-wave riding—is that these particular few dozen people are the ones who, by means in-born or learned, are able to master the technique of underwater relaxation. Don't panic underwater, conserve oxygen, and you'll come up. It's the first and simplest big-wave principle, yet for the enormous majority of surfers it's an impossible order. Surfers who train themselves in swimming pools to stay underwater for three minutes—long enough to survive even a three-wave hold-down—will likely find themselves on the outskirts of panic just ten seconds into a full-throttle big-wave wipeout. If they even get that far. Bryce Ellis and Gary Green, two top-rated pros, pulled out of a world tour contest in 1986 when the event was relocated to Waimea Bay. Nat Young, 1966's world champion—perhaps the most influential surfer of the century; rangy, fit, and aggressive, with enormous stamina, long, fast-paddling arms, and an outsize ego that would seemingly *demand* big-wave performance—could not bring himself to ride waves over twenty feet. "I've only done it once, on one wave," Young said in the 1967 surfing film *Fantastic Plastic Machine*, "and I don't ever wish to do it ever again. If those guys can enjoy themselves while their hearts and guts are falling down a mineshaft, then I respect them and their courage. I just don't think I could ever express myself while scared out of m v wits."

Evan Slater HAD THROWN HIS heart and guts down the big-wave mineshaft with gusto and pleasure, but as of midafternoon, December 22, 1994, he'd had enough. His duffel bag was packed and loaded into his van, and he was about to drive to Southern California for the Christmas holidays. Physically, he was fine. He'd assembled a fantastic collection of wipeouts over the past week—balanced by an equally fantastic set of completed rides—but had avoided injury. Mentally, though, he was washed out. Slater had ridden Maverick's for seven straight days, including that morning, and while he'd moved to San Francisco to become a full-time on-call Maverick's surfer, he'd hit a saturation point. Even as Slater was getting ready to leave, Maverick's was producing smooth, well-shaped fifteen-footers, and the thought of it left him—not *indifferent*, quite, but not exhilarated, either. It felt strange. Good big surf was usually so hard to find, and big-wave supply had never before outstripped Slater's big-wave desire. Two days in a row of big surf was a treat, three was rare, four almost unheard of. *Seven* consecutive days of big surf was beyond comparison—almost beyond comprehension. Slater had gorged himself, sometimes driving between Ocean Beach and Half Moon Bay twice a day, living a big-wave existence that had shifted from thrilling and pure to surreal.

He needed a break. He walked through his flat once more, checking to see if he'd forgotten anything. The phone rang and Slater answered. After a short conversation with Ben Marcus, managing editor at *Surfer*, he hung up and spent a few contemplative seconds staring out the window. Tomorrow was going to be a big deal, Marcus said. He'd been getting calls all afternoon. Mike Parsons, Southern California's best big-wave rider, was driving up from San Clemente. Brock Little was flying in from Los Angeles. Ken Bradshaw and Mark Foo were taking the red-eye from Hawaii. The Santa Cruz guys would be on it, of course, plus all the photographers. The surf was getting bigger, and the warm weather was going to hold.

Slater's hit-the-road resolve began to flag. He was a professional big-wave rider, which he took as an honor as well as a vocation, and that carried obligations. But that wasn't really it. Nobody was going to dock his pay if he passed on tomorrow's session. No, Slater admitted to himself, it was an ego thing. Maverick's wasn't his spot the way it was Jeff Clark's, but he'd been a fixture in the lineup for three months, and now felt, correctly, that he had a reputation to uphold. Foo, Parsons, and Little—all friends of Slater's—would be riding Maverick's for the first time. Slater felt he should be there when they arrived, as a welcoming gesture, yes, but also as a member of the home team. His take on his fellow big-wave surfers was in line with that of nearly all his professional peers: never antagonistic, usually friendly, always competitive.

Slater was boxed in. His Maverick's experience thus far practically demanded he see things through to tomorrow. It wasn't that he wanted to stay; it was just pretty much impossible to leave. He walked outside and began unloading the van.

overleaf
Santa Cruz surfers
Darryl Virostko (left)
and Zack Wormhoudt
ride together at
Maverick's, 1994.

MACHINE AGE

big-wave surfing

beyond waimea

1991–

1994

The 1990 Quiksilver/Eddie Aikau contest appeared to be an unqualified success. Waimea Bay was shown off to huge, beautiful, dramatic effect; Keone Downing was a popular winner (and fifty-five thousand dollars richer); and lavish media coverage followed. Thousands of white-on-black Quiksilver contest promo stickers were stuck onto car bumpers, each bearing the cryptic declaration that "Eddie Would Go." Surfers understood and loved the message. Eddie Aikau, Hawaii's sainted big-wave master, had stylishly charged his way into enormous North Shore waves, and by doing so (and by dying young in a 1978 boating accident) had become a surf-world icon. Martin Potter, reigning world champion in 1990, could bend the laws of physics in surf up to fifteen feet, and was brutally charismatic in the bargain—but not many surfers were going to slap a "Martin Would Go" sticker on their pickup. The Quiksilver/Eddie Aikau contest perfectly distilled the idea that big-wave riders were made of tougher, deeper, more fascinating stuff than other surfers.

Nonetheless, some people, including a few contestants, viewed both the 1986 and 1990 Quiksilver events as acts of big-wave sabotage. Surfers encouraged by Quiksilver's record-breaking prize-money checks—so the argument went—had settled into the Waimea lineup like locusts. Forty-five riders were counted at Waimea on a January afternoon in 1988, sitting in a take-off zone that shouldn't hold more than twenty. A *Surfer's Journal* photograph from 1990 shows ten surfers paddling for a single wave, and fourteen more floating over the top. Surfing's basic wave-possession rule—one surfer/one wave, with right-of-way going to the surfer closest to the curl—was selectively or comprehensively ignored. "The [Quiksilver] money hype just brought out the worst people," Darrick Doerner remembers. "It gave the place a *Rollerball* feel. It was a sad thing." Doerner quit riding Waimea unless it was over twenty-five feet—big enough to scare the crowd off. Ken Bradshaw didn't give up so easily. "If just *one* of you guys drops in on my next wave," he roared to a cowed group of Waimea novitiates, "I'm sending *all* you motherfuckers to the beach!"

By 1990, the North Shore had become a surf-world Rorschach blot, revered by some, reviled by others. Much of its back-country character—the unbroken fields of pineapple and sugarcane, the two-lane roads trimmed with small, independently owned shops, the slowly developing harbor town of Haleiwa—was virtually unchanged from the time Greg Noll first drove his oil-burning '37 Plymouth over from Makaha in the midfifties. The North Shore surf, meanwhile, remained the magnetic center of the surfing universe, attracting the best

riders, world championship–deciding contests, the latest board designs, and the surf media. There was a naturalness in the way surfers migrated each winter to the North Shore—like salmon swimming upriver to the headwaters. Nowhere else in the world did the sport manifest itself with such range and variety in such a compact area.

The North Shore had also become shamelessly oversold and overused. In high season, on any given day, no more than one-quarter to one-half of the roughly fifty North Shore breaks will produce ridable waves, and of those breaks perhaps just three or four will be really firing. About five thousand surfers were in regular North Shore rotation in December of 1990, including world-tour pros and pro hopefuls, resident non-pros, and peripheral members of the surf press and surf industry, the majority of them easily marked as loud, zealous, well-muscled, territorial young adult males. Peace, for the most part, was maintained through an unstated Darwinian-style social hierarchy. Everybody pretty well understood their rank and position, and lines weren't often crossed. But violence and mayhem—or the *suggestion* of violence and mayhem—hung in the air like sea-spray, and intersurfer communication was often reduced to a series of postures, flexions, stares, grimaces, and exclamations. Ken Bradshaw, in other words, could threaten to deport an entire lineup of Waimea surfers with virtually no chance of having to start in with any real knuckle-popping demolition work.

Big-wave serenity, though, had practically evaporated. When forty-five surfers were paddling and riding in a tight weave across the Waimea lineup in 1988—"just a full pig-pile," as Bradshaw put it—everyone went home feeling beaten down, if not beaten up.

On January 22, 1990, the day after he'd placed second in the Quiksilver contest, Brock Little packed two surfboards into a huge, cigar-shaped foam-padded travel bag, flew from Honolulu to Los Angeles, and headed south for Todos Santos, a rock-fringed big-wave break at the northwest tip of Todos Santos island in Baja Mexico. Never before had a big-wave surfer *left* Hawaii during the winter season. It felt strange, Little thought, but he liked the idea that Todos might be an anodyne to the North Shore surf-crowd chaos.

Nobody lived on Todos Santos. Nobody vacationed there. Surfers who visited, nearly all of them from southern California, didn't stay for more than a few hours. Little had been wondering about Todos since 1987, when he saw photographs of California surfers Dave Parmenter and Tom Curren in "The Biggest West Coast Waves Ever Ridden"—or so *Surfing* magazine declared in the article that helped introduce Todos Santos to the surf world. "There wasn't a soul out," Parmenter wrote. "Huge, perfect waves completely empty!" Parmenter called it fifteen feet, but one of the photos showed Curren paddling up the face of a cresting Waimea-size twenty-footer.

This was a genuine and original big-wave surprise. Surfers were caught off-guard. Big-wave riding was essentially and traditionally Hawaiian, and for thirty years it had been defined by a single place: Waimea Bay. There were second-tier breaks—Sunset Beach, Makaha, and Hanalei Bay in Hawaii; Lunada Bay and Steamer Lane in California; Easter Reef in Australia; Outer Kom in South Africa; and Pico Alto in Peru—but what came below Waimea didn't really matter. Waimea defined the genre. So in 1987, to stare at a magazine photograph of Curren clawing through a twenty-footer at a nearly uncharted surf break in Mexico—and doing so in a full neck-to-toe wetsuit, the water color a frigid cobalt-blue instead of an embracing tropical cyan—was to view nothing less than the first cellular division of big-wave surfing. No magazine hype this time. These were the biggest West Coast waves ever ridden, and if Todos wasn't a Waimea replica, it was awfully close.

Brock Little was mildly skeptical of Todos's building big-wave reputation, but confident enough with the updated wave forecast to believe he was about to score some oversize—if not gigantic—surf. Wave forecasting, during Little's twelve years in surfing, had graduated from wet-finger-to-the-wind conjecture to a hard science. Using new computer programs to help order wind and swell data from ship reports, satellites, and Pacific Ocean weather buoys, a southern California phone service called

SurfLine, headed by oracular surf prophet Sean Collins ("The Prince of Tides," as the *Los Angeles Times* labeled him), was able to forecast not just where and when good surf would arrive but its duration and quality. Little, in fact, didn't leave for Todos Santos until the itinerary was vetted and approved by Collins. Fifteen-to-twenty and clean as a whistle—that was the prediction.

Now, in the predawn hours of January 23, Little drove with a carload of surfers to the harbor town of Ensenada, one hundred miles below the California/Mexico border, where a fishing boat was hired for the one-hour, eight-mile trip out to the small cactus-and-scrub-covered Todos Santos island. Motoring into the channel adjacent to the break, Little—cold, baggy-eyed, and slightly nauseous from the boat engine's diesel fumes—watched a dozen or so eight- to ten-foot waves peel across the reef. Nothing to get sour over, but hardly worth a three-thousand-mile journey. Collins, this time, Little figured, blew the call. But the surf grew all morning, and by midday Little was harvesting twenty-footers one after the other. "Todos," he said afterward, coming around to offer the ultimate big-wave benediction, "reminded me a lot of Waimea."

Todos reminded everyone of Waimea—the two waves seem to be cast from the same geologic mold. Both take form over a compact ridge of reef and break to the right, and both produce a straightforward and relatively short ride. Waimea falls apart at thirty feet; so does Todos. Waimea hits twenty feet a little more often (about five times a year to Todos's four), and breaks with more force, but its similarities to Todos are more obvious than its differences.

Todos Santos was a revelation for southern California's two dozen big-wave devotees. Mike Parsons, Evan Slater, Joe and Terrance McNulty, Allan Sarlo, and Marty Hoffman—most of whom had been flying each winter to the North Shore to pick off strays at Waimea—now reveled in the solitary Todos wave field. When

147

Brock Little returned to Hawaii, he gave an enthusiastic report to his neighbor Mark Foo, who then made the Todos trip himself. In 1992, Little and Foo traveled to Todos together. The surf was twenty feet and sun-drenched, but Foo remembered the jet-setting experience as an endurance test. "I'd just surfed for two days at Waimea, then we had a day of traveling, no sleep, got off the plane at like 2 A.M., then drove straight to Ensenada. After four or five hours in big waves in a full wetsuit, I wanted to take a break. But the waves were unreal, and I didn't want to leave while Brock was still in the water. We surfed for seven hours that day." Late in the afternoon Little aced a twenty-five footer, and Foo rode one nearly as big. A photo of both surfers riding together was turned into a *Surfer* cover with the gibing caption, "Dueling egos: Brock Little and Mark Foo at Todos Santos."

The still-expanding big-wave world was in fact treating both surfers well. More places to surf. Bigger sponsors' paychecks. Lots of magazine coverage and plenty of ego gratification. Foo and Little talked and laughed as they boated from Todos to Ensenada, then slept like babies on the flight back to Honolulu.

Todos Santos should have alerted

the surf world to the possibility of more overlooked Mainland big-wave breaks, but it didn't, and in mid-1992, after Santa Cruz surfer Richard Schmidt was photographed on a twenty-five-footer at a just-revealed spot called Maverick's, hundreds of thousands of surfers bent back the pages of surf magazines and goggled anew at this strange and terrible wave as if it had suddenly burst up steaming from the earth's crust.

Schmidt's wave was larger than anything yet seen at Todos Santos. It was also double the length, faster, stronger, and more hostile. Schmidt had barreled along at top speed for more than

fifty yards, in perfect trim—long past the point where he would have been home-free at Waimea or Todos—when the wave abruptly flared up, wound itself into a sepulchral mist-spitting tube, and deleted Schmidt in an instant.

Waimea had been matched. Or outmatched. No one yet knew exactly how a twenty-five-foot wave at Maverick's would spec out against a twenty-five-footer at Waimea. For atmospheric menace, though, as *Surfer* writer Ben Marcus noted in his 1992 Maverick's-debuting article "Cold Sweat," Half Moon Bay's "gray, gloomy, isolated" big-wave break was in a class alone.

Maverick's radiates danger. The reef is surrounded by deep water, and lies naked to every nasty thing above and below the Pacific: Aleutian swells, northwest winds, southeast storms, aggro elephant seals and wilder things that snack on aggro elephant seals. The place reeks of *Jaws*. The shoreline is craggy rocks backed by sheer cliffs. Paddle out from the north and you skirt a twisted bowl section that makes brave men nauseous. Paddle from the south and you fight a current that sweeps through the rocks, then turns out to sea [near Pillar Point harbor] and becomes one of the worst navigational hazards on the California coast.

Maverick's location itself was slightly bizarre. Todos Santos was geographically closer than Maverick's to surf-crazed southern California—Los Angeles to Ensenada is about 200 miles; Los Angeles to Half Moon Bay is about 350—but Todos seemed like another world. Getting there required provisioning, a border crossing, and an open-ocean boat ride. Maverick's all but spills onto the highways and backyards of metropolitan California. Maverick's turning up where and when it did, as the *SF Weekly* put it, "was like finding a lost species of animal in downtown San Francisco."

No more than five hundred surfers, outside of Half Moon Bay, had heard of Maverick's by early 1992. Fifty or so had watched from the cliff, or paddled out for a closer look, perhaps even sampling a wave or two, before deciding it wasn't for them. About ten surfers were surfing Maverick's regularly, and when "Cold Sweat" was published, another ten or fifteen were set to join them.

Jeff Clark, the original Maverick's surfer, said in "Cold Sweat" that he was glad for the company. In truth, he'd been ambivalent about going public with his still-cloistered big-wave break. Santa Cruz surfers Tom Powers and Dave Schmidt didn't tell anybody for months about their 1990 Maverick's experience, Powers said, "out of respect to Clark." When *Surfer* ran a short profile on Clark in 1991, he was identified as "the unofficial guardian of a true secret spot." Maverick's was named, but vaguely located, at Clark's insistence, "somewhere between Santa Cruz and the Golden Gate Bridge."

Vince Collier, Peter Mel, Josh Loya, Darryl Virostko, the Schmidt brothers, and Mark Renneker were all mentioned in "Cold Sweat," which opened properly enough with a two-page shot of Clark dropping into a bleak, beautiful, empty Maverick's wall. The "Cold Sweat" prose, bantering in places, also sounded some cautionary notes. "I've witnessed some of the most frightening wipe-outs there," said Mark Renneker, "and my prediction is there's going to be some major injuries, perhaps deaths."

"I took Flea Virostko and some other kids out at Maverick's last January," Santa Cruz rogue Vince Collier said, "and Flea got caught inside on a huge set and was just scared shitless. I felt like Uncle Al Bundy. No, actually, I really was worried that those kids were going to get hurt—or worse. I think only a certain amount of people are going to want to ride this place. Anybody can paddle out. But to paddle out time after time, year after year, they got to either have something, or lack something. I can't quite put my finger on it."

What *didn't* worry Renneker, Collier, or any of the other Maverick's regulars was the idea of being attacked by a shark, despite the fact that the Farallon Islands, twenty-five miles west of San Francisco, are a white shark breeding ground. Local legend was full of shark stories. Santa Cruz surfer Craig Rogers, in the summer of 1987, once watched in paralytic silence as a fifteen-foot white shark bobbed up, luridly opened its mouth, clamped onto the front section of his surfboard, then swam off uninterested, leaving Rogers with a cut hand and empirical evidence that "you can't scream and breathe at the same time." But the Maverick's surfers also knew that just one person had ever been killed while surfing off the California coast, and that all nonfatal attacks on California surfers—about thirty, total—had occurred in small waves.

By mid-1992, with the introduction of Todos Santos and Maverick's, big-wave thrills had become democratically parceled out among three major breaks, and the entire pursuit was broader and more engaging than ever before. But two fundamental things hadn't changed: the ride was the same dead-ahead race to the channel it had always been, and most frustratingly, the twenty-five-foot size barrier had proven all but inviolable. Greg Noll's thirty-footer in 1969 now seemed to be not quite a *fluke*, but extraordinary and perhaps unique. Surfers before and after Noll had caught waves measuring between twenty-five and thirty feet, and even made some progress down the face, but always to a bad end. The base-to-apex rush of water was too much. It was true for George Downing, Pat Curren, and Buzzy Trent, and it was still true for Brock Little, Darrick Doerner, and Mark Foo. Even Noll, on his giant Makaha wave, hadn't done anything more than make it to the trough, where he was atomized. "You have to believe that it's mind over matter," Little once said in reference to high-end big-wave surfing. "But sometimes there's just too much matter."

Little was right: Mind over matter

wasn't enough to get a surfer in full trim across a thirty-footer. Mind and *machine*, though—that was a different story. On a bright blue North Shore afternoon in 1992, Darrick Doerner, Buzzy Kerbox, and Laird Hamilton loaded up Kerbox's inflatable Zodiac boat and motored out to a North Shore break called Backyards. Three conventional big-wave surfboards were stacked across the bow, and a thirty-foot length of nylon water-ski rope was tied off at the stern and lay coiled on the floorboard. The surf at Backyards was a moderate twelve to fifteen feet, but this was just a preparatory exercise.

Kerbox, driving, slowed the Zodiac down about one hundred yards beyond the Backyards lineup, the rope was tossed out, and Hamilton picked up his board and knifed smoothly into the water. He and Kerbox had been working on this routine for the past few months; Doerner was the newcomer. Hamilton got to his feet and gripped the plastic handle at the end of the rope as the Zodiac, in a holding pattern, made a few lazy low-speed circles. When Hamilton gave a hand signal, Kerbox turned for shore and opened the throttle, placing the Zodiac

Surfer, June 1992.

COLD SWEAT

a big-wave secret spot for 30 years, northern california's maverick's emerges from the mist.

just ahead of a mounting but unbroken wave. Hamilton flexed, crouched, and leaned back, the rope taut as a wire as his board chattered across the water. Then, as the boat angled off toward the channel, Hamilton dropped the rope and glided for five full seconds before the swell crested, at which point he inscribed a long calligraphic turn across the wave face, and then ran high and fast along the curl line. The control was absolute. The thirty-mile-an-hour, sling-shot entry allowed Hamilton to settle into a rhythm and pace that carried all the way through his forty-five-second ride, and when he arrived in the channel, Kerbox and Doerner, already standing by, towed him immediately back to the starting position out past the surf line. Five minutes later Hamilton was again up and riding.

Waimea warhorse Ken Bradshaw stood on the beach with a pair of binoculars, watching and trying to figure out what to make of things. Hamilton was *wailing* across those faces, no question there. Big, deep, carving turns, too. Hamilton *damn* sure knew how to bury a rail, Bradshaw mused. But something was wrong. The boat and the rope—it just looked weird. Frivolous, kind of. Or worse. Bradshaw lowered the binoculars, unfocused his gaze for a moment, and stropped his jaw with a well-callused thumb as two words floated to mind: *they're cheating.* Then Hamilton was tearing into another wave and Bradshaw whipped the binoculars back into place.

In February 1993, Hamilton, Kerbox, and Doerner towed each other into twenty-footers for the first time, and rode nearly without a hitch. Each surfer got ten to fifteen waves an hour, and about fifty rides were completed, against just two wipeouts. No energy was wasted on paddling; everything was poured into the ride itself. (A paddle surfer, in similar conditions, would have caught two or three waves an hour and completed only half to three-quarters of the rides.) Tow-in surfing, as it would come to be known, was born, and the progenitors knew

exactly what they wanted.

"We're preparing to ride some of the biggest waves of our time," Darrick Doerner said. "We're just getting our timing down, figuring the whole thing out, because one day a thirty-foot set's gonna come in, and we're gonna be ready for it."

The tow-in choreography was obvious from the beginning. The driver had to accurately place the surfer on the wave, veer off without leaving a ride-disabling wake across the surfer's path, then monitor the action from about twenty-five yards away. Contingencies were planned for, and rescue drills were invented and practiced. Wipeouts were expected—horrific wipeouts—as they continued to push into bigger surf.

Hamilton and Kerbox moved to the north coast of Maui in 1993, next to a cataclysmic big-wave break called Jaws, a place that could hold thirty-five-foot surf, maybe bigger. Seventies Pipeline idol and Maui resident Gerry Lopez, along with a few other surfers, had been keeping an eye on this remote big-wave location for twenty-five years. "But we never surfed it," he wrote in *Surfer's Journal.* "Sometimes we dragged our boards down the cliff trail to the rocky beach, [then] back up the trail we went, tails between our legs. It was called Atom Blaster back then, because we thought it broke like an atom bomb."

In the early nineties, Maui locals Mike Waltz, Rush Randle, Mark and Josh Angulo, and Dave Kalama began riding Jaws on their sailboards, using wind power to give them a running start, just as Hamilton, Kerbox, and Doerner were using the Zodiac to the same purpose at Backyards on the North Shore. When Hamilton and Kerbox began tow-in surfing fifteen- to twenty-footers at Jaws in late 1993, these sailboarders, and a few others—Gerry Lopez included—joined the tow-in fold.

The Maui group made two big changes right away. They replaced the Zodiac with a pair of diesel-burning two-stroke 650cc Yamaha Wave Runner III jet skis. An easy switch: The nimbler skis were much better suited to darting into the surf zone for rescues, and the water-jet propulsion system was safer than the Zodiac's prop-driven outboard motor. And they overhauled tow-in board design top to bottom. Wave-catching speed was no longer the primary requirement—it wasn't a requirement at all. For the first time ever boards were built for riding only, and when Hamilton stripped away all paddling features for his 1993 big-wave model, he ended up with a board just seven feet, ten inches long and sixteen inches wide. Other boards were even smaller and narrower—"like a cross between a regular surfboard and a water ski," as Kerbox put it. Some had lead plates embedded into their midsections for added weight and stability. Rubber-covered sailboard foot straps were bolted into the deck to prevent slipping, to help leverage turns, and to allow a rider to hit a chop at high speed—always a possibility in big surf—get airborne, and stay together for landing. The straps were easily disengaged when necessary; the last thing a surfer needed underwater was to be within striking distance of his board. Ankle leashes were discarded for the same reason. Risk was mitigated in that the tow-in surfers rarely wiped out, and every ride was monitored by at least one rescue-trained jet-ski driver. But it was well understood that the giant waves in the soon-to-be-entered "unridden realm" were inherently more dangerous than the more familiar twenty-five-footers that had, so far, marked the far perimeter of the big-wave world.

These and other developments were the result of what amounted to a tow-in cooperative involving perhaps twenty surfers. Everybody pitched in. Everybody looked out for the other guy. Photographers had already flown to Maui to document the fast-evolving tow-in project, and when the surfers gathered for the obligatory group portrait, they smiled and slouched easily over their boards and jet skis in a no-first-among-equals pose.

That said, Laird Hamilton, from the beginning, rendered his tow-in partners and associates all but invisible. Raw good looks didn't hurt (Hamilton's steel-bending physique earned him a mideighties modeling assignment with Brooke Shields and photographer Bruce Weber), but meant nothing next to the fact that he'd become the decade's breakaway big-wave rider. He was featured in twenty-seven of the twenty-eight tow-in shots in *Surfer*'s 1994 "Power Surfing" article. He was the only tow-in surfer introduced by name in Bruce Brown's *Endless Summer II*, released that spring. Solidarity among the tow-in crew was destined to fissure and split, but in the early years the surfers

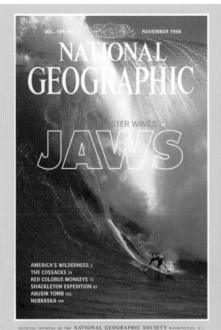

Hawaiian tow-in virtuoso Laird Hamilton featured in the November 1998 issue of *National Geographic* and the June 1994 issue of *Outside*.

themselves praised Hamilton regularly and lavishly. "He's an animal," Darrick Doerner said. "Me and Buzzy are riding the waves; Laird just casually plays with them."

That's just how it looked to *Endless Summer II* audiences across the country, including hardcore surf-world cinemaphiles, all of them craning their heads up to the screen like baby birds as Hamilton made his blazing Technicolor entry into a choleric twenty-footer at Jaws. He's strapped to a yellow-and-red toothpick of a surfboard, feet spread wide, thighs and knees slightly turned out, and as the wave gobbles and spits just a few yards behind him, he cuts a flaring sideways S across the face, and does it again—fusing big-wave riding and high-performance surfing like he

was buttering toast—then launches off the crest of the now-spent swell, arcs through the air, and softly touches down in flat water. "We all felt that big waves could be ridden better than they've been ridden," Hamilton said later. "We dreamed about it. Then we figured out a way to do it."

Hamilton's adventure in tow-in

surfing, superhuman as it appeared to the world at large, was in fact nothing more than an obvious, almost predictable, extension of a life that had already been nothing but oversized, fortuitous, and just flat-out gnarly. He was the stepson of sixties' surf icon Bill Hamilton, and an "absolute holy terror" as a child, according to his mother. The kindergarten-age Hamilton would run screaming past a row of sunbathing women and rip off their bikini tops. When his second-grade teacher asked that he not cut in line, he slugged her in the stomach. After completing a father-son hike up to the top of Waimea Falls, Laird, age eight, walked to the edge, looked down, looked back at his stepdad, and jumped sixty feet to the small freshwater lake below. As a teenager, Hamilton was already a fearless and hugely talented surfer. A few years later he began long-distance paddling—from England to France, from Oahu to Molokai, and across the Mediterranean Sea. He wrestled a tiger. He set sailboarding speed records. In his street luge debut (high-speed, supine-posture, downhill skateboarding), he went head-first, instead of feet-first, just to unman the local pros. At age thirty he jumped from a 125-foot cliff, broke a rib when he hit the water, coughed up blood for fifteen minutes, then went back a few weeks later to try again.

"That was fun," he said of the cliff-jumping episode. "I love the whole idea of going up there with a few other guys, and we'll see who will jump the highest. The challenge is super clear. Perfectly defined. Not like, 'Well, I *could* have . . .' *No.* No. Did you do it or not?" Vigorous declarations of machismo had already become a Hamilton trademark. "It's real simple," he told *Outside* in 1994, stating his tow-in surfing aspirations. "Big monster. Go ride it."

Hamilton, in *Outside,* is described as a reliable and jovial friend to the rest of the Maui tow-in group, as well as a much-loved local celebrity. Even today, north coast Maui crop farmers, along with surfers, sailboarders, and even some crystal-stroking New Agers, all wave, smile, and shout greetings at Hamilton as he drives his giant, red, mud-splattered Ford pickup through the streets of Paia, near his home. Still, none of Hamilton's friends or acquaintances would disagree with stepfather Bill, who, with a resigned smile, told *Surfer's Journal* in 1997 that Laird can be "mean and arrogant, to the point where you want to slap him upside the head." Pause. "Except you don't, because he'd beat the shit out of you."

This might help explain why tow-in surfing critics have for the most part carefully avoided any mention of Hamilton, aiming their remarks instead at the practice itself. Tow-in surfing, the argument goes, stomps all over many long-cherished surfing standards and practices. "Leave your trips and hang-ups on the beach" was the sixties' phrase—that is, strip down and merge, *flow*, with the elements. Beauty follows simplicity; this is surfing's gospel. Thrumming, smoke-bellowing jet skis are anything *but* simple, and the same can be said for walkie-talkies, tool boxes, support boats, trucks, trailers, and the rest of the tow-in auxiliary gear, as well as the coordinated platoon-style method of attack.

Surf writer Dave Parmenter compared this apparatus-loaded version of the sport to rhino hunting while strapped into the bucket seat of a customized four-wheel pursuit truck. The process is ruined. Big-wave riding, Parmenter said, is "having the rhino charge *you*. And you're there by yourself in a pair of trunks." The purity of the sport, he argued, was more valuable than creating a new, artificially enhanced performance standard. And purity meant paddling. The surfing aesthetic developed as much from paddling—back-breaking at times, soothing at others—as it did from riding waves. North Shore big-wave veteran Peter Cole agreed. "Paddling into the thing; that's the challenge. Just getting in yourself and charging straight down." A motorized running-start, Cole thought, made big-wave riding too easy. "Hell, these guys are missing the best part."

The tow-in project was unaffected by criticism. And perhaps rightly so. From the beginning, Laird Hamilton and the rest of the tow-in partisans described their version of the sport as a second genre, virtually unrelated to traditional surfing. ("Hey, I've paddled from Oahu to Molokai," Hamilton said in 1993, looking irritated. "I've paddled the English Channel. I'm *sick* of paddling.") Tow-in and paddle-in surfing almost never overlapped, as tow-in riders, ultimately, were interested in waves that otherwise went unridden.

The big-wave guild was shaken out and reordered. Some big-wave surfers at first dismissed the tow-in project as cheating, then converted. Others dismissed the tow-in project as cheating and *didn't* convert, then stood by and watched with a visceral churn of disgust, righteousness, and wonder as the infidels set and reset the boundaries on the big-wave frontier. Maverick's surfer Grant Washburn insisted that "it's *more* special, and *more* magical, to be out there with just your board, and your own strength and stamina"—but

his remarks seemed filled with an abject, almost *pleading* subjectivity. Conventional big-wave surfers rode for their own reasons. So did tow-in surfers. And any larger big-wave schism was avoided as both orders flourished throughout the decade. Evidently the sport was big enough to handle the split.

And, as Darrick Doerner predicted, when the giant waves came, the tow-in surfers were ready. A *Surfer*-published photograph taken from a low-flying helicopter on December 20, 1994, shows Dave Kalama stuck like a refrigerator magnet on the face of a colossal dark-blue Jaws wall. "Measure Kalama's body with your fingers," the *Surfer* caption instructs, "then count how many times it is to the top of the wave, and do the math. Optical illusion, or the biggest wave ever ridden?" By most people's finger measurement, Kalama's wave comes out to about fifty or sixty feet high on the face. Surfers of course don't measure wave height by the face, and the prevailing code of cool kept *Surfer* from identifying Kalama's wave as thirty or thirty-five feet. But that's what it was. With great noise and even greater flair, by means legitimate or otherwise, the tow-in surfers had quickly driven around Greg Noll's once-immovable big-wave record.

maverick
down
december 23 1994
g

ken

Bradshaw AND **MARK FOO** were puffy-eyed and a bit faded as they walked through the United Airlines terminal at San Francisco International Airport. It was 5:20 A.M., which meant 2:20 Hawaiian time. Bradshaw led the way to the baggage area. He told Foo he'd deal with the car, then rolled off toward the Alamo booth. Foo located the "odd size" luggage depot, wrestled his enormous two-surfboard travel bag from the metal chute, set it against the wall, then stretched out alongside and closed his eyes. Bradshaw hadn't brought any boards, as he had one stashed in Mark Renneker's garage. A half dozen times over the past two seasons he'd flown from Honolulu to San Francisco to ride Maverick's—just six days earlier, in fact, he'd made the same trip. The big-wave chase was kind of exciting, Bradshaw thought. Then again, it was a lot simpler and less expensive when the whole thing pretty much began and ended on the North Shore.

Just after 7 A.M., Renneker handed Bradshaw a cup of green tea, and both men stood in front of Renneker's third-story dining room window and looked out to the twelve-foot Ocean Beach surf. Maverick's would be bigger; how much was hard to say. Bradshaw lowered his gaze to the rental car, where Foo was curled up in the back seat. "Foo-Foo," he said, with a dismissive shake of the head. "Look how excited he is."

The tone was sarcastic, but not cutting. The Foo-Bradshaw hostilities had been over for two or three years. Neither surfer had officially stepped down, resolution hadn't been sought or acknowledged, but the nastier accusations and insults—not to mention the chest-hair tweezing and underwater headlocks—were a thing of the past. Foo had toned down his act, which helped. In fact, at age thirty-six, he was now a tenured member of the same big-wave establishment he'd once ignored— or railed against. He could even be magnanimous, neatly and honorably defining his peers in a *Surfer* magazine interview as "artists, athletes, and professionals."

Foo and Bradshaw's new rapport was authentic, but limited. They didn't go out to dinner, or make coffee and lounge around the kitchen table, or discuss much of anything aside from big-wave riding. They called each other when the swell was up and arranged to surf together. It was as much a vocational alliance, in fact, as a newfound friendship. Time and circumstance had put Bradshaw and Foo in the same career bind: both were dedicated, early-middle-age big-wave huntsmen (Bradshaw was then forty-one), and both were now defending their reputations and professional viability not just against a younger set of surfers but against an entirely new big-wave practice. Laird Hamilton's monstrous tow-in achievement at Jaws had them both feeling a little out of it. Bradshaw had initially dismissed tow-in surfing. Foo had been neutral. Now they were talking about going partners on a jet ski.

Foo, Bradshaw knew, could still be breathtakingly crass. His "photogenic looks and athletic prowess," as noted in Foo's two-page, four-color 1994 resume, were key to his "spiraling media career as a print, radio, and TV personality." Elsewhere in his c.v., Foo declared himself "surfing's preeminent big-wave rider" as well as "surfing's consummate living legend." Bradshaw would sigh and wearily rub his eyes at this kind of florid PR work. Then again, Bradshaw, like Foo, always kept his appointments with the surf magazine photographers, and Bradshaw's brightly colored boards, like Foo's, were dappled with surf company logos. The sport had long ago become a pleasure/business fusion for both men.

And so, on December 22, when Bradshaw heard that the surf at Maverick's was due to come back up, he called Foo and suggested an overnight strike. Ninety minutes later Foo was able to book a pair of airline tickets, but the plane left in three hours, so they had to move fast. Bradshaw packed a bag and drove to Foo's house near Waimea Bay, then stood in the driveway talking with Foo's fiancée Lisa Nakano— a twenty-eight-year-old former model and a marketing department employee for Levi Strauss in Honolulu—while Foo shouldered his boards into the car. Nakano watched with a tight little smile. *This is what Mark does,* she told herself, accepting his odd vocation with its fire-drill departures but not liking it much at the moment. Christmas Eve he'd be back. Surfed-out and worthless, probably. But happy.

Foo tossed a duffel bag onto the back seat and was ready to go. Nakano looked at Bradshaw as she gestured toward Foo. "Take care of him," she ordered. "Make sure he gets back okay." Nakano told Foo to take care of Bradshaw, too, and after a fast round of good-bye hugs and kisses, it was full-speed for the airport.

Foo revived AS BRADSHAW STEERED into the dirt parking lot at Maverick's, just behind Renneker's van. It was almost 9 A.M. The weather, again, was lovely—sharp blue skies and a gentle offshore wind. Foo, suddenly energized, bounded outside and unloaded a gaudy yellow-and-purple airbrushed surfboard from the top of the car. He crouched, rested the board perpendicularly across his thighs, and vigorously rubbed a bar of traction-enhancing wax back and forth across the deck, perfuming the air with a sweet chemical-coconut scent. Not too cold, he said to Renneker. How about the water, though? Should he wear a wetsuit hood? Hold on—maybe he was waxing the wrong board. Switch to the nine-six,

overleaf
Mark Foo's last wave:
December 23, 1994.

or stay with the ten-footer? Which way was the tide going? Leave the clothes here, or bring everything to the beach? Hey, is that Jeff Clark's van? Foo often got this way before riding big waves, especially at a place he'd never before surfed. Not nervous, exactly, but restless and chattering, the staccato-voiced questions following one after the other. He'd never fit the low-key, slow-grinning big-wave archetype. Or he didn't on land. In the surf he always leveled out.

Thirty minutes later, as they paddled through Maverick's north channel, Renneker began doing most of the talking, explaining to Foo in a lively, helpful, somewhat pedantic voice about the Boneyard, the rocks, the Second Bowl section. Both surfers watched an empty twelve-footer lift up into the familiar pyramidal shape. Sunlight was absorbed into the blue face, then blindingly reflected off the frosted-white crest. The curl hit the trough with a low tearing sound that seemed to emanate from behind the surfers as well as in front of them—a strange aural deception that sometimes happens in big surf. "Some juice there, huh?" Foo noted. The waves were beautifully cast, but no bigger than fifteen feet. Maybe an eighteen-footer every hour or so, Foo hoped. Renneker didn't quite apologize for the smaller-than-expected surf, but did preface a comment or two by saying, "On Monday and Wednesday, when it was *big* . . ."

Foo and Renneker approached the takeoff area, where a dozen surfers were loosely clustered and waiting out a lull. Josh Loya was talking to Peter Mel. Jay Moriarity sat and looked out to sea, his schoolboy features arranged in a dreamy, almost beatific expression. Pacifica surfers Shaun Rhodes and Matt Ambrose were positioned slightly to the north—Ambrose excelled in these kinds of pearly smooth conditions, and had been first in the water at 7:30 that morning. Steve Dwyer, also from Pacifica, was paddling through the south channel. Evan Slater had recovered his big-wave *esprit* and was now happily recording his eighth consecutive day at Maverick's. Jeff Clark sat near the center of the group, but was already thinking about returning to the beach, as the lineup was getting crowded, the between-set lulls were getting longer, and Clark wasn't in the mood to hustle waves. He also wanted to watch the morning unfold from a distance. Five years earlier he'd ridden alone on days like this. Now the big-timers, all at once, were arriving at his break. Ten minutes later, Clark rode to the beach, pulled on jeans, a sweatshirt, and a pair of wool-lined Ugg boots, and assumed a kind of mayoral position on the cliff.

Foo wasn't the only big-wave surfer making his debut at Maverick's; Mike Parsons and Brock Little were as well. Parsons, from San Clemente, had been an amiable pro tour journeyman during the eighties and early nineties, but over the past few years had changed his focus to Todos Santos, and was now southern California's premier big-wave rider. He'd arrived in Half Moon Bay the night before, late, after a droning, seven-hour, coffee-fueled drive up Highway 101. Hawaii's Brock Little had also arrived the night before, flying in from Los Angeles. He wiped out on his first two Maverick's waves, breaking his leash on the second, which forced a long board-retrieving swim to the harbor jetty about a half mile from the lineup. Little would nonetheless describe the surf as relatively mild. "Pretty easy for the most part," he said. "A beautiful day. A nice size to check the place out."

All attending surfers, in fact, were content to settle into what looked to be a bright and airy morning of moderately big waves. The locals were wrung out after a fortnight of oversize surf. The newcomers, as Little said, were happy that their Maverick's introduction was being conducted under such pleasant conditions.

Visiting members of the surf press, however, were a little disappointed. Twenty-four hours earlier this had been shaping up as a real big-wave summit. The surf was going to rise, the weather would hold. Surf magazine editors moved photographers and writers to Half Moon Bay like chess pieces, and big-wave captains Foo, Little, Parsons, and Bradshaw were expected to gather for the laying-on of hands. Now everyone was in place, the color was perfect, but the surf was five or ten feet smaller than it needed to be to produce any atmosphere-crackling big-wave drama.

Or so it seemed. At about 9 A.M., as Foo, Bradshaw, and Renneker were walking down the trail toward the beach, Shaun Rhodes fell on a twelve-footer and was jostled downward until his wetsuit-covered feet brushed the reef. Rhodes was startled; in three years of riding Maverick's, he'd never touched the bottom. He swam up and ducked three more waves, the last of which again pushed him to the reef— except this time his left leg, just above the knee, suddenly wedged tight into a narrow crevasse. Rhodes twisted his hips and lower torso, but the leg held fast. Reaching down to brace his hands on the rocky ledge, he pushed, kicked, kicked again, and came free. Back to the surface a moment later, freaked out and short of breath, Rhodes reeled in his surfboard and paddled for shore. Nobody on the beach asked him about it. Nobody had noticed.

Mark Foo PROMPTLY CAUGHT three waves, none spectacular, but invigorating just the same. "It's *good*," he told Ken Bradshaw. "I'm stoked. Glad we came." Then the nearly requisite add-on, one gnarly big-wave vet to another: "Wish it had a little more size, though." Over the next hour, Foo rode one wave with Bradshaw, another with Little, and got two or three more to himself.

A lull settled in about 11, and the lineup became almost pool-like. The surfers' black neoprene wetsuits absorbed and distributed the sun's midmorning warmth, and everyone went deeper into an assortment of relaxed positions, sitting or laying on their boards. Conversations were easily picked up and just as easily dropped. Mostly it was quiet.

The hundred-or-so cliffside spectators—Maverick's biggest crowd yet—were also relaxed. Some were standing, others were sitting in the dry scrub grass, arms back for support, eyes closed, faces tilted up to the sun. Nearly everybody had shed at least one layer of clothes, and a few men were shirtless. Fifteen minutes passed without a single breaking wave, at which point, surf videographer Eric Nelson, standing behind his camera, squinted out across the level blue ocean and said to a friend, "Guess that's about it." Sometimes the surf just shuts off like that. Nelson hunkered down, picked at the grass, and began thinking about lunch.

At 11:20, he straightened up and murmured, "Here comes something," as the distant water stirred and changed color slightly. A minute passed. An underdeveloped first wave went unridden, but the second wave was bigger—about fifteen feet—and Nelson pressed "record" as Bradshaw and Foo both turned and paddled. Bradshaw was about five yards north of Foo, deeper in the peak, and thus holding priority. But he was *too* deep and pulled back at the last moment. Foo stood, rode halfway down the steepening face, then dropped off the right side of his board. Still filming, Nelson aimed again for the takeoff area, where Mike Parsons and Brock Little were paddling hard for the third wave, another fifteen-footer. Both surfers got to their feet at the same time—so few waves had come in over the past hour that riders were doubling up—and Nelson muttered "Go, go, *go*" under his breath. Parsons, though, caught an edge and fell on his back, arms and legs in the air and scrambling uselessly as the falling curl drove scythelike through his torso. Little continued for another ten yards before being erased by whitewater. Three more waves passed, all too small to catch, then Bradshaw got a long ride on the final and best wave of the set.

Just after Bradshaw's wave, people on the cliff noticed that Little and Parsons were being swept through the Boneyard toward the rocks. Five or six waves rushed over and around the ridges and crags, spume bouncing up, then settling into a mist, and there was no telling from this distance just what was happening with Little and Parsons. Surfers usually were flushed directly through the rocks into the lagoon, but not always; most of the Maverick's locals remembered two years ago when Jeff Clark had been pinned atop a room-sized rock for nearly an hour. Now it looked as if Parsons and Little were both trapped somewhere on the west side of the rocks—but, no, here came Little's surfboard bouncing into the lagoon, with Little just a few yards behind. Then another wave and Parsons washed through as well. Both surfers got to their feet and began walking through the lagoon's tidal zone, moving slowly, but apparently unhurt. Little went back out and continued surfing. Parsons, done for the day, paddled for *The Deeper Blue*, the hired fishing boat he'd rode out with that morning.

Surf filmmaker Steve Spaulding extended a hand and helped Parsons into the boat, then listened with surprise as Parsons described his tour through the rocks—which had in fact nearly killed him. Parsons's leash had snagged on an outcropping. For two consecutive waves he'd been pinned underwater, then a quick breath, then back down for another two waves, this time thrashing wildly for the surface. Little, fifty feet over, was strung up in near-identical fashion. Then Little's urethane cord sawed through as it rubbed against the rocks, and Parsons's Velcro-lined ankle strap, through no doing of his, somehow pulled open—an amazing bit of almost simultaneous good luck. "I thought for sure I was dead," Parsons told Spaulding, who had turned on his camera. "Brock, too. Both of us." Spaulding commented that the wipeout looked pretty heavy as well. Yeah, it was, Parsons answered, but more so for Little "because I was coming up, and I could feel Brock underneath me, banging up underneath me—he was still down there, really deep."

Parsons was a reliable and plain-spoken big-wave surfer, and Spaulding was impressed. "Words of advice for anyone thinking about surfing

Maverick's?" he asked. "Avoid the rocks," Parsons answered with a wan smile, trying to keep it light.

Spaulding kept the tape rolling as he tried to think of another question. Nothing came to mind. Just an afterthought: "So where's Foo?"

Mark Foo WAS FACE-DOWN in the ocean, drifting idly to the southeast, his water-filled lungs keeping him low on the surface. Wavelets rippled over the back of his head. His arms and legs were slightly open, like a paper-doll cutout, and the tail section of his broken surfboard was still tied to his ankle. Nobody had looked for Foo after what seemed to be an unremarkable wipeout on an unremarkable wave, and now his dead body floated out of the Maverick's line-up without notice or comment.

"You have to fight to hold onto consciousness," Foo said in 1986, after he nearly drowned during a two-wave hold-down at Waimea Bay. "That's a fallacy, you know—when people say to relax and go with it. That's a crock of shit. First you relax, but after a while you have to fight. You gotta have your eyes open. You have to find out which way's up, where it's bright and green, not black. You actually look at death in those situations, [and] if you just relax and go with it, the wave's going to hold you down forever."

Brock Little, one year later, had his own close call at Waimea. "I think I know what it would be like to drown," Little reported afterward. "A desperate fight—then peacefulness as you black out."

An hour after Spaulding asked about Foo, Evan Slater spotted the purple-and-yellow surfboard fragment floating near the Pillar Point harbor entrance. Slater, Parsons, and Spaulding were gathered near the cabin of *The Deeper Blue*, motoring back to the harbor after an onshore wind had roughed the ocean surface and cleared the lineup. They watched Foo's board for a moment or two as it rocked gently in the current. Everyone knew Foo had broken his board after his late-morning wipeout—the nose section had turned up right away. Foo had no doubt swum to the beach and gone back to the parking lot for his reserve board; it was a process that could easily keep him out of the water for an hour or more.

Slater blinked at a shadow next to Foo's board. Adrenaline bombed through him, and he yelled for the boat driver to turn back. Thirty seconds later he and Parsons jumped into the water and with an awkward tandem effort got beneath Foo and lifted him up to the others, all of them now swearing and shouting high-pitched instructions. Foo was laid on his back across the engine housing, his half-open eyes staring up blankly. Somebody pressed his sternum and water flowed from both sides of his mouth, splashing onto the deck. The boat captain radioed the harbormaster, sped past the breakwater, then throttled back as two harbor paramedics intercepted *The Deeper Blue*, jumped aboard, and began a half-hour's worth of diligent but pointless resuscitation efforts.

Brock Little didn't see Mark Foo's blanket-covered body as it was lifted onto a stretcher and placed in an ambulance bound for the San Mateo County morgue, but it looked as if somebody had posed Foo in such a way as to illustrate Little's notion of life-ending struggle and peace. His hands were clenched fists, the knuckles and tendons pushing out against the skin. His face, though, was composed and untroubled. When Ken Bradshaw arrived at the harbor, just before Foo was taken away, he pulled the blanket down from Foo's head and shoulders. It was a surreal, heartbreaking sight, but not grotesque. Foo had a small cut over his right eye and a light abrasion across his forehead, but neither injury was serious, and he was otherwise unmarked.

Bradshaw kept looking. The corners of Foo's mouth, he noticed, were slightly turned up in what looked like a wry smile. Bradshaw rested a hand on Foo's shoulder. "Then I kneeled," he remembers, "and held him, and prayed, and just kept saying, 'Why, why, why?'"

Six days later, ON DECEMBER 29, Mark

Renneker phoned Peter Benson, pathologist for the San Mateo County Coroner's Office, to ask about Foo's autopsy. The two small injuries to Foo's head, Renneker learned, almost certainly weren't enough to knock him unconscious. There was no skull fracture or brain contusion, or any other sign of severe head trauma. It was possible, Benson said, but not likely, that Foo's head injuries contributed to his death. It was possible, too, that he'd had the wind knocked out of him early in the wipeout and was unable to swim for the surface. Benson also noted in his report that Foo had an 80 percent narrowing in one of his heart arteries—although there was no evidence of a heart attack.

The forensic details of Foo's death were of great interest to Renneker and the rest of the Maverick's surfers. If Foo drowned *after* being struck unconscious, by his surfboard or from hitting the bottom, then it wasn't really a Maverick's-specific fatality; it could have happened in three-foot surf. But that probably wasn't the case. Benson thought Foo had died from a "suffocation by submersion," which meant he'd been held down until he blacked out, at which point his throat relaxed and water was inhaled into the lungs, probably killing him within five minutes. Because Foo wasn't washed through the rocks along with Parsons and Little, and because the tail section of his board was smashed and laced with thin strands of sea-grass, it seemed likely that Foo had been tethered to the bottom, just below where he'd wiped out, by either his board or his leash. At some point he floated to the surface—released from the bottom by a small underwater eddy, perhaps, or a shift in the current—and drifted off toward the harbor.

This quickly became the standard and accepted version of Foo's death. Maverick's, plainly put, did him in. Surfers didn't get lashed to the bottom at Waimea, Sunset Beach, or Todos Santos. And it wasn't just Foo, the Maverick's group reminded each other. Shaun Rhodes had been trapped on the reef as well.

Three nearly identical videotape recordings of Foo's last ride were watched and rewatched in the days and weeks after his death. Foo pushes up into a crouch. The wave inflates slightly and grows steeper, throwing Foo off balance to his right. He straightens and lifts both arms into a V-shape above his head as he tries to realign himself over his board. Lowering back into a crouch, however, he's still listing to the right, and he falls forward—his right hand touching the water first, then the left, then his chest. Foo's head is raised to the last moment, then it tucks down just before he disappears into the wave face. Viewed in regular motion, about two seconds pass from the time Foo gets to his feet to the moment he falls. Two seconds after that, as the wave hollows into a tube, Foo unexpectedly reappears, shadowy and indistinct, suspended within the curl as it drops toward the trough. This flickering moment, this terrible sign-off—unnoticed as it took place; freeze-framed in every video replay—lent a focal point to his death. Foo's there, phantomlike, encased in water, then he's gone, erased by the countervailing explosion of white foam. The jolt was strong enough to break Foo's surfboard into three pieces.

In each of the three recordings, the camera then swings out to Parsons and Little, who wipe out in tandem on the following wave. Both of their heads are seen bobbing in the aftermath. Foo is underwater somewhere between them—a point that was ghoulishly underscored when Little said he hadn't hit anyone during his wipeout, which meant the surfer who'd been "banging up underneath" Parsons was Foo.

Foo's fiancée Lisa Nakano later asked, bitterly and tearfully, "Whatever happened to the buddy system?" She had a point. Everyone's guard was down when Foo died, for reasons that, in hindsight, seem pretty thin: the warm, soothing weather; the vastness of the Maverick's wave field; the waves being *only* fifteen to eighteen feet.

On the other hand, Foo's wipeout, as it took place, looked no more severe than a half dozen others that morning—and infinitely *less* severe than the calamitous series of wipeouts earlier in the week. Also, it might not have made a difference if Foo had floated up immediately, unconscious but revivable, as Parsons and Little had drawn everyone's attention for the next few minutes while they were siphoned through the rocks. And finally, there didn't really seem to be any *need* for a buddy system. Skilled big-wave riders never died in action. Never. So it didn't seem particularly callous or unreasonable when Jeff Clark responded indirectly to Nakano's question by saying, "Mark just slipped through the cracks." Evan Slater agreed. "It was a freak thing," he said. "Nothing more."

In the days that followed Foo's death, a provincialist view developed among some of the older Maverick's surfers, the gist being that *their* big-wave break was plainly more dangerous than any other, that local surfers knew to approach Maverick's with due respect and restraint, and that anyone bounding into the lineup for the first time thinking they'd set the place on fire and get their photo taken in the bargain—well, hey, sorry, but no way. Look what happened. Foo, Parsons, and Little: one dead man and two close calls. You don't travel all night and then ride big waves,

the Maverick's surfers told each other. You don't launch from deep in the Bowl the way those guys were—and there had indeed been a lot of wipeouts that morning—without knowing the break a lot better. "I can tell you unequivocally," Mark Renneker said, "that they [the visiting big-wave riders] were so far past the rules of Maverick's. Those of us who surf there regularly were saying to ourselves, 'Look at those guys over there, the best big-wave riders in the world, and they're behaving like fools.'" Renneker then urged his big-wave colleagues to wear crash helmets and to think twice about overnight jet-setting surf travel. And, most importantly—try to wipe out less often.

Ken Bradshaw, and most other big-wave surfers, thought this was nonsense. Foo, to begin with, Bradshaw said, was prepared to surf that morning. The red-eye flight was tiring, but he was rested enough to ride. In any case, the Santa Cruz gang, it was pointed out, were known to surf Maverick's hungover; Renneker himself sometimes arrived at dawn after working the night shift at Laguna Honda Hospital. Also, Foo hadn't charged out there hell for leather. He'd asked questions. He'd been watchful. And of *course* the visiting pro surfers were taking off later and deeper than what was deemed prudent by some of the older local surfers. "But that's just the nature of the thing at this level," Brock Little said. "We're a bunch of competitive fools, and it's been that way forever. So yeah, we were taking off too deep. And what always ends up happening is that someone gets an insanely good ride."

Finally, as Bradshaw noted, Foo himself had been riding carefully. True, his last wave was steep and a bit dicey. It was also smooth, well shaped, and entirely makable, and ten, fifteen, even twenty feet smaller than some of the waves that had periodically thrashed him over the years. Foo's death, in other words, as Bradshaw, Little, and most other big-wave surfers viewed it, was a terrible shame—and attributable to nothing more than dumb bad luck.

Two memorial SERVICES, one at Maverick's and one at Waimea Bay, were held simultaneously on December 30. About seventy people gathered at the base of the Pillar Point headland as furrowed, black-bottomed storm clouds blew in from the northwest and ragged twelve-foot waves collapsed over the reef. The wind was bitterly cold, and some in the crowd stood shivering during Mark Renneker's late-afternoon commemoration. He'd been thinking a lot about Mark Foo's death, Renneker said, and decided that it was perhaps best placed in a Native American spiritual context, which meant that there were "important messages and meanings—not all of which may be immediately obvious." To say that Foo died doing what he loved to do, Renneker continued, was to miss the point. A kind of "mass intoxication" had fallen over the Maverick's lineup that day—partly because the surf was so gorgeous, but also because so much attention was being directed toward Maverick's; the implication was that Foo was the victim of some kind of energy overload. Renneker then described, in nearly hagiographic detail, what Foo looked like in death: the becalmed expression on his face, the jade Chinese medallion around his neck, the perfect musculature. He looked, Renneker finished, "like a fallen warrior."

The service at Waimea Bay's sun-warmed grass field, just a few hundred yards from Foo's house, was bigger, more elaborate, and more grief-stricken than the one taking place at Pillar Point. Roughly half of those gathered at Maverick's had been slightly acquainted with Foo; the rest had never actually met him. At Waimea it was Foo's family, thirty or forty close friends, and a few hundred more ancillary friends, associates, and partisans. Warm, moving testimonials were offered one after the other, and by the time Lisa Nakano, the day's last eulogist, walked to the rostrum and reminded everyone about Foo's emotional generosity, and how he said "I love you" easily and often, nearly everyone was in tears. Two hundred people then paddled into the middle of the bay, sat up on their boards, grasped hands, and formed an enormous circle. Nakano, Brock Little, Ken Bradshaw, Mark's sister SharLyn, along with Dennis Pang, Clyde Aikau, Richard Schmidt, and a few others, formed a second, smaller interior circle. Flowered leis and garlands were cast toward the middle of the circle. Foo's name was chanted three times, and everyone beat the sea with their hands. Pang then removed an urn from his backpack, opened it, and let Foo's ashes float out onto the water.

During a BRITISH BROADCAST CORPORATION interview in May 1994, Mark Foo said that dying in big surf "would be a glamorous way to go; a great way to go." He told *Surfer* that "it's not tragic to die doing something you love." But nobody who knew Foo believed he had a genuine death wish. He left for Maverick's engaged to be married. He talked about having children. He was excited about upcoming work projects. Furthermore, as defined by big-wave standards, Foo was a courageous but not reckless surfer. Jose Angel, a North Shore notable from the sixties, would paddle into a twenty-five-foot wave and purposely back-flip off the tail of his board, straight into the vortex, just to see what would happen. Foo wouldn't dream of such a thing. He rode huge waves with deliberation and calculation. Dying in big waves was something he talked about the way other people talk about dying in their sleep—as a preferred choice against other types of death, not as something to be wished for, or planned for, or acted upon.

But it probably wasn't something he was scared of, either. And of course he was right—death by big-wave misadventure was indeed a glamorous way to go. "Dennis Pang and I sat under a tree at Waimea the other day," Bradshaw said just after the Foo memorial service, "and Dennis looked at me and said, 'Mark's just *laughing*. He couldn't have done it any better.' And he's right. Mark rode a ton of big waves, he surfed all over the world, he got to be famous, and he went out in a big way. He wanted to be a legend. And, boy, is he ever going to be a legend now."

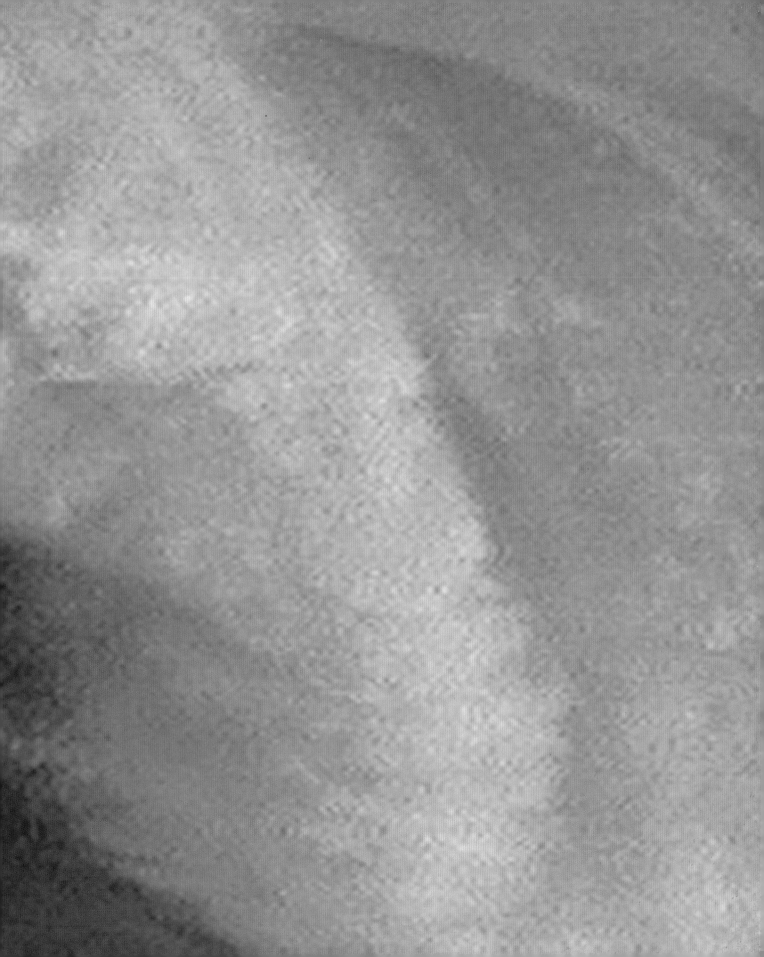

BIGGER, RICHER, FASTER, HARDER

big-wave surfing

circa 1995–2000

"Mark Foo's Last Ride," the title of

Jon Krakauer's May 1995 *Outside* magazine feature story, is printed in 100-point drop-shadow type across a grainy two-page photo of a surfer racing along a deep blue Maverick's wall. "A life and death woven through with dark ironies," the caption reads. "Foo, earlier on the fateful day at Maverick's." What *Outside* rendered as dark irony, though, became light comedy to most Maverick's surfers, who knew at a glance that the rider shown was Brock Little, not Foo. In "Searching for the Perfect Wave and Finding Death," meanwhile, the *New York Times* defined "Mavericks" not as a location but as an especially hazardous classification of wave, and reported that Foo died after failing to notice that "the wind had shifted." Where the *Times* compared the typical Maverick's wave to a two-story building, *Rolling Stone's* "The Last Wave" raised it to three stories, and *San Francisco Focus's* "The Last Ride" jumped all the way to five. *Spin's* "Killer Wave" settled on four stories, but went the extra metaphoric yard by asking readers to imagine the structure pulling loose from its foundations and giving chase. "You turn on your heels and run, but the building gathers speed, gains ground. In desperation you jump feet-first on the hood of a taxi. The taxi takes off down the street as you fight to keep your balance. You're now moving at 45 mph, the building still in hot pursuit. If you slip and fall, it will crush you . . ."

And so it went in the days, weeks, and months after Foo's death, with feature articles in the *Los Angeles Times*, *Paris Match*, Britain's *Independent*, the *Sydney Morning-Herald*, and dozens more international newspapers and magazines. *Dateline* and *NBC Nightly News* produced full-length segments on Foo and Maverick's, as did *MTV Sports*. Tom Hanks, *Movieline* reported, was teaming up with Krakauer to write and produce a Universal film about Foo and Jeff Clark, with Keanu Reeves, Brad Pitt, Brendan Fraser, and Leonardo DiCaprio cited as a possible ensemble cast.

Surfing, in a way that would have thrilled Foo to no end, had become a news and entertainment sensation. "I've always tried to give something back to surfing," Foo said in 1986, "mostly by creating more public awareness and appreciation for what we do." Alive, he'd made some modest advances toward this goal. Dead, it looked as if he'd single-handedly delivered the sport from the faddish fringe to the warm and embracing center of mainstream media popularity.

This sudden upswing was actually part of a decade-long, ongoing, all-fronts renegotiation between the surfing and nonsurfing worlds—a process

that began in 1992 with William Finnegan's lengthy Mark Renneker profile for *The New Yorker* and that extended to other national magazines (including feature stories in *The Nation, Harper's, Sunset*), to corporate advertising (Toyota, Crest, Kodak, Ralph Lauren, Kellogg's), to academia (in 1999, Drury College in Springfield, Missouri, offered a "Surfing: American Culture or Sub-Culture?" honors course), and to high-end literature, both fiction and nonfiction (Kem Nunn's 1997 noir big-wave novel *Dogs of Winter* and Dan Duane's 1996 surfing memoir *Caught Inside* were both well reviewed). Documentary films were made on senior surfers, women surfers, world-champion surfers, surf filmmakers, and surf breaks. Surfing museums opened. Antique wooden surfboards sold at auction for ten thousand dollars. The Surfboard was aesthetically parsed along with Blue Jeans, Lipstick, the Baseball Bat, and eight more culturally freighted everyday items in the San Francisco Museum of Modern Art's 1996 "Icons: Magnets of Meaning" exhibit.

If the sport remained open to hackneyed, sniggering, heavy-handed interpretation, its societal currency was on the rise like never before. Surfing had always been seen as colorful and thrilling, but its cultural significance had been more or less equated with marathon dancing and Love-Ins. In the nineties, surfing began to support weightier ideas and themes. Fulbright scholar and longtime surfer Thomas Farber, in his 1994 book *On Water*, went so far as to place surfing at a bright spiritual nexus between life, death, earth, and religion:

In early 1991, a seventy-two-year-old retired electrical engineer died while surfing off Spanish Beach in northern California. "That's what he did," his widow said. "He surfed. He'd just go out there and wait for the waves."

What a way to go, no? Right on the face of the waters. ("In the beginning God created the heavens and the earth. The earth was without form and void, and darkness was upon the face of the deep; and the Spirit of God was moving over the face of the waters.") When I die, please, scatter my ashes on the face of the waters. Warm waters, too. Let me cycle and recycle in the tropics forever and ever. And don't mourn for me. I'll be in touch—when it rains. When it pours!

From *Gidget* to Genesis in just over thirty years. Surfing's thrills were still accounted for, but now so was the poetry. "A game without sacrifice of anyone or anything," Farber writes, describing a group of surfers at Makaha. "A rare interaction of humans and the environment. One's life passes before one's eyes. That is, just how much would you give to be in such a medium in such a way?"

This new intellectual and artistic ballast was being demanded, consciously or not, by an expanding class of adult surfers, many in their fifties, sixties, seventies, and older, people who had found in surfing something beyond youthful recreation and diversion—something therapeutic, steadying, cleansing—and wanted the sport to be newly defined as such. In the 1999 documentary *Surfing for Life*, eighty-five-year-old Woody Brown, a figure of kinetic mental and physical good health, rides at a stately clip toward shore at Waikiki atop a powder-blue longboard. "Sometimes the wind would hold its breath and the sea would get glassy calm," Brown says in a croaking but animated voice, reminiscing about his days as a hot curl big-wave rider. "And then all of a sudden out of nowhere these mountains of blue water would come, you know— and it was *beautiful*." Brown's walnut-lined face opens into a joyous grin. "And, by golly, we'd go out there and *live* in that stuff!"

In the first half of *Surfing for Life*, sixty-seven-year-old Fred Van Dyke bluffly recalls the challenge of pioneering big surf in the fifties, but later, as he talks about the challenge of *quitting* big surf, he slips into melancholy, the feeling's more difficult. Van Dyke remembers paddling for a twenty-five-footer at Waimea Bay in the late seventies that in years past he would have bulled into without hesitation. But this time he pulled up, "blown away" by fear, and soon realized that he no longer belonged in the Waimea lineup. After that, he limited himself to waves under ten feet. "I lost friends that way," Van Dyke says, trying to smile past the thought. "None of them would admit it, but I wasn't one of the big-wave gang anymore. It bothered me. It hurt. I was like the castrated cat in the neighborhood; all the other cats beat up on you because they know something's different."

Buzzy Trent and Greg Noll quit big surf before Van Dyke; Noll after his great Makaha wave in 1969, and Trent a year or two later. Unlike Van Dyke, Noll and Trent both describe their respective exits with brawny old-boy fondness. "I said to myself, 'This is the last wave I ride. This is the way I go out,'" Trent told *Surfing* magazine in 1990. "So I went to the top of the point at Makaha, caught a beautiful wave, rode to the beach, and that was it. I never surfed again. Sold my board and quit—cold turkey."

Van Dyke, a different kind of retired big-wave rider, or a more honest one, can't leave it at that. "I'm supposed to be this macho tough surfer guy," he says in *Surfing for Life*. "But I'm not. I'm really a wuss inside. Just—totally." The anxiety Van Dyke banished so effectively as a young big-wave toreador on the North Shore has changed shape and returned, stronger than ever. Tears now fill his eyes. "The bullshit that comes out of most men, about 'Oh, I'm not afraid of death; I'm not afraid of anything.' Well, you're looking at me right now, and I'm scared shitless. The fear comes up continuously. It's hard to deal with."

Death regularly stirred through the big-wave world in the midnineties. Hawaii's Jim Broach, age forty-five, drowned beneath a set of twenty-five-footers at a North Shore break called Phantoms on January 31, 1993. Foo died in 1994. One year to the day after Foo's death, on December 23, 1995, twenty-five-year-old Donnie Soloman from Ventura, California, paddled through a looping Waimea wave and was pulled back over with the curl and held underwater until he drowned.

"I say this all the time," North Shore harlequin Todd Chesser told *Surfer* in late 1994, "you're only afraid of what you don't know." Chesser, twenty-five, was at that point famous in Hawaii for riding the outer reefs alone on twenty-foot-plus days and for sprinting nude on a semi-regular basis across public beaches and thoroughfares. "The situation is only as dangerous

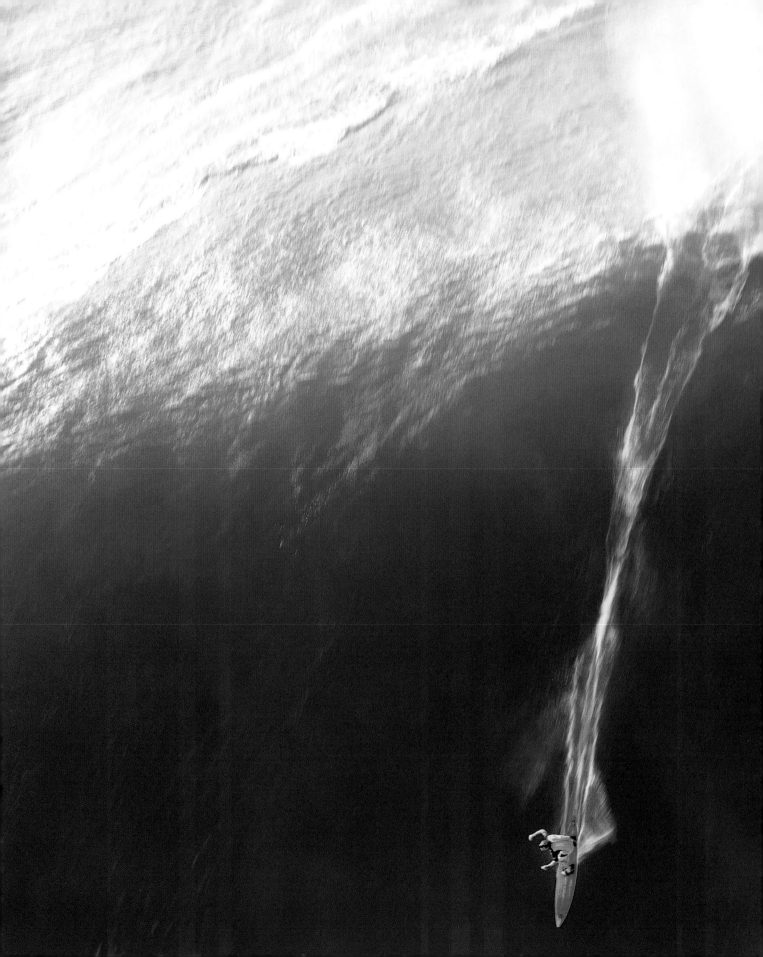

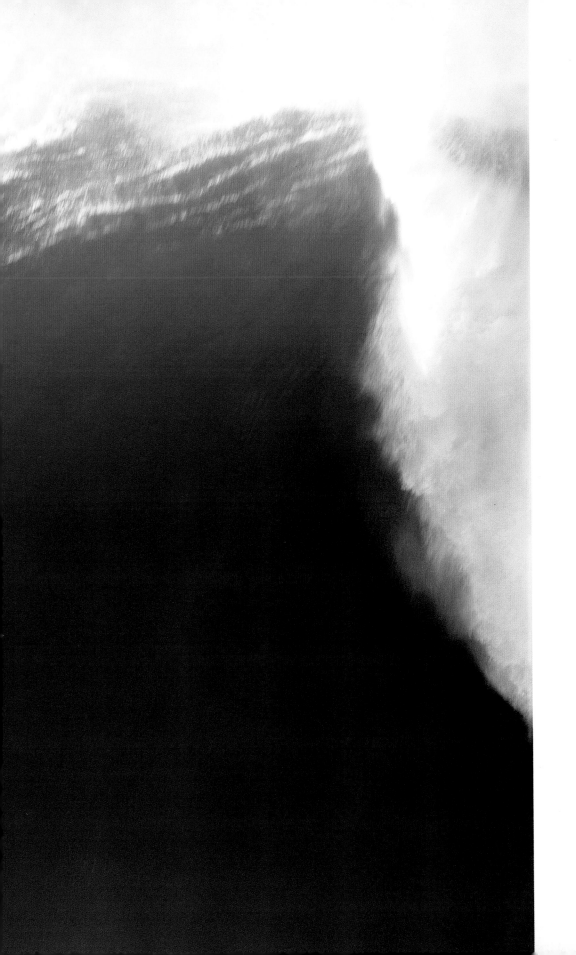

Ken Bradshaw,
Outside Log Cabins,
Hawaii, 1998.
"How can I ever get
that high again?"
Bradshaw said after-
ward. "How can I ever
feel that good again?"

as your mind perceives it to be," he said, "[and] if you know the basics, the danger is minimal. Once someone pushes you out there, you realize how easy it is."

With his shaved head and muscle-packed torso and arms, spinning his usual raunchy line of banter, Chesser indeed looked fully at ease waiting out a lull with Cody Graham and Aaron Lambert at a North Shore big-wave break called Outside Alligator Rock on February 13, 1997. Then a deviate set of thirty-footers rolled through and all three surfers were caught inside. Graham was bleeding, vomiting, and sobbing by the time the final wave passed, his arms and hands weakly dog-paddling through a white skein of residue foam. The ocean had gone perfectly still. Graham turned to face shore and mewled in his throat as he saw Chesser, ten yards distant, floating facedown and motionless. It took three-quarters of an hour for Graham and Lambert to paddle their friend's body through the surf to the beach. Lambert left with Chesser in the ambulance. Graham stood next to Kam Highway in shock. "I'm done riding big waves," he announced a week later. "I left my board on the beach that day and just walked away. Todd Chesser was solid as a rock. He was one of the fittest men on the North Shore. I don't know why he drowned and I didn't. But I quit."

The peculiar disproportion between big-wave fear and big-wave danger suddenly appeared to be leveling out. Four deaths in four years—the numbers were plain enough. Maybe the big-wave anxiety, even dread, most surfers felt was justified after all. Soloman and Chesser (and probably Broach), it was noted, hadn't been knocked out or tethered to the bottom, but simply held underwater until they expired. These weren't surfing deaths that happened to take place in big waves, in other words. These were deaths that could only take place in big waves.

The rising body count seemed to have little or no effect on Laird Hamilton, Brock Little, Peter Mel, and the rest of big-wave surfing's ruling class. Some began to train harder. Makaha's Brian Keaulana would dive thirty feet to the sea floor, pick up a sixty-pound boulder, and run a series of slow-motion underwater sprints. Jay Moriarity, son of a Green Beret, began a demanding off-season regimen of swimming, running, and long-distance paddling. Most big-wave surfers, however, just carried on as before, either accepting the new, shorter mortality odds or looking at the 1993–97 casualties as an aberration. This included the tow-in surfers, who were now catapulting into waves far more powerful and longer-boiling than anything that could ever be paddled into. Hamilton and his tow-in posse were undoubtedly the fittest big-wave riders ever. Jet ski drivers had only improved and tightened their post-wipeout search-and-rescue drills. But the next big-wave fatality, it was generally assumed, would be a tow-in surfer.

left
Hawaii's Noah Johnson, Waimea Bay, 1999.

In the four years since Laird

Hamilton's screen-burning cameo in 1994's *Endless Summer II*, tow-in surfers had tracked ever-deeper into what Mark Foo had once described as the "unridden realm." Another two dozen big-wave riders had paired up—each team buying its own eight-thousand-dollar jet ski—and more previously unridden (or under-ridden) big-wave breaks were being surfed. Never mind that jet skis had been singled out as a safety hazard (9 people died and 161 were injured in California jet ski accidents in 1998) and an environmental scourge (one-third of each fuel load is dumped unburned through the exhaust into the air and water). Never mind, too, that *Time* listed the jet ski, along with Muzak, Barney, telemarketing, and aerosol cheese, as one of "The 100 Worst Ideas of the Century." Surfers—a majority of them—didn't care. They'd come to accept the jet ski as the necessary means to real or vicarious high-end big-wave thrills. Laird Hamilton was a surfing icon. Jaws was the terrifying and wondrous new big-wave capital. Tube-riding, once the rarest of events in big-wave surfing, always the most sublime, was so much easier in the tow-in format that it became a semiregular occurrence.

Ken Bradshaw didn't begin tow-in surfing until 1995. He was forty-two years old and had been riding big surf for twenty-one years, but his reputation by then was based more on longevity and seniority than on any recent big-wave exploit. Bradshaw had paddled for, then backed out of, the huge glory-drenched wave Brock Little rode in the 1990 Quiksilver contest, and that seemed to encapsulate the latter half of his career: always in the thick of things, but slightly off the mark at the crucial moment. Few would have picked him to take the next step into the great big-wave unknown. Bradshaw himself may have been a little surprised, on January 28, 1998, to find himself rocketing down the face of a North Shore wave fifteen feet larger than anything he'd ever ridden, and at least five feet beyond anything *anyone* had ever ridden. "I just know I caught a really big one," he said that evening, "and I was just trying to get out of its way."

Bradshaw's wave was generated by an enormous near-stationary North Pacific storm and delivered into a cloudless, windless Hawaiian setting. Waimea Bay was overwhelmed. Ten years earlier, such conditions would have produced a small exodus to Makaha. Instead, seven jet-ski teams, including Bradshaw and tow-in partner Dan Moore, set out for a monolithic and rarely ridden break known as Outside Log Cabins—"the Everest of the North Shore" *Surfing* called it— one mile northwest of Waimea.

Ken Bradshaw, strapped into a bright orange seven-foot, ten-inch surfboard and taking full advantage of a 30-mph running start, opened with a twenty-five-footer, then followed up with his sky-scraping leviathan. How big was it? *Surfer* predictably demurred—the surf media's aversion to measuring wave height in the tow-in era has been both comical and pathetic—saying only that the wave was "the biggest ever ridden on the North Shore." But as seen in North Shore filmmaker Bill Ballard's 8-mm footage, the wave appears to be at least seventy feet on the face. Bradshaw himself finally decided, for the record, a few days after the event, that his wave was forty or forty-five feet. Nobody argued.

Afterward, Bradshaw fell into a debilitating post-partum big-wave funk. Clean forty-foot surf is a rarity of the highest order, and he knew the chances were slim-to-nonexistent that he'd connect with another wave that big and that refined. "It was like, 'How can I ever get that high again? How can I ever feel that good again?'" Bradshaw said, months later. Australian Layne Beachley—female tow-in pioneer, 1998 women's world tour champion, and Bradshaw's live-in girlfriend at the time—said he was "a little nuts to be around. He basically waited twenty-five years for that day. And afterward—he just wasn't doing very well."

The depression had passed by the next winter season. But immediately after his Outside Log Cabins ride, Bradshaw carried the rare burden of owning an achievement that seemed both perfect and project-terminating.

In keeping with the spirit of the times, Bradshaw's ride became the dramatic highpoint of Bill Ballard's new *The Moment* video, and a Bradshaw poster was rushed into print. Big-wave surfing, hotter than ever, was being packaged, marketed, and sold at a furious rate. Bradshaw, in fact, had barely dried his hair after the big day at Outside Log Cabins when the spotlight wheeled around to Todos Santos, in Baja California, for the unplanned merger of two corporate-backed events, the K2 Big-Wave Challenge and the Reef Brazil Big-Wave Team World Contest.

The K2 promotion was the baldest imaginable play to surfing avarice—and a flat-out marketing masterstroke. Fifty thousand dollars, winner take all, to the paddle-in surfer photographed on the biggest wave of the 1997–98 North Pacific winter season. "Big-wave riders finally get what they deserve," read the K2 ad copy, which also pointed interested parties to the Big-Wave Challenge website. Meanwhile, the Reef Brazil sandal company had scheduled a conventional single-elimination event at Todos Santos. On February 16, 1998, during the Reef contest semifinals, San Diego surfer Taylor Knox pocketed the fifty-thousand-dollar K2 prize money after dropping cleanly into a twenty-five-footer. "Taylor Knox, into the Money Pit," read the *Surfer* cover, which showed Knox in perpendicular descent on his cash-winning wave. This uniquely bold piece of surfing commerce, with its mercenary coloration—one giant wave, one giant check—briefly put Knox on the defensive. "I just love surfing [Todos Santos]," he said in *Surfer*. "I've felt that way about it for years, and it'll be that way for years to come, whether or not there are cameras or anything. Anyone who thinks I rode that wave for the money is on glue."

Fifty-thousand-dollar paydays, as all big-wave riders know, exist just this side of fantasy. Earning a living from big surf is difficult, and nobody understands this better than Jeff Clark. So when Quiksilver approached Clark with their new, first-of-its-kind, Maverick's-designed Men Who Ride Mountains event—scheduled to run sometime during the 1998–99 season—and asked him to sign on as contest director, he agreed. Clark enjoyed the work. Or most of it. At age forty-one, he remained a superb Maverick's rider, but his temporary administrative position with Quiksilver meant he wasn't allowed to enter the contest itself. He'd have to watch everybody else surf while he acted as the Men Who Ride Mountains host, spokesman, and referee. Frustrating, but that was the deal he'd struck.

Surfing

the **$50,000** shot

taylor knox's **plunge** into the green

right
California's Taylor
Knox, winner of the
K2 Big-Wave
Challenge. *Surfing,*
July 1998.

far right
Maverick's in the
video age.

newspaper in 1997 that, as a carpenter getting squeezed by the late-eighties' economy, he'd finally decided to "put down my hammer and follow my heart." Originally this meant designing and building a Maverick's-named line of surfboards, but other Clark-related ventures soon followed, including the Maverick's Surf Shop, the Maverick's Roadhouse Cafe, and a line of Maverick's logo-screened T-shirts, sweatshirts, and stickers. In 1998 Clark registered the Maverick's name. In 1999 Clark's agent struck a deal with Universal Films for the movie rights to his life story. Very little happens with regard to Maverick's—in the water or in the media—that doesn't involve Clark to one degree or another. "It's Jeff Clark's spot," as *Surfing* magazine said in 1995. "He owns it, and what he says goes."

Four years had passed since Clark had jogged into the Maverick's parking lot to relay the news of Mark Foo's death to Ken Bradshaw and Mark Renneker, and since then Clark's relationship to surfing had grown more complex. He was in demand as a big-wave authority, and his steely presence figured in every post-Foo Maverick's media offering. "Maverick's is the most dangerous surf spot in the world," Clark told southern California's *Daily Breeze* newspaper. "Only the wise and bold should be out there." For *MTV Sports* he wore a pair of black wraparound sunglasses and spoke with his usual soft-voiced aplomb. "Maverick's has no conscience." Pause. "Your mistake is its gain."

And Maverick's gain, indirectly, was Clark's gain too, as his once-private big-wave preserve developed quickly into his place of business. His financial stake in Maverick's wasn't really a secret. Nor was it something he talked about on record, either, beyond his comments to a local

Clark's sovereignty has played out in two ways. Most colleagues and observers see him as a hardworking and tribute-worthy patriarch. Some think he's crassly exploitative. He was all but sainted in a well-reviewed documentary titled *Maverick's,* then condemned in Jack Boulware's *SF Weekly* cover story titled "The Selling of a Wave." Boulware wrote that Maverick's was "approaching maximum surfing usage. Some say that it's already ruined, and all signs point to Jeff Clark as the person most responsible. . . ."

194

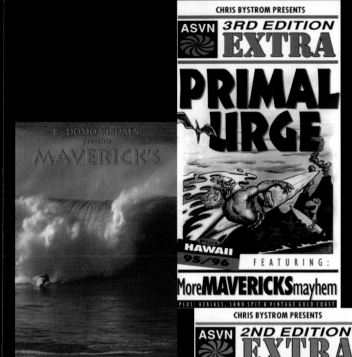

E-DOMO VISUALS
presents
MAVERICK'S

HIGH NOON
AT
LOW TIDE

CHRIS BYSTROM PRESENTS
ASVN 3RD EDITION
EXTRA
PRIMAL URGE
HAWAII 95/96
FEATURING:
More MAVERICKS mayhem
PLUS: AERIALS, SAND SPIT & VINTAGE GOLD COAST

KNOW FEAR

MAVERICKS WINTER 98/99

A Film by Mark Rivera & Eric W. Nelson
A POWERFILMS PRODUCTION

HEAVY WATER

MAVERICKS
Winter 94/95

E-DOMO VISUALS PRESENTS
Twenty Feet Under
A VIDEO BY ERIC W. NELSON

MAVERICKS
Winter 97/98

CHRIS BYSTROM PRESENTS
ASVN 2ND EDITION
EXTRA
GRAVITY SUCKS
plus HAWAII 94/95
FEATURING:
MAVERICKS The real story
AUSTRALIA . HAWAII & HUGE CALIFORNIA

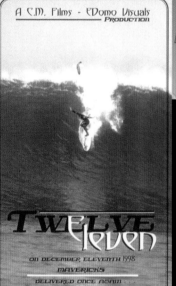

A C.M. Films - EDomo Visuals
PRODUCTION

TWELVE Eleven
ON DECEMBER ELEVENTH 1998
MAVERICKS
DELIVERED ONCE AGAIN

MAVERICK'S
a documentary film

Seven years in the making, this comprehensive epic
documents the most incredible discovery in modern
surfing. A must see for surfers and non surfers alike.

www.mavericks.com

SHIFTING PEAKS

A
CM FILMS
PRODUCTION

ean Wave Direction 12 H FCST
'98

MAVERICKS
100 SHADES
OF BLACK !
OCT./NOV. '98

Except some of the signs don't point that way at all. Implicit in the *Weekly* article is the idea that the commercialization of Maverick's was somehow avoidable. But with or without Clark, Maverick's was destined to be located, mapped, surfed, filmed, written up, gawked at, raved over, and merchandised; it's a natural wonder, a marvel—powerful, inspiring, and humbling—like the Grand Canyon or the Northern Lights. Jeff Clark didn't sell Maverick's as much as Maverick's, once presented to the world, sold itself. (It's worth noting, too, that Maverick's hasn't yet approached "maximum surfing usage." The lineup is jammed on occasion, but usually the crowd is manageable, even friendly, and often it's just three or four surfers out alone. Empty waves roll through every time Maverick's breaks.)

If anything, Clark's dissipated business style has probably spared Maverick's from *worse* mercantile degradation. Clark, ten years into his diversified Maverick's-based career, hasn't in fact earned much money. He's a craftsman by nature and training, not a businessman, and while the Maverick's Roadhouse does fine (owned and operated by Clark's second wife, Katherine), the Maverick's Surf Shop was turned over to Clark's ex-girlfriend in early 1998 (and renamed Coastside Surf and Skate), leaving Clark's Maverick's-label

surfboards without a retail outlet. "Jeff's kind of scattered," one friend says. "He works super hard, but can't focus for too long on any one thing."

Finally, Clark himself seems deeply ambivalent about how things have turned out. "Big-wave riding," he said during a 1998 Outdoor Life Network interview, "used to be about challenging the ocean for personal gratification. When you dangle that money out there . . ." Clark stops, the idea too repellent to complete in words, grimacing instead to show his displeasure. But it seems to be his own cross he's describing. At the very least, it must be difficult to reconcile the "personal gratification" of big-wave surfing with his role as Quiksilver contest director. Or his trademarking of the Maverick's name.

Jeff Clark, in some sense, does indeed own Maverick's, and his life is no doubt broader and more interesting for it. And yet it's easy to imagine him as a happier person before Maverick's became his workload as well as his great passion. When Outdoor Life asked if he got lonely riding those huge cold-water waves by himself for so many years, he visibly softened. "I surfed alone, yeah, but really got so that I enjoyed the solitude. It was just me and the ocean, and I could focus completely on what I was doing. So it never really felt so much like loneliness. More of a peacefulness, actually." Ownership, whatever else it's brought, seems to have put a fairly high tax on his sense of peacefulness.

left
A closely monitored ride during the 1999 Men Who Ride Mountains event, the first Maverick's-designed competition.

Clark stood on the deck of the sixty-five-foot *Wild Wave* cruiser on February 17, 1999, contest day, along with most of the twenty Men Who Ride Mountains invitees, five contest judges, and assorted support personnel. The *Wild Wave* was by far the plushest boat to ever drop anchor at Maverick's. Quiksilver, Clark knew, was spending money as only a large corporation could. The Men Who Ride Mountains media kit said that the company's European and American sales totaled 271 million dollars in 1997, so what was chartering a midsize cruiser, staking a fifty-thousand-dollar prize, and putting another two hundred grand or so into contest advertising? It certainly wasn't going to break the bank.

The *Wild Wave* was positioned in Maverick's south channel, adjacent to the surf. It was almost noon. A thick apron of fog had just lifted, revealing a pewter sky and a burlap-textured Pacific. Scaly, wind-ruffled fifteen-foot waves, grouped in twos or threes, rolled up about four times an hour, spiked with the occasional eighteen-footer—challenging enough, but not the kind of "spectacular . . . epic" stuff promised in the media kit. Maybe half of the regular Maverick's surfers would have ventured into the wind-bitten surf had there been no contest. The rest would have passed.

Six more boats floated in loose confederation around the *Wild Wave*, which unfurled a pair of bright red-and-white Quiksilver banners over its gunwales. Two helicopters circled overhead. Seven two-man jet-ski rescue teams throttled aimlessly between the boats and the Maverick's lineup, waiting for the competition to begin.

At a signal from Clark, the five Heat One competitors stepped off the Wild Wave's stern and paddled a hundred yards to the lineup. Each wore a solid-colored competition jersey—hot pink, lime green, yellow, blue, or purple—the Quiksilver logo stamped front and back, and down each arm.

A five-second airhorn blast signaled the beginning of the contest. Nothing happened. One actionless minute led to the next, the five surfers floating in the lineup like candy-colored buoys, and Clark began to worry. A rising tide could easily ruin the already marginal waves, and the wind could blow it to rags. But hold on,

here was a set—two fifteen-footers, both ridden, followed by an eighteen-footer that throbbed up and actually scared off a competitor—and Clark exhaled in relief.

The contest rolled on from there. Each surfer in the first heat got his three-ride minimum, as did those in the second heat, and at 2:30 in the afternoon Darryl "Flea" Virostko from Santa Cruz feathered his way down a craggy eighteen-footer, going airborne in the process, to earn a near-perfect 98 out of 100 score. Clark whistled, cheered, and clapped at Virostko's ride along with the rest of the *Wild Wave* company, then stole a look at the Quiksilver marketing director standing nearby, who was pumping a fist in the air. Clark felt great. He'd delivered. Quiksilver was already talking about a Men Who Ride Mountains return date, and with these guys paddling out and catching air, and with reporters from *Esquire*, the *Chronicle*, the *Examiner*, and the *Los Angeles Times* all scribbling purposefully in their spiral notebooks, presaging a full complement of media coverage—well, Clark didn't see any way Quiksilver could not come back in 2000. And come back even bigger and richer.

The Men Who Ride Mountains event was another small PR masterstroke for Quiksilver, and just minutes before Darryl Virostko stepped forward at the post-contest awards banquet to accept his enormous first-place trophy—dressed for the occasion in black leather gloves and a zip-up blue jacket with "Counter Culture" printed across the chest, his close-cropped hair bleached white and dappled with jet-black leopard spots—a Quiksilver executive announced that the contest would indeed return the following year.

It was hard to begrudge Quiksilver its commercial success. In the sprawling sun-baked world of "beach lifestyle" commerce—a 1.5-billion-dollar-a-year interest in the late nineties—Quiksilver had justly earned a reputation as the model surf company: their clothes were handsome and well made, surfing was graciously depicted in their ad campaigns and promo videos, and Quiksilver-sponsored competitions had long been the class events of the world pro tour.

Still, the Men Who Ride Mountains contest, as a small but indignant percentage of surfers viewed it, had overstepped. "The selling [of Maverick's] is a very sad turn of events," Marin County's Rocky Vannucci wrote in the *Surfer* letters column, two months before the contest took place. "They just can't let the beast be. It's not about the wave anymore; it's about the money. It's the final bastardization of what Northern California surfing used to stand for: man against the ocean in adverse conditions. Nothing more, nothing less."

Greg Noll, two weeks after the Maverick's event, offered the pungent metaphor that big-wave contests "are like a giant turd sitting on top of the whole deal," while Gerry Lopez, addressing the surf-competition topic with his usual rigor and grace, weighed in a few months earlier. "Competition," he said, "doesn't really lend itself to what surfing's all about. The idea is to glide around smoothly, you and the wave, and when you're out there trying to squash your opponents—that doesn't do much for the smooth approach." Lopez, a two-time Pipeline Masters champion, and a 1974 Smirnoff entrant, allowed that contests can function as showcases and social gatherings. "But once you get a little further into surfing," he concluded, "you see that the challenge is in fact a lot deeper than what you'll find in contests. And a lot more personal."

At daybreak, February 18, the morning after the Quiksilver contest, the Maverick's setting was personal to an exquisite degree. One surfer floated alone in the chill gray lineup, peering into the middle distance and waiting for an opening ride. The waves were twelve to fifteen feet, thick and raw and slate-blue in the diffuse morning light.

Mark Renneker had paddled out by himself, in part because he was locked in a fatuous and hugely enjoyable contest with Grant Washburn and John Raymond to see who could ride Maverick's the most days over the course of the 1998–99 season. Washburn's tally stood at forty-four, Raymond's at forty-three. Renneker had forty-six days and was about to go to forty-seven, and because there was a good chance the other two wouldn't show up before the already-faltering swell shut down altogether, he might be the only one to get a score for the day.

Renneker was also looking for—and finding—signs of post-Quiksilver restoration. The normal, ambient sounds had returned. A northwest wind brushed atonally past Renneker's neoprene-covered ears, and waves beat against the Boneyard rocks, but the thrumming helicopters, the atmosphere-rending airhorn, the two-stroke choral drone of the jet skis—all gone, and mercifully so, along with the spectators and photographers, the boats and banners and bright-pink competition jerseys. Maverick's had also regained its scale and proportion. Yesterday it had been oddly compressed into a two- or three-acre wave field. Now the lineup was once again of a piece with the outer waters, the sky and clouds, and even the fog-shrouded coastal hills and valleys.

Renneker's sense of relief was greater than he'd expected. Not that the Men Who Ride Mountains contest had been such a terrible affront to his big-wave sensibilities. Never would he have called Quiksilver's event the "final bastardization" of northern California surfing. Renneker had been riding waves for thirty-five years and had further immersed himself in the sport as a collector, writer, and critic, and he understood, perhaps better than anyone, the enormous amount of play between surfing as it was marketed and sold—contests included— and surfing as it was lived and practiced. The disparity usually didn't bother him. In fact, he often leapt into the breach with great irony-fueled enthusiasm; he had surfing games, puzzles, and toys lined up on his office shelves (including a plastic spinning top that played "Wipeout" as it twirled), and he'd cackled and honked his way through three big-screen viewings of 1998's horribly overwrought big-wave film *In God's Hands*. He'd accepted his Men Who Ride Mountains invitation largely because

competition was the one part of surfing that, so far, he'd had absolutely nothing to do with. And he'd had a great time yesterday. The close-quartered *Wild Wave* crowd was loud and rude and matey. He loved cheering on the other guys, and he loved hearing them cheer for him. As it turned out, Renneker performed way above the form book, placing twelfth in a field of twenty, and he'd turned *that* into a game, calling thirteenth-place finisher Evan Slater, who had taken the event a lot more seriously, to offer some competition pointers. "So, Evan, listen," Renneker said, in his warmest, most condescending voice. "Let me tell you a little bit about contest surfing. You got your lefts, see? And then you got your rights . . ."

But sitting out here now, alone, Renneker reviewed what had taken place the day before with a feeling of disquiet. Big-wave surfing—the actual ride itself—was impervious to commercialization. Renneker believed this. You laughed at the hype and the schlock, or you ignored it, and hopefully understood that the ads, videos, and contests did nothing more than blow like litter across the periphery of the big-wave experience. But the Quiksilver contest had taken Renneker out of his accustomed role as commercial observer and made him a commercial participant. It felt strange. Certainly he'd been caught off guard at the banquet the night before, to hear his name called as the winner of the Mark Foo Commemorative Award—although he recovered quickly, accepting the trophy (a glass-fronted wooden box with a color photo inside of Foo smiling) with a short and thankful extemporaneous speech.

And yet, Renneker found it difficult to pinpoint exactly which of Foo's qualities were being commemorated and, furthermore, exactly what he'd done to earn the award. Perhaps it was nothing more than empty corporate sentimentality, Quiksilver drafting on Maverick's best-known and most notorious episode. The snide view, voiced by some, was that the award celebrated both Foo's and Renneker's deep and abiding love of the spotlight. A kinder interpretation—one that Quiksilver should have articulated but didn't—was that Renneker and Foo both were "high-profile," vocal, persuasive, and often eloquent champions of big-wave surfing. They engaged the sport at all levels. They absorbed its science, design, and technology. They riffed on it and scat-talked it, jumping from punch line to punch line—Renneker always howled when repeating a seriously phrased question Grant Washburn had asked him after one of Washburn's first visits to Maverick's: "Okay, say you're caught in the Pit and a twenty-footer is just sucking dry and about to break right on you. Any way it could be strong enough to actually tear your head off your shoulders?"

Both Foo and Renneker also sought to articulate a kind of big-wave epistemology. What exactly was so compelling about riding oversize surf? How could it be so all-consuming? Brock Little liked to say that big-wave surfing was "just the funnest thing ever," but Foo and Renneker knew it went deeper, and they sifted the topic constantly, alone and in conversation with others. It had something to do with a curious set of balances and quotients: air, water, wind, and swell; energy stored and expelled; the ninety-nine parts anticipation against one-part release; the slow, metered pulse of a trans-Pacific swell against the apocalyptic flash of a huge breaking wave. The equipoise at work here, Renneker thought, was absolutely ruined by tow-in surfing, and perhaps nothing in the sport saddened him as much as the fact that the Santa Cruz surfers were buying jet skis and getting ready to launch at Maverick's. Foo, more interested than Renneker in cracking wave-height barriers, no doubt would have towed in with them—that was a difference between the two.

Foo's death at Maverick's didn't change in the slightest Renneker's notion that riding big surf was essentially and continuously life-affirming. A 1989 back injury had threatened to put an end to his surfing days, and coming back at full strength nearly a year later seemed to produce within him an ever-replenishing sense of gratitude and wonder. Foo had a similar experience in 1986, after recovering from a neck injury. "I never appreciated the act of riding waves more," he wrote, describing his reentry into the surf. "Not only because I came so close to losing the pleasure forever, but because I realized once again how, for those time-warped seconds, life is pure. There is no confusion, anxiety, hot or cold, and no pain; only joy."

overleaf
Maverick's, 1998.

201

Renneker dropped smoothly to his stomach as he came to the end of his one and only Maverick's wave of the morning, and from a prone position he aimed toward shore, just ahead of a powerful but dissipating embankment of whitewater. The sense of speed was greatly amplified riding at sea level, and drops of water sheared off from the nose of Renneker's surfboard and rifled past either side of his face. He contentedly drummed his hands on the deck of his board. Nice to get another mark in his season-to-date column, of course. Nice, too, to look up and see an empty cliff and an empty beach.

It wasn't yet nine in the morning, which meant he'd hit traffic driving home, but the thought flew past like another water drop. Then another thought: The Men Who Ride Mountains event could get by without him next year. His contest career was over. Renneker closed his eyes and listened while his board skimmed and chattered into the calm water of the lagoon.

SOURCES BY CHAPTER

Introduction

Finney, Ben, & James Houston. *Surfing: A History of the Ancient Hawaiian Sport.* Rohnert Park, CA: Pomegranate Artbooks, 1996.

Marcus, Ben. "Cold Sweat." *Surfer,* June 1992, 56–61.

Surfer's Journal: Great Waves, Volume 6. Produced by Ira Opper. Opper Sports, 1998. Video. Interview with Ken Bradshaw.

"The 25 Greatest Moments in Big-Wave Riding." *Surfer,* Dec. 1992, 42–50.

Chapter One   SURFACING

Douglas, Peter M., ed. *California Coastal Resource Guide.* Berkeley, CA: University of California Press, 1987.

Gravity Sucks. Chris Bystrom Films, 1995. Video.

Gualtieri, Kathryn. *Half Moon Bay: The Birth of a Coastside Town.* Half Moon Bay, CA: Spanish Town Historical Society, 1988.

"Island Big-Wavers Sound Off." *Petersen's Surfing,* Sept. 1964, 20–21. Interview with Buzzy Trent.

Marcus, Ben. "Cinderella vs. Godzilla." *Surfer,* May 1995, 80–83.

Morrall, June. *Half Moon Bay Memories.* El Granada, CA: Moonbeam Press, 1978.

"Really Big Wave, Really Bad Wipeout." *New York Times Sunday Magazine,* 26 Feb. 1995, 17. Photo caption information contributed by Steve Hawk.

"Sixty Days That Shook the Pacific." *Surfer,* May 1995, 60–95.

Slater, Evan. "Learning Maverick's." *Surfing,* May 1995, 51–54.

Smith, Jason. "The Apprenticeship of James Moriarity." *The Surfer's Journal,* spring 1996, 104–9.

Chapter Two   HOT CURLS AND BLUEBIRDS

Ball, J. H. "Surf-Boarders Capture California." *National Geographic,* Sep 1944, 355–62.

"Big-Wave Guns." *Peterson's Surfing,* Feb. 1964, 32–35.

Blake, Tom. *Hawaiian Surfriders.* Published as *Hawaiian Surfboard.* Honolulu, HI: Paradise of the Pacific Press, 1935; reprint, Redondo Beach, CA: Mountain and Sea Publishing, 1983.

Carroll, Nick. "Sons of Makaha." *Surfing,* May 1991, 99–108.

Church, Ron. "Waves of Waimea." *Surfer,* Apr. 1963, 24–30.

Finney, Ben, & James Houston. *Surfing: A History of the Ancient Hawaiian Sport.* Rohnert Park, CA: Pomegranate Artbooks, 1996.

Ford, Alexander Hume. "Riding the Surf in Hawaii." *Collier's,* 14 Aug. 1909, 17.

Gartner, Paul W. "Surfboard Riding: These Simple Hints Will Help You Learn." *Popular Science,* July 1937, 24–25.

Gault-Williams, Malcolm. "Fran Heath: The Forgotten Hot Curler." *Longboard,* Mar. 1997, 34–41.

———. "Surf Drunk: The Wallace Froiseth Story." *The Surfer's Journal,* winter 1997, 94–109.

———. "Woody Brown: Pilot, Surfer, Sailor." *The Surfer's Journal,* fall 1996, 94–107.

Hall, Sandra, and Greg Ambrose. *Memories of Duke: The Legend Comes to Life.* Honolulu: The Bell Press, 1995.

"Hitch-hiking on the Big Waves." *Popular Mechanics,* Feb. 1942, 72–75.

Hoffman, Flippy. "The Wild Frontier." *Surfing,* May 1992, 40–54.

Hynd, Derek. "The Big Thick Book of Lists." *Surfer,* Aug. 1989, 143. Biographical information on Wally Froiseth.

Jenkins, Bruce. "Makaha: The Forgotten Wave." *Surfer,* Apr. 1991, 44–53.

Kampion, Drew. *Stoked: A History of Surf Culture.* Los Angeles: General Publishing Group, 1997.

London, Jack. *The Cruise of the Snark.* New York: Macmillan, 1911.

Lueras, Leonard. *Surfing: The Ultimate Pleasure.* New York: Workman Publishing, 1984.

Lynch, Gary. "Joe Quigg and the Shape of Things to Come." *Longboard,* Feb. 1995, 27–35.

Marcus, Ben. "I'd Rather Eat Life: A Brief History of Woody Brown." *Surfer,* Nov. 1993, 58–61.

Orbelian, George. "Give It the Axe: Early Development of the Modern Gun." *Surfer,* Oct. 1989, 104–5.

Parker, Sarah. "Band of Californians Here to Ride Twenty-foot Makaha Surf." *Honolulu Star-Bulletin,* 7 Jan. 1954.

Stecyk, Craig. "Hot Curl." *The Surfer's Journal,* summer 1994, 64–73.

Trent, Buzzy. "Makaha, Home of the Kings." *Petersen's Surfing,* Sept. 1964, 9–13.

"The 25 Greatest Moments in Big-Wave Riding." *Surfer,* Dec. 1992, 42–50.

Van Dyke, Fred. *30 Years of Riding the World's Biggest Waves.* Kailua, HI: Ocean Sports International, 1989.

"Waimea Bay: The Heavies." *Surfer,* 1960 (premier issue), 16–19.

"Walter Hoffman's Scrapbook: Tales of Town and Country." *The Surfer's Journal,* summer 1993, 78–97.

Warshaw, Matt. "John Kelly: 20th Century Radical." *The Surfer's Journal,* spring 1995, 28–39.

Chapter Three   H3O (HEAVY WATER)

Beck, Lawrence, "Maverick's." *The Surfer's Journal,* winter 1993, 6–25.

Grigg, Ricky. *Big Surf, Deep Dives and the Island.* Honolulu, HI: Editions Limited, 1998.

Junger, Sebastian. *The Perfect Storm.* New York: W.W. Norton, 1997.

Maverick's. Produced by Lili Schad and Grant Washburn. Clearwater Films, 1998. Video. Interview with Jeff Clark.

Morris, Vic, and Joe Nelson. *The Weather Surfer.* San Diego: Grossmont Press, 1977.

"Sixty Days That Shook the Pacific." *Surfer,* May 1995, 60–105.

Slater, Evan. "Learning Maverick's." *Surfing,* May 1995, 48–60.

Surfer's Journal: Great Waves, Volume 5. Produced by Ira Opper. Opper Sports, 1998. Video. Interviews with Grant Washburn, Darryl Virostko, and Mark Renneker.

Vansant, Amy. "East Coast Halloween Swell: Trick or Treat, It's Ten Feet." *Surfer,* Apr. 1992, 62–67.

Warshaw, Matt. "Surf's Down." *Interview,* Jan. 1991, 45. Interview with Brock Little.

Chapter Four   BULL MARKET

Ball, John. *California Surfriders.* Los Angeles: Norman B. Whale, 1946. Reprint, Redondo Beach, CA: Mountain and Sea Books, 1979.

Barilotti, Steve. "Heavy Weather: Field Notes and Lost Photos from the Swell of '69." *Surfer,* Dec. 1992, 72–75.

Brady, Leonard. "Seven Mile Miracle." *Surfer,* Apr. 1989, 134–39.

Burdick, Eugene. *The Ninth Wave.* New York: Houghton Mifflin, 1956.

Chapey, Paul. "Mass Media Waves." *Surfing,* May 1970, 74–79.

Church, Ron. "The Waves of Waimea." *Surfer,* Apr.–May 1963, 24–31.

Editorial. *Surfer,* summer 1961, 1.

The Endless Summer. Bruce Brown Films, 1964. Film.

"First Annual Surfing Illustrated Poll Awards." *Surfing Illustrated,* June 1965, 20–25.

Gidget. Columbia Pictures, 1959. Film.

"Gidget Makes the Grade." *Life,* 28 Oct. 1957, 111–14.

"Greg Noll's Scrapbook." *The Surfer's Journal,* summer 1997, 34–63.

Grigg, Rick. "The Great Waves of December, 1969." *Surfer,* Aug. 1971, 72–79.

Holmes, Paul. "The Mongoose at Sixty: The Life and Times of Mickey Munoz." *Longboard,* Nov. 1997, 34–43.

Houston, James D. *A Native Son of the Golden West.* New York: The Dial Press, 1971.

James, Allston. "The Bay." *Surfer,* Sept. 1990, 70–89.

Kohner, Fredrick. *Gidget.* New York: Putnam, 1957.

Lynch, Gary. "The First Surfers on the North Shore." *The Surfer's Journal,* summer 1995, 92–95.

Noll, Greg, and Andrea Gabbard. *Da Bull: Life Over the Edge.* Berkeley, CA: North Atlantic Books, 1989.

"Personalities." *Surfer,* Dec 1963, 68. Interview with Pat Curren.

Pezman, Steve. "The Curren Gun Project." *The Surfer's Journal,* fall 1994, 76–81.

Ride the Wild Surf. Columbia Pictures, 1964. Film.

Search for Surf. Produced by Dana Brown. Da Bull Productions, 1992. Video. Compiled from Greg Noll's original *Search for Surf* films from 1958 to 1961.

Severson, John. "Riding the World's Wild Giants." *Saturday Evening Post,* 14 July 1962. Photo essay.

Silk, George. "Riding the Wild Waves." *Life,* May 1963, 36–43. Photo essay.

Stange, Mike. "Waimea Tamed." *Surfing,* Feb. 1965, 40–45.

"The Surfer's Cross." *Time,* 22 Apr. 1966, 81–82.

Surfers: The Movie. Bill Delaney Films, 1990. Film.

"The Surfing Problem." *Surfing Illustrated,* winter 1962, 5.

Surfing the '50s. Bud Browne Films, 1994. Video.

"Surf's Up!" *Time,* 9 Aug. 1963, 49.

Van Dyke, Fred. "The Peril of Surf." *Life Australia,* 1 Apr. 1968, 42–46.

Warshaw, Matt. "Vision/Revision." *Surfer,* Nov. 1992, 48.

Chapter Five   SINGULAR ACHIEVEMENT

Batstone, Donald. "Secret Swell: Outing Northern California's Monster Wave." *San Francisco Bay Guardian,* 10 Aug. 1994.

Beck, Lawrence. "Perspectives on Maverick's." *The Surfer's Journal,* summer 1995, 58–75.

Collins, Ken. "Westside the Flea." *Surfing,* July 1999, 45–46.

George, Sam. "The Evolution of Soul: How Surfboards Got from There to Here." *Surfer,* Apr. 1996, 90–95.

—. "Maverick Man: Who Is Jeff Clark, and Why Is He Always Surfing Giant Waves by Himself?" *Surfer,* Nov. 1993, 62–65.

"Gun Show." *Longboard,* summer 1993, 50–55.

Kampion, Drew. "The Life and Work of Richard Brewer." *The Surfer's Journal,* spring 1999, 72–95.

Marcus, Ben. "Cold Sweat." *Surfer,* June 1992, 56–61.

—. "Peaking." *Surfer,* July 1998, 76–83. Profile of Peter Mel.

—. "People Who Surf: Jeff Clark." *Surfer,* Dec. 1991, 95.

Orbelian, George. "Toys in the Attic: A Look at the Enduring Art of Gun Design." *Surfer,* Oct. 1989, 106–11.

"Sheer Agony." *Surfing,* Sept. 1992, 73–74.

Surfer's Journal: Great Waves, Volume 5. Produced by Ira Opper. Opper Sports, 1998. Video. Interview with Jeff Clark.

Wright, Allan. *Surfing California.* Redondo Beach, CA: Mountain and Sea Books, 1973.

Chapter Six   ATHLETES, ARTISTS, PROFESSIONALS

Abellira, Reno. "It Leaves You Breathless." *Surfer,* Feb. 1975, 28–33.

Baker, Bernie, with Jim Kempton. "Is There a New Matador?" *Surfer,* Mar. 1979, 28–39.

Brady, Leonard. "Dinner at Charlie's: Hawaii Monster Surf." *Surfer,* July 1983, 78–91.

—. "The Return of Big-Wave Competition." *Surfer,* July 1986, 118–22.

—. "Whatever Happened to Big-Wave Riding?" *Surfer,* May 1983, 40–49.

Carroll, Nick. "The Legend of Eddie Aikau." *Surfing,* May 1990, 65–82.

—. "Profile: Richard Schmidt." *Surfing,* July 1990, 120–27.

Carter, Chris. "Conversations." *Surfing,* Oct. 1982, 71–74. Interview with Mark Foo.

Foo, Mark. "Occurence at Waimea Bay." *Surfing,* June 1985, 66–69.

—. "Out There." *Surfer,* Dec. 1994, 68–71.

—. "The Unridden Realm." *Surfer,* Sept. 1990, 98–99, 138–40.

Hemmings, Fred. *The Soul of Surfing Is Hawaiian.* Honolulu, HI: Sports Enterprises, 1997.

—. "Professionalism Is White!" *Surfer,* Nov. 1969, 64–65.

Hollinger, Kimo. "An Alternative Viewpoint." *Surfer,* Aug. 1975, 38–40.

Hopewell, Deb, and Elizabeth Glazner. "Margo Would Go." *Wahine,* Mar. 1997, 16–17, 40.

James, Allston. "The Bay." *Surfer,* Sept. 1990, 70–89.

Jenkins, Bruce. *North Shore Chronicles: Big-Wave Surfing in Hawaii.* Berkeley, CA: North Atlantic Books, 1990.

—. "Waterman: Darrick Doerner Seeks Perfection in the Danger Zone." *Surfer,* Sept. 1990, 110–13.

Kampion, Drew. "Dueling for Dollars." *Surfing,* Apr. 1975, 34–53.

—. "The Edge." *Surfer,* Oct. 1989, 90–101.

Kempton, Jim, and Corky Carroll. "Margo." *Surfer,* July 1981, 36–43.

Krakauer, Jon. "Mark Foo's Last Ride." *Outside,* May 1995, 64–72.

Little, Brock. "Pressure Drop." *Surfer,* May 1990, 118–24.

Lockwood, Craig. "World Contest, Puerto Rico." *Surfing,* Mar. 1969, 27–41.

Surfer's Journal: Great Waves, Volume 6. Produced by Ira Opper. Opper Sports, 1998. Video. Interview with Mark Richards.

Surfing, Sept. 1993. The "Big Waves" issue.

Tales of the Seven Seas. Produced by Scott Dittrich, 1982. Film.

Trent, Buzzy. "Big Waves Are Masculine, Women Feminine." *Surf Guide,* Nov. 1963, 23.

Warshaw, Matt. "The Dueling Kings of Big-Wave Surfing." *Outside,* May 1988, 56–63.

—. "The Man Who Loved His Work." *Surfer,* May 1995, 106–10. Profile of Mark Foo.

—. "The Ultimate Thrill." *Surfer,* Feb. 1987, 58–65. Interview with Mark Foo.

Wilkinson, Peter. "The Last Wave." *Rolling Stone,* Apr. 1995, 56–66.

Chapter Seven   WHEEL OF FEAR

"Big-Wave Danger: Real or Hoax?" *Surfer,* Dec. 1994, 72–81.

The Fantastic Plastic Machine. Produced by Eric Blum and Lowell Blum. Crown-International, 1969. Film.

Finnegan, William. "Playing Doc's Games." Parts 1 and 2. *The New Yorker,* 24 Aug. 1992, 34–59; 31 Aug. 1992, 39–58.

"Greg Noll's Scrapbook." *The Surfer's Journal,* summer 1997, 34–63.

Hall, Stephen S. "Fear·Itself." *New York Times Magazine,* 28 Feb. 1999, 42–47.

Maverick's. Produced by Lili Schad and Grant Washburn. Clearwater Films, 1998. Video. Interviews with John Raymond, Grant Washburn, and Josh Loya.

Nash, J. Madeleine. "The Personality Genes." *Time,* 27 Apr. 1998, 60–61.

Renneker, Mark, Kevin Starr, and Geoff Booth. *Sick Surfers.* Palo Alto, CA: Bull Publishing, 1993.

Van Dyke, Fred. "The Peril of Surf." *Life Australia,* 1 Apr. 1968, 42–46.

Van Dyke, Peter. "Big-Wave Danger: A Hoax!" *Surfer,* Jan. 1966, 74–77.

Warshaw, Matt. "Surf's Down." *Interview,* Jan. 1991, 45. Interview with Brock Little.

Chapter Eight   MACHINE AGE

Baker, Bernie, and Matt Warshaw. "The Crunch at Waimea." *Surfer,* July 1988, 102–11.

Benning, Jim. "The Prince of Tides." *Los Angeles Times Magazine,* 18 Jan. 1998, 20, 36–37.

Borgeson, Will. "The White Album." *Surfer,* Apr. 1997, 62. Book review.

"California's Nuclear Winter." *Surfer,* June 1992, 54–79.

Duane, Daniel. "Something Wicked This Way Comes." *Outside,* May 1998, 92–98.

Endless Summer II. Directed by Bruce Brown. New Line, 1994. Film.

"Full Throttle." *Surfer*, June 1995, 62–67.

George, Sam. "In the Land of the Giants." *Surfer*, July 1996, 104–11.

Jenkins, Bruce. "Laird Hamilton: 20th Century Man." *The Surfer's Journal*, fall 1997, 84–121.

——. "The Next Realm." *Surfer*, Dec. 1993, 48–55.

Little, Brock. "Todos Maximus." *Surfing*, June 1990, 104–13.

Lopez, Gerry. "Quantum Leap: Jet Assisted Take-Off." *The Surfer's Journal*, spring 1995, 82–103.

Lyon, Charlie, and Leslie Lyon. *Jaws Maui.* Waialua, HI: Jaws Maui Ltd., 1997.

Marcus, Ben. "Cold Sweat." *Surfer*, June 1992, 56–61.

——. "People Who Surf: Jeff Clark." *Surfer*, Dec. 1991, 95.

McFeeley, Patrick. "Into the Teeth of Jaws." *National Geographic*, Nov. 1998, 58–71.

McMahon, Bucky. "The Hydroponic Dreams of Laird Hamilton." *Outside*, June 1994, 76–84.

Parmenter, Dave. "Big Time." *Surfing*, July 1987, 90–103.

"Power Surfing, Take II: The Next Realm." *Surfer*, Sept. 1994, 52–61.

Surfer's Journal: Great Waves, Volume 5. Produced by Ira Opper. Opper Sports, 1998. Video. Interview with Grant Washburn.

Chapter Nine   MAVERICK DOWN

Boulware, Jack. "The Selling of a Wave." *SF Weekly*, 14 Oct. 1998.

Carroll, Nick, with Mitch Varnes and Jamie Brisick. "The Passing of a Waterman." *Surfing*, May 1995, 24–37.

Ciaffardini, David. "His Final Ride." *Penthouse*, May 1995, 55–60.

Epstein, Edward, with Rob Haeseler. "Huge Waves Kill Famous Surfer." *San Francisco Chronicle*, 24 Dec. 1994.

Gravity Sucks. Chris Bystrom Films, 1995. Video.

Jenkins, Bruce. "Tragic Death of a Surfing Legend." *San Francisco Chronicle*, 26 Dec. 1994.

Kampion, Drew. "The Edge." *Surfer*, Oct. 1989, 90–101.

Krakauer, Jon. "Mark Foo's Last Ride." *Outside*, May 1995, 64–72.

Little, Brock. "Fade to Black." *Surfer*, Oct. 1989, 112–13.

Renneker, Mark. "Lessons Learned: A Postmortem on the Death of Mark Foo." *Surfer*, July 1995, 38–42.

Warshaw, Matt. "The Final Charge: Understanding Mark Foo's Last Day." *Surfer*, May 1995, 96–102.

Wilkinson, Peter. "The Last Wave." *Rolling Stone*, Apr. 1995, 56–66.

Chapter Ten   BIGGER, RICHER, FASTER, HARDER

Baker, Bernie, & Ben Marcus. "A Death at the Bay." *Surfer*, May 1996, 50–52.

Batstone, David. "Killer Wave." *Spin*, June 1995, 58–61.

Boulware, Jack. "The Selling of a Wave." *SF Weekly*, 14 Oct. 1998.

"Dropping in On . . ." *Surfing*, Nov. 1990, 48–49. Interview with Buzzy Trent.

Duane, Daniel. *Caught Inside: A Surfer's Year on the California Coast.* New York: North Point Press, 1996.

Farber, Thomas. *On Water.* Hopewell, NJ: The Ecco Press, 1994.

Fish, Peter. "Surf Cities." *Sunset*, Aug. 1998, 70–77.

Foo, Mark. "Toi-Toi Atoll." *Surfer*, Apr. 1986, 88–91.

Foo, Mark. Obituary. *The Independent* (London), 12 Jan. 1995.

Fried, Stephen. "The Last Ride." *San Francisco Focus*, Feb. 1996, 32–37.

Friend, Tom. "Searching for the Perfect Wave and Finding Death." *New York Times*, 29 Dec. 1994.

Gahahl, Jane. "The Wild Bunch–Surf Style." *San Francisco Examiner*, 18 Feb. 1999.

Heavy Water. CM Films, 1995. Video.

Hoffman, Brian. "Jeff Clark: Big Wave Maverick." *San Francisco Examiner*, 31 Aug. 1997.

Jenkins, Bruce. "The Biggest Buzz: Flea Steals the Show at the Quiksilver/ Men Who Ride Mountains Contest." *Surfer*, July 1999, 58–62.

——. "Big Surf's Up at Maverick's." *San Francisco Chronicle*, 18 Feb. 1999.

——. "Condition Black." *Surfer*, July 1998, 86–99.

——. "The Gutsiest Surfer There Ever Was." *Surfer*, Dec. 1992, 66–71.

——. "Rediscovering the Old Stoke." The Surf Column on the SF Gate, 1998. Available at www.sfgate.com/sports/Jenkins/surf/columns/surfcol19. html. Internet.

——. "Surf's Up For Maverick's." *San Francisco Chronicle*, 25 Nov. 1998.

——. "Tragic Death of a Surfing Legend." *San Francisco Chronicle*, 26 Dec. 1994.

Johnson, Pete. "The Knockout Punch." *Surfing*, June 1998, 28–60.

Krakauer, Jon. "Mark Foo's Last Ride." *Outside*, May 1995, 64–72.

Marcus, Ben. "A Good Man Is Gone." *Surfer*, June 1997, 54–56.

——. "A Thousand Bucks a Foot." *Surfer*, Aug. 1998. Pull-out poster interview.

——. "Exer-psychos." *Surfer*, Mar. 1996, 74–81.

——. "Not Fade Away: Todd Chesser Is Gone, but the Smile Lives Forever." *Surfer*, July 1997, 42–50.

Mendoza, Martha. "Beepers Ready, Surfers Wait for the Big One." *The Daily Breeze*, 5 Dec. 1998.

Muir, Frederick. "Surfing Secret Catches a Wave of Notoriety." *Los Angeles Times*, 31 Dec. 1994.

Murgatroyd. "Surf's Up." *Movieline*, Nov. 1998, 24.

Nakaso, Dan. "Slaying the Giant." *Honolulu Advertiser*, 2 Nov. 1998.

Nieves, Evelyn. "Half Moon Bay Journal: Big Water a Big Lure to Surfers." *New York Times*, 4 Dec. 1998.

Noll, Greg. Telephone interview by author. Crescent City, CA, 25 Feb. 1999.

Nunn, Kem. *The Dogs of Winter.* New York: Scribner, 1997.

"The 100 Worst Ideas of the Century." *Time*, 14 June 1999, 37.

Pennybacker, Mindy. "Surfin' Safari." *The Nation*, 7 Sept. 1998, 38–41.

Slater, Evan. "Casca Grossa: Perserverance Pays at Todos Santos' First Big-Wave Event." *Surfer*, July 1998, 66–75.

——. "Intro." *Surfer*, July 1999, 16.

——. "Learning Maverick's." *Surfing*, May 1995, 51–54.

Surfer's Journal: Great Waves, Volume 5. Produced by Ira Opper. Opper Sports, 1998. Video. Interview with Jeff Clark.

Surfer's Journal: Great Waves, Volume 7. Produced by Ira Opper. Opper Sports, 1998. Video. Interview with Gerry Lopez.

Surfing for Life. David L. Brown Productions, 1999. Documentary.

Surfing, Apr. 1998, 69. K2 Big-Wave Challenge advertisement.

The Moment. Produced by Bill Ballard. Billygoat Productions, 1998. Video.

Thomas, Pete. "High Rollers: Maverick's Likely Spot to Catch $50,000 Breach." *Los Angeles Times*, 23 Jan. 1998.

——. "Maverick's Newfound Popularity Not So Swell." *Los Angeles Times*, 6 Feb. 1998.

Vannucci, Rocky. "Maverick's in a Bottle." *Surfer*, Apr. 1999, 38. Letter to the editor.

Wilkinson, Peter. "The Last Wave." *Rolling Stone*, 20 Apr. 1995, 56–66.

Wong, Edward. "Fame Shatters a Surfer's Solitude." *Los Angeles Times*, 26 Nov. 1998.

ACKNOWLEDGMENTS

The following PEOPLE, BY VARIOUS

means and methods, direct and indirect, offered their help, inspiration, or comfort during the writing of this book, and I'll stand everybody here a drink or a set wave, their choice: The Warshaw, Blau, and Kalland families (Helen, Michael, Mimi, Chris, Susan, Katie, Jo, and Gene); Claudia Sóle; Anne, David, and Jacob Eisenmann; Dan Duane and Liz Weil, August Hidalgo and Stasia Lord, Nate Brostrom and Lisa Capps; *agent provocateur* Wendy Burton-Brouws; and the old-school Taraval crew, including (but not limited to) Three-Piece, Martini, Nabob, G-Man, Doc, the Bad Lieutenant, Bluey, Pee-Wee, Yawny, Kevin, Thomas, Steve (Iron Leg) Dwyer, (Downtown) Colin Brown, Clay the Sponge, and the Mayor. Evan Slater and Bruce Jenkins held up well under an early telephone barrage of fussy little detail-obsessed questions, and I appreciate their time and patience. Caroline Herter and Sarah Malarkey pulled this book together and patted my hand as needed, and I'm deeply indebted to them both. Thanks to Martin Venezky for making it look so wonderful. Extra special thanks to editor Jeff Campbell, for his patience, precision, and professionalism (*Matt: lose the alliteration?*). Steve and Debbee Pezman once again lent a nice, calm presence to the proceedings—Steve, in fact, you get *two* set waves. Thanks as always to Uncle Dan for pushing me across the pool on his T-band Hobie in 1965. And, finally, for her encouragement and patience, and for pulling me out of a riptide or two, my everlasting gratitude to Ellen Cart.

PHOTOGRAPHY CREDITS

Original BLACK-AND-WHITE PHOTOGRAPHS

commissioned from and copyright © by **DAVID PERRY:** pp. xiv, 36, 78, 81, 86, 92, 96–97, 99, 124, 162, 196, 202–3. *David Perry Studio*, 607 Laurel Street, Vallejo, California 94591. Tel: 707-649-2760; Website: www.davidperrystudio.com.

Cover photograph reprinted by permission of and copyright © by **FRANK QUIRARTE.** Photographs pp. i, 56, 71, 103 reprinted by permission of and copyright © by **JOHN SEVERSON.** Website: www. surferart.com. Photographs pp. 5, 9, 13 reprinted by permission of and copyright © by **BOB BARBOUR.** Photographs pp. 16, 29 reprinted by permission of and copyright © by **BUD BROWNE.** Photographs pp. 19, 20, 63, 72–73 reprinted courtesy of *SURFER MAGAZINE.* Photograph p. 21 reprinted by permission of and copyright © by the **BISHOP MUSEUM.** Photograph pp. 22–23 reprinted by permission of and copyright © by **DOC BALL.** Photographs pp. 26, 27 reprinted by permission of and copyright © by **WALTER HOFFMAN.** Photograph pp. 32–33 reprinted by permission of and copyright © by **BRUCE BROWN.** Photograph p. 38 reprinted by permission of and copyright © by **NASA.** Illustration p. 41 reprinted by permission of and copyright © by **GRANT WASHBURN.** Photographs pp. 46–47, 53, 84–85, 87, 140–41, 185 reprinted by permission of and copyright © by **LAWRENCE S. BECK.** Email: Lbeck@primitive.com; Website: www.primitive.com/beck. Photographs pp. 51, 93, 136–37 reprinted by permission of and copyright © by **VERN FISHER.** Photographs pp. 54, 60–61, 106-7 reprinted by permission of and copyright © by **LEROY GRANNIS.** Photographs pp. 100, 114–15 reprinted by permission of and copyright © by **MERKEL FILMS.** Photographs pp. 110–11, 148–49, 151 reprinted by permission of and copyright © by **JEFF DIVINE.** Photograph p. 113 reprinted by permission of and copyright © by **KWOCK.** Photographs pp. 120, 123, 160–61, 182 reprinted by permission of and copyright © by **ERIK AEDER.** Tel: 808-572-0443; email: eba@maui.net. Photograph pp. 128–29 reprinted by permission of and copyright © by **TERRY WAY.** Tel: 831-464-0939; Website: www.terryway.com. Photograph p. 131 reprinted by permission of and copyright © by **DARRELL RAY JONES.** Photograph p. 132 reprinted by permission of and copyright © by **BERNIE BAKER.** Photograph p. 142 reprinted by permission of and copyright © by **ART BREWER.** Tel: 949-661-8930; email: abrewerphoto@home.com. Photograph p. 145 reprinted by permission of and copyright © by **TOM SERVAIS.** Photograph p. 155 reprinted by permission of and copyright © by **JOHN BILDERBACK.** Video stills pp. 167, 171, 177, 181 reprinted by permission of and copyright © by **STEPHEN SPAULDING.** Photograph pp. 188–89 reprinted by permission of and copyright © by **FRED FOTO.** Photograph p. 190 reprinted by permission of and copyright © by **DON KING.** Photograph p. 210 reprinted by permission of and copyright © by **ROB GILLEY.**

INDEX